MW01274648

August 4, 2013

For Norma,

   My friend through some hard
times and a lot of fun times.
Thank you!

          Betty Moorhead

# To Travel Is To Live

### A Southern Girl's Life of Love, Adventures, Travels and Tragedy

**Betty Sexton Halsey Moorhead**

"To breathe, to fly, to float
To gain all while you live
To roam the roads of lands remote
To travel is to live."

Hans Christian Anderson

# DEDICATION

This book is dedicated to my children, Chip, Steve and Heidi, and my grandchildren, Paige, Riley, Michael, and Alexander and those to come. You've returned my love many times over and made my life rich and fulfilling. Thank you for sharing my adventures. I wish you a happy, adventurous life shared with those who love you.

# CONTENTS

*Daddy and Mama*
*Golden Anniversary - 1961*

# Prologue

## Going Home

While in Atlanta recently my niece's husband said to me, "Bett, why did you come?" The question startled me and my response was not immediate. I was thinking how I would answer. Atlanta is the place in the world that I've called "home" ever since leaving it sixty years ago. During those years I've created a new family and "homes" in many places.

What is it that draws me back to Georgia frequently? Why do I call Georgia "home" when I actually live in Washington? What is a "home," anyway?

Much has been written about "home" and there are many definitions. The simplest definition is that it is the physical structure that shelters you. Forty-two physical structures have sheltered me in seven states and two different countries and few of them lure me back to visit. Home is where we go for love, comfort and nurturing and age has nothing to do with wanting to go there. Sometimes we go to give those same things to others more than we seek them for ourselves.

I grew up with seven siblings and several of their children, as well. The bonds I formed with them run deep into who I am. In creating my own small family I eagerly immersed them into my original family and they developed their own bonds. They also feel the pull towards Georgia and family there.

Atlanta is a beautiful city but very different from the small place it was in the 1930's and '40's. The city itself is not what I seek on my visits. I want to revisit old memories and feelings, find comfort and love in arms that are no longer there – Daddy and Mama, Hazel and Jack, Evelyn and Dean, Lillian and Elmo and Larry, Taylor and Edna, Bill and my baby brother, Jimmy. Our family was not physically affectionate but I always felt the love. Now that I am more open to physical affection, I hug more easily and can even say "I love you." I need to hug those that are still there and feel them hug me.

I finally answered the question posed to me – "Bett, why did you come?"

"This is my home. This is my family. I just want to see them and be with them once in a while."

My nephew, David, then responded to the question "And she's always welcome!"

That's what I'm talking about – I can feel the love that sustains me from all of them.

As Anais Nin wrote "We write to taste life twice, in the moment and in retrospection."

It's amazing that a little girl growing up in the depression years in the Deep South lived such an exciting, adventurous life. Setting off on my first independent travel while still in kindergarten, I always felt that I was in charge of my life. I acted on every opportunity that passed my way whether it was in the next county or half way around the globe. A voracious appetite for the world literally took me around it. Always far from rich, I was privileged to travel at times on private planes and private yachts. A restless soul, my life has been filled with love, heartbreak and tragedy. I've outlived two husbands named "Chuck," both pilots. I've cared for a chronically ill child. I benefited from having three sisters so much older than me. They were all "additional mothers" to me and continued to be all of their lives.

Blessed with children and grandchildren and an abundance of friends I say, "I wish I could do it all again!"

# Part One

## Growing Up

Bett - 2 years old

# Chapter One

## Earliest Years - Snapshots
### 1930 - 1934

In my mind's eye I see a tiny girl sitting on a curb eating an orange. At just over two years of age I'm filled with anticipation waiting for the ambulance bringing home Mama and Maxine, my new baby sister. I'll soon have a playmate. Taylor, eight, and Bill, six, are too old to play with me and Hazel, fifteen, Evelyn, thirteen and Lillian, eleven, are practically grown up.

My birth certificate identifies me as Charlotte Betty Sue Sexton, born in Grady Hospital in Atlanta, Georgia December 9, 1930. Weighing less than five pounds, with thick dark hair, Mama later told me I looked like a rat! My family calls me "Bett." Daddy is Howard Sexton, 37 years old, city policeman. Mama is Susie Moon Sexton, age 35, housewife.

Home is 100 Dahlgren Street in Atlanta, the first house my parents bought, and we lived there until I was almost five. Although the country struggled in the depths of the Great Depression, our family was better off than many.

Policemen weren't paid well in those days, but Daddy had a secure job and later received a promotion to detective.

Mama read in bed at night. She stretched one arm wide and Maxine and I would lie there with our heads on Mama's arm looking at our own books. Sometimes Bill lay down with us. We all wanted to be close to Mama. She held her magazine in her other hand and managed to keep us all close at the same time. I felt loved and secure.

Our best friends lived across the street. They had three older girls the same ages as Hazel, Evelyn and Lillian and the youngest girl, Mildred, was my age. Mildred and I pushed doll carriages up and down the sidewalk, played paper dolls and rode tricycles together. Maxine was taking a long time to get big enough to play with me! Mrs. Loveless babysat me sometimes and one day when I was three, she served butterbeans for lunch. Scowling, I said "I don't like butterbeans!"

"Well, that's what we're having for lunch, so eat them."

"No! I don't like butterbeans!" Picking up my spoon Mrs. Loveless force-fed me until, choking and gagging, I cleaned the plate. When she let me down, I had the last word, "I'll never eat butterbeans again!" I was on my way to being a lifelong finicky eater.

Down the hill behind our house a stream gurgled, tempting us to come play. Taylor, Bill and I caught crawdads and the boys caught frogs but I wouldn't touch a frog. It was fun playing in the mud and water. Several children lived on our block and we all roamed freely.

Mr. and Mrs. Warner were neighbors who became lifelong friends. With no children of their own, they loved the neighborhood kids. They treated us with kindness and respect and had a knack for making each of us feel special. The Warner's talked and played games with us and invited us inside for cake or cookies.

We moved from the neighborhood shortly after I started kindergarten but throughout elementary school Mr. Warner occasionally worked at my school and brought me a piece of cake or cookies Mrs. Warner had baked. I felt special when he walked into my classroom to give it to me. Several times a year Mrs. Warner walked five miles to visit us, always bringing a big bag of candy orange slices, still one of my favorite candies.

Lillian started going to Inman Park Baptist Church with her best friend. On Mother's Day when I was three years old Mama decided to go to church with Lillian. As she was dressing Daddy said, "Susie, where are you going?"

"I'm going to church with Lillian," Mama responded.

"Wait. I'll go with you," Daddy said. They took me along and I saw Mama awarded a large basket of flowers for being the mother with the most children, nine, two deceased. Her first two children were stillborn. For several years our entire family attended Inman Park Baptist Church for Sunday morning and evening services.

Church played a big part in our lives. We attended revival meetings a few times a year. Held in a tent or a borrowed church visiting preachers dramatically preached "fire and brimstone" sermons strongly encouraging everyone to come forward and "take Jesus as your Savior." The best part, for me was the rousing music designed to stir up many emotions. Groups of singers traveled a circuit singing at revivals and, occasionally, during regular Sunday services. The Waters family, "shirttail relatives" of ours, was my favorite. At age three, I was in love with James Waters, a young teenager. One night after they sang, Mama took me by the hand and walked up to talk to the family. She told them I loved James! I felt so embarrassed I hid behind Mama! I was really mad at her for telling them!

From my earliest years I enjoyed all kinds of music, especially piano music. I wished we had a piano. Extended family members had pianos but even though Mama played "by ear" we never had one. When we visited relatives who had a piano they usually let me "play" it. One day when I was four, a big truck stopped in front of our house and men began unloading something big, dark and heavy! Excited, jumping up and down, I clapped and yelled "Piano! Piano! Piano!" Such a big disappointment when Mama said the large oak buffet would go in the dining room.

Our radio was on for hours every day, mostly hillbilly music, some of it now called "bluegrass." Saturday nights in the 1930's, sitting close to the radio; we listened to the Grand Ole Opry, broadcast from Nashville, Tennessee.

When I was four, five year old Shirley Temple became America's darling, a star in moving pictures. With a head full of beautiful curls she sang and danced her way to fame and fortune. I had blue eyes and light brown hair that Mama wet and wrapped around her finger every morning to form long curls and, according to Lillian, sometimes people commented that I resembled Shirley. But singing and dancing were never among my talents!

As Maxine grew older my curls caused her a lot of resentment. She wanted long curls too! Her hair was a beautiful dark brown and everyone commented on her big brown eyes. She was much prettier than I was but that didn't keep her from wanting curls. So, when Maxine was three years old and I was five, Lillian and Evelyn took us to a beauty salon and Maxine got a permanent. No one realized the three year old expected to come out with long curls and, of course, that is not possible. When Maxine saw short, tight frizzy curls all over her head she was furious and immediately took both hands and messed up her hairdo as thoroughly as she could!

Easy-going with a sunny disposition, I was the recipient of much love and attention and special treats. My earliest years laid a firm foundation on which to build my life and gave me the confidence to do it.

*Mama, Bett, Maxine and Jimmy*

# Chapter Two
## More Snapshots
### 1934 - 1935

Anticipation reigned high. Excited and nervous, finally my first day of school had arrived! Almost five, I started kindergarten at Whiteford Elementary School on Whiteford Avenue in Atlanta, half a mile from our house.

Wearing a new blue dress and brown oxfords, I felt like a big girl as Mama and Mrs. Loveless walked to school that day with Mildred Loveless and me. Mr. Warner came over and gave each of us a nickel before we left for school. In those years, to a little girl who was not yet five, a nickel seemed like a lot of money! I could buy a sack of penny candy for a nickel or an ice cream cone or maybe I'd buy a toy - a bolo bat, jacks with a ball, a yo-yo or marbles.

I loved watching the birds flying overhead. I envied their freedom, thinking they could go anywhere they wanted, anytime.

Shy and small for my age, didn't keep me from loving school. My teacher was as sweet as she looked and I loved learning new things and having new playmates. Before the first week was over I set out on my first independent adventure. I wanted to see the world, or at least the part that I could walk to. I knew a classmate, Frankie Fecter, from Sunday School and talked him into going for a walk with me after school one day. We took the long way around but eventually got to his house which was several blocks in a different direction than mine. Not knowing my way home I got lost for a while and by the time I got within a block or so of my house, I heard Lillian yelling for me and learned almost the whole family was worried and out searching for me. Apparently I hadn't been afraid for later in life I was lost in several cities or countries I'd never been to before.

After getting off to such a good start I felt sad when we moved a few weeks after school began. Daddy had let the bank foreclose on our house on Dahlgren Street. Many of our neighbors let their houses go back to the banks also. They were no longer worth the debt owed on them.

We moved to Bouldercrest Drive in east Atlanta in November, 1935. With no school bus service in the city and no public bus service in our area, I walked at least a mile to John B. Gordon School. Sometimes I walked the last half with a classmate or if I got to her house in time, her father drove us to school on his way to work. My fifth birthday was in December. No party that year, just the family and a cake that Mama baked and one or two small presents.

Christmas, the most anticipated holiday of the year, came a couple of weeks after my birthday. Bill, Maxine and I excitedly awaited a visit from Santa Claus. He never let us down and brought us two or three presents each plus there were a few presents from family members. We all looked for the longest stockings in the house to hang. Usually, they belonged to Daddy. What Santa put in the stockings repeated year after year including the ever present apple and orange. A few pecans and/or walnuts and several small toys from the five and dime rested in the middle and a candy cane always topped the stocking.

Mama spent the week before Christmas baking the same kind of cakes she baked every year - Southern and Japanese fruitcakes, coconut, chocolate and peppermint cakes. Japanese fruitcake and peppermint cake were my favorites. She also baked cookies; my favorite, called "tea cakes," – a plain vanilla similar to a sugar cookie but not as sweet.

Soon after Christmas snow started falling. We children were excited and eager to get out and play. By Atlanta standards, it was a big snowstorm - a foot of snow on the ground that lasted for several days. Mama made snow ice cream, a rare treat. Brothers Bill and Taylor, who were about nine and eleven, got into trouble when they and other boys threw snowballs at passing cars. One evening Mama and I went next door to visit neighbors. On the way

10

home I dropped a beautiful handkerchief, a Christmas gift. We retraced our steps but couldn't find it in the snow and dark. Mama said we'd probably find it when the snow melted. We didn't and I couldn't figure out how my handkerchief could just vanish! Handkerchiefs, one or a box of four, usually beautifully embroidered, were a popular gift in the 1930's and 40's.

The school year was divided into two semesters. The first semester of kindergarten was called "low" kindergarten and the second semester was called "high" kindergarten. The second semester started about the first of February. At John B. Gordon, low kindergarten finished at 11 AM and high kindergarten started soon after in the same classroom with the same teacher. After I passed into high kindergarten, Mama had a hard time keeping me home until time for high kindergarten to start. An eager student, I got to school early each day because Mama couldn't hold me back! Although I arrived early, the teacher had to let me in. Finally she pinned a note on my dress, asking that Mama not allow me to get there so early! Almost every day at school we had Jello for a treat. I liked plain Jello but one day the Jello had fruit cocktail in it and I didn't want to eat it. Just by looking I knew I wouldn't like fruit cocktail but felt I had to eat it so I did and then got sick. I haven't eaten fruit cocktail since!

Winters in Atlanta are cold. The long walk to school was hard for a five year old. Daddy got a German shepherd I claimed as mine. We named her "Lady." Lady walked with me every morning and then returned home until Mama told her to go get me. When I came out the school door Lady would be waiting. One day she wasn't there and I worried about her. Even though Daddy was a police detective, he never solved that one!

On the coldest mornings Mama stood beside the road and flagged down cars until someone agreed to drop me at school. I felt a little uncomfortable in the car with strangers but I always got in! The only time I was afraid was one time when there were two men in the car. I can't remember why I was afraid except it had something to do with a gun. Maybe I saw a gun in the car or maybe a gun was mentioned in conversation; whatever, I always remembered that ride.

For those readers who grew up after the 1930's and 1940's I know that putting a five-year-old girl in a car with strangers must sound unbelievable. In the '30's no one questioned personal safety. Most people never locked a door. We usually didn't even have a key. That's just the way things were, a much safer time.

When spring came, the weather warmed and we played outside most of the time. We made kites out of newspapers and sticks, tore up rags to make a tail and, if lucky, Daddy brought us butcher paper to use instead of newspaper. It made a stronger kite and we thrilled to see our kites soaring into the wild blue yonder. A kite cost a nickel but nickels were hard to come by.

Behind our house we dug clay from the banks of a stream and molded figures of all kinds. Georgia clay is known as among the best in the country and is highly desired by artisans. A big tree next to the creek supported a long vine. Hanging on for dear life, it was great fun to swing out over the creek.

Before the school year ended we moved to Stone Mountain, a small town 20 miles from Atlanta named for the massive stone mountain that dominates the landscape for miles around. Daddy grew up in the area and my grandparents and many relatives lived nearby so the mountain has always been a fixture in my life. Today a large state park surrounds the mountain and hordes of tourists visit every year.

It was close to the end of the school year when we moved so I didn't complete kindergarten. Shortly after moving, on May 21, 1936, when I was five and a half, Mama gave birth to her last child, a boy named Jimmy. While she was recuperating, 16 year old Evelyn did laundry using our wringer washing machine on the back porch. Fascinated by the hard rubber rollers going round and round squeezing water out of the clothes, I inched closer and closer. A fingernail size chip was missing from one roller and every time that spot rolled around I quickly touched it with my finger. Suddenly my fingers slid between the rollers and then my arm, right up to my elbow! Evelyn panicked, jumped off the porch and ran, leaving me screaming with the rollers moving rapidly up my arm! Mama heard me yelling and rushed to the porch and hit the release bar on top of the rollers rescuing me.

Wrapping my flat, purple arm in a towel she sent 12 year old Taylor running to Uncle Ezron's house, a mile or so away going through the fields instead of by road. Telephones were just beginning to be available for average families but we didn't have one. Uncle Ezron was home and came at once to drive me to the hospital in Atlanta. He had a telephone and called Daddy at the Police Department. By the time Uncle Ezron and I reached Avondale, the half way point between Stone Mountain and Atlanta, a police car met us and escorted us to Grady Hospital with siren blaring. I remember telling Uncle Ezron to make them stop the noise because it made my arm hurt more. I was glad to see Daddy waiting at the hospital. No bones were broken but the skin was bleeding in a few small places and the arm badly bruised. I still have scars on my left arm.

We lived in Stone Mountain only for the summer. Daddy's sister, Ela, and her family lived nearby as did Uncle Ezron, and his family, so we had cousins as well as neighbor kids to play with.

Shortly after school started we moved back to Atlanta into a three bedroom brick house at 207 Arizona Avenue. Since we kids were a few days late starting school at Mary Lin Elementary, and I was still small and less than six years old, the principal wanted me to repeat kindergarten. Mama convinced her to let me "try" first grade and never another word was said about kindergarten.

# Chapter Three
## Elementary School
### 1935 - 1942

Curly brown hair, warm blue eyes, sweet, kind and generous, Mrs. Falls was an ideal first grade teacher. I loved her and loved school. I developed a lifelong passion for learning. It was fun being one of the first kids to read and do arithmetic. Working hard for Mrs. Falls became a habit that continued throughout my school years.

Every year we had spring holidays, a Thursday and Friday. If the school reached a designated percentage of children who had visited the dentist and received a certificate of dental health, then we had Wednesday off. A lot of pressure was on the children to bring in that certificate and we wouldn't know until the last minute if we'd get the extra holiday. Mrs. Falls' husband, a dentist, helped out.

As time was growing short Mrs. Falls obtained permission from parents to take a few students to her husband for dental care, at no cost to the parents. She took us in a group to have our teeth cleaned and examined. Never having been to a dentist before I felt nervous, but having my teacher with me helped. She took me back two more times and all of my cavities were filled. Filling teeth in the 1930's was a painful process. Drills were much slower than they are today and it took a long time to drill out the cavity without the use of a pain killer. Thanks to Mrs. Falls and her dentist husband, our class was one of the few that achieved 100% dental health certificates. The school met the required percentage so we had Wednesday, Thursday and Friday off for our spring holidays.

Mrs. Brooks, my second grade teacher, was as nice as Mrs. Falls and I enjoyed another successful year. An avid reader, I learned how to use the school library and borrowed many books.

14

Arithmetic was my second favorite subject, after reading. Numbers came easy to me and I enjoyed working with them.

A lovely woman who had taught some of my older brothers and sisters, Mrs. Callier was my third grade teacher. She walked the class on a field trip to Carnegie Library, a mile or so from our school. I felt as if I'd discovered a hidden treasure! All of those books were available to me just for the asking! I got a library card that day and became a frequent borrower.

The most exciting thing that year was just before my eighth birthday I became an aunt! My sister Hazel gave birth to my first niece, Jacqueline, always called Jackie. I loved her so much and enjoyed playing with the baby and taking care of her and helping Hazel so I learned to travel alone across Atlanta to spend weekends with Hazel, Jack and Jackie.

The first time I made the trip two ladies on the street car started a conversation with me. They asked where I was going and I told them I was going to the shoe shop where Jack worked, two blocks from where I'd get off the street car. After we got off the street car I walked away in the opposite direction. The ladies saw the shop and realized I'd gone the wrong way. They ran back and found me and took me Jack's shop. Jack took me across the street and put me on a bus to Techwood, where they lived. He told the driver where to put me off the bus and gave me instructions on how to find the apartment. I made the trip alone many times over the next few years.

When I was eight, Daddy bought a house and we moved to 1490 Iverson Street, only a mile from Mary Lin School. I enjoyed learning about anything and everything. If I didn't know it, I wanted to learn it. Still shy, I rarely had confidence enough to raise my hand to volunteer an answer. Mrs. Koffee, my fourth grade teacher, had also taught several of my siblings. That year I transitioned from "little kid" to "big kid." A year of discovery about myself, I learned how competitive I was academically and athletically. A chart on the wall listing each student's name had a gold star for every book read. As my line of gold stars got longer and longer Mrs. Koffe kept adding paper to make the chart wider. I read 153 books that year, more than any of the other students.

In fourth grade we studied geography and I enjoyed learning about other countries and where they were. At that time I couldn't imagine ever visiting a foreign country. We also memorized the multiplication tables through twelve's. Second in the class to recite them perfectly, only beat out for first place by Jerry Turner, a bright Shirley Temple look-alike, who grew up and married my cousin, Don Aderhold. My athletic ability began to show itself as well; always one of the first picked for any team, frequently I was chosen team captain. For years I'd played with neighborhood kids after school and we played a lot of backyard softball. I was as good as most of the boys and I finished fourth grade with more confidence in myself.

With a dozen neighborhood kids I played *kick the can, hide-n-seek* and *fox and hounds, marbles* and board games - *Monopoly, checkers, dominoes and others*. Outside games were played in the street in front of our house or in Bobby Longino's back yard. Bobby's yard, the biggest in the neighborhood, had a huge, old oak tree. Underneath the tree we played with Bobby's collection of toy soldiers and miniature cars. Digging in the dirt we'd create cities and roads for the cars or hills and bunkers for playing soldiers.

In Atlanta's hot, humid summers, we kept an ear out for the iceman who gave us chunks of ice to chew on. Many families still used iceboxes to keep food cold and a truck delivered ice. By the late 1930's we had a refrigerator but during World War II, it broke down and couldn't be repaired. Manufacture of new ones ceased during the war so Daddy borrowed a large Coca Cola icebox from a friend who owned a gas station. Most gas stations had such boxes filled with cold drinks they sold for a nickel. We used that Coca Cola ice box until new refrigerators were available again.

Mrs. Williamson gave me a lot of grief in fifth grade. The only teacher I ever had I thought did not like me. I surely did not like her! A large stern looking woman with a gruff voice, she thought my penmanship was terrible. It was! Compared to others in my class, my handwriting was ugly! Mrs. Williamson compounded my embarrassment by making me write every paper over at least once that entire year. I couldn't make my penmanship good enough or neat enough no matter how hard I tried. I practiced writing exercises but my handwriting never improved. I was so happy to finish fifth grade and move on to sixth.

The highlight of fifth grade included participating in a festival with elementary students from all over the city. Fifth and sixth graders danced the *Virginia Reel* and a square dance in Georgia Tech's football stadium. For easy identification each school wore different color costumes. Mary Lin School girls wore red muslin dresses. Georgia Tech was several miles across Atlanta from my home. Lillian, and her husband, Elmo, drove me to the stadium but we didn't leave early enough and were caught in a big traffic jam.

Long past time to report to my teacher on the field, we finally arrived and made our way into the crowded stadium. My class stood on the field which indicated they had not yet danced. Spotting a cousin in sixth grade, Lillian convinced me to make my way to Toby. He was happy to see me as Mrs. Williamson had prevailed upon him to dance in my place with the fifth graders.

Mrs. Shepherd, my sixth grade teacher, had a sweet disposition and a warm smile. She also had taught several of my brothers and sisters. Mrs. Shepherd never said a word about my penmanship or neatness. A terrible thing happened during that year. The JAPS (as they were referred to) bombed Pearl Harbor! Our country was at war! It was very scary and changed our way of life. About this time I decided I'd like to be a stewardess because I wanted to fly but girls couldn't be pilots unless they were rich like Amelia Earhart. I always said if I were an animal, I'd be a bird.

Performing with sixth graders in the annual spring festival in1942, after WWII had begun, Mama, the only one available, took me to Georgia Tech. At my insistence, we left home hours before the event, took the streetcar downtown and transferred to a bus the rest of the way. When we arrived at the stadium, we saw we were the first ones there! The performances went well and I felt proud. At year's end I headed off to junior high, seventh through ninth grades, with confidence.

*Bett and Lillian - Mobile 1942*

# Chapter Four

## Summer By The Bay
### 1942

During the summers of my childhood Mama and the four younger children spent a few weeks visiting Mama's siblings and their families, all farmers in Gwinnett County. Daddy would drive us to one home and leave us. After a few days our uncle would take us in a horse drawn wagon to visit another family. Spending time with our aunts, uncles and cousins was a lot of fun.

There was usually a creek or pond nearby where we'd play in the water and once in a while we'd go to Yellow River where we could really swim. At night we'd sleep on homemade quilt pallets in the living room where we'd tell true family ghost stories after the kerosene lanterns were turned off. Electricity didn't get to the rural areas until after World War II. I'd help out sometimes by hoeing weeds from the cotton fields or vegetable gardens. With my cousins I'd walk long distances carrying water to the men working in the fields. Some summers after Mama and the other kids returned to Atlanta I'd be left with one family for a week or so and then be taken to another family's house where I'd visit for a few days.

The summer of 1942, six months after Pearl Harbor was attacked by the Japanese and the United States plunged into World War II, was different; it turned into the best summer of my childhood.

Eleven years old and looking forward to junior high I was overjoyed when my sister Lillian invited me to visit her and Elmo in Mobile, Alabama. Elmo worked in a shipyard and even though they lived in a rented room they invited me to spend a week with them. I rode the Greyhound bus alone from Atlanta to Mobile, feeling very grown-up. Lillian was waiting at the downtown bus station when I arrived, and after lunch at Woolworth's counter, showed me around town. A couple of days into my visit Elmo announced we were moving to Fairhope to share a house on Mobile Bay with his coworkers. Fairhope was a small town 20 miles from Mobile, so small it did not have a Post Office and we had to drive a few miles to Daphne to pick up mail.

The house was located on a very large lot, facing Mobile Bay. A family's summer home for many years it was abandoned after rumors a German submarine had been spotted in the bay. Driving down the long sandy driveway, approaching the house from the back, one could see straight through the large center hall to the dock and bay. The kitchen and a big screened porch, where we ate all meals, were across the back. From the porch you entered a wide room that ran through the house to the front porch. On one side of this big hall were two large bedrooms. A family with one or two children occupied each one. Because of the war living space was costly and hard to find which is why so many of us shared the house. On the opposite side of the big hall were a large bedroom and a smaller room and a bathroom. Lillian and Elmo and I shared the big front bedroom until the single man occupying the smaller room moved out, then I moved into that room and Lillian and Elmo let me stay the rest of the summer.

Everyone shared the common spaces and we all pitched in to prepare meals and clean the house

A leaky old rowboat lying neglected in the front yard enticed us kids. We turned it over and with a little elbow grease cleaned it up and put it in the water. The leak was small and slow so we rowed and bailed all summer. Swimming in the warm water of the bay every day, fishing with shrimp we bought for bait for twenty cents a pound, and learning to catch crabs, kept us occupied. Painfully stung by a jelly fish while swimming one day taught me to keep watch and when I saw jellyfish, out of the water I'd go.

A Negro woman, who came in to help with the cleaning and cooking, showed us how to catch all the crabs we could eat. The butcher gave us meat scraps and bones that we tied securely with heavy string, and hung them from a nail on the edge of the pier. A few hours later there were usually several crabs hanging on and we'd just pull them from the water. Our fishing poles were bamboo rods with line and a cork between the pole and the fishhook. The idea was to let the cork float. When a fish grabbed the bait the cork would sink and we'd pull the fish in.

At the municipal dock I saw my first stingray. It was lying on the dock, and was about 12"-15" across and at least 30" long. It was flat and felt kind of like the sandy bottom of the bay. If you were unfortunate enough to step on one, its long sharp tail would inflict serious injury.

Slot machines in grocery stores and gasoline stations exposed me to gambling for the first time. Lillian frequently gave me a few nickels to try my luck. When I was lucky enough to bring up two or three cherries in a row and win a few nickels I felt rich!

As the other families began to leave we had room for Mama and Maxine and Jimmy to join us. Still young, I enjoyed the last carefree summer of my childhood. I'm sure the adults were wondering if this might be our last happy time as war was building in the Pacific and in Europe. It wasn't long before our family members joined those already fighting.

By the end of summer Lillian, Elmo and I were the only family left. We spent our evenings on the dock, swimming and enjoying the cool breeze while Elmo sang to us. He had a beautiful voice and loved to sing and we loved listening. He sang all of the popular songs of that era but my favorite was "Sailboat in the Moonlight." I've never heard it since without thinking of Elmo.

Many times at night when we were on the dock, we'd look back at the house and think we saw someone. After I rode the bus back to Atlanta at the end of summer, Lillian and Elmo were the only ones left in the house. Elmo had two experiences with ghosts that frightened him. Both times he was awakened by someone bending over him as he slept. He described a man dressed in dark clothes with only his white shirt collar and cuffs and his gold wrist watch clearly showing. The second time Elmo was frightened so much that he and Lillian went next door and woke the neighbors and asked them to come over and help search the house. Of course no one was found. Elmo knew he would be drafted soon and go to war and he believed the ghost was an omen, that he would die in the war.

Lillian and Elmo returned to Atlanta, leaving their yellow Pontiac with a rumble seat in the yard by the house. It needed new tires and because of the war, they were not available. It wasn't long before Elmo was drafted into the Army Air Corps and left for training. He gave the car to a friend who owned a gas station and had tires he could use to drive down and get it. The fun-filled summer was over and I started junior high.

# Chapter Five
## Junior High School
### 1942 - 1945

In September 1942 when I started junior high, the country at been at war for nine months. Evelyn's husband, Dean, and Lillian's husband, Elmo, were off fighting or training to fight. At home many things were rationed, including meat, butter and other foods, gasoline and, even shoes. Each person had a ration book with stamps in it that were removed when you bought a rationed item.

Large collection bins were placed around the city. We deposited all things made of metal, including tinfoil from gum packages. All rubber went to the war effort so rubber bands were no longer available and we learned to tie things together with string. Underwear and pajamas no longer had elastic around the waist, only drawstrings or buttons, which sometimes failed! Margarine was created to replace butter. Looking like lard, no one wanted to eat it on bread so manufacturers began packaging it with a small packet of yellow dye that we mixed in at home.

Everyone had to practice "blackouts" in case we were attacked by bombers. When air raid sirens sounded all lights were extinguished. If the Air Raid Captain saw light coming from a house, he issued a warning. At school we practiced what to do in case of an air raid. At the sound of the alarm, all children sat on the floor in the halls with heads lowered until the "all clear" signal. German submarines were sighted off the coast of Georgia and in Mobile Bay where I'd just spent the summer with Lillian and Elmo. Almost every house had a small flag in the window showing a blue star to represent each family member in uniform. Gradually, some of those stars were replaced with a gold one, which meant a family member died in the war.

Patriotism propaganda was prolific. Signs and posters everywhere urged us to buy "war bonds" and to contribute in as many ways as possible to the war effort. The most memorable poster for me was a big colorful one of a beautiful, shapely young woman with a bandana around her hair, flexing her muscles, titled "Rosie, the Riveter." A picture of Uncle Sam with his finger on his lips and the message "Loose Lips Sink Ships," served as another reminder to be careful what we talked about. The enemy was always listening and we must not give them information they could use against us.

When we went to the "show" (the expression we used then for movies), at some point the lights always came on and baskets were passed around to collect money to fight infantile paralysis, later called "polio." Our beloved President, Franklin D. Roosevelt, was paralyzed from infantile paralysis. His winter home in Warm Springs, Georgia became a treatment center for thousands of victims. Infantile paralysis was a huge problem, especially in the south, as the germ, carried by mosquitoes, made many children sick each summer, including children at my school. We were all fearful of contracting it and many children were left paralyzed.

I remember how frightening all this was. I worried about family members and friends fighting in the war. I learned to carry those worries in a special place in my mind and think of them as tied up in a little box. Worries were always there but tucked into this special place so I could go on living my everyday life and laugh and have fun.

Grades seven through nine were spent at Bass Junior High, a large, imposing building on top of a hill. Located a mile from my home, several blocks from our church and a couple of blocks from Carnegie Library, I knew the neighborhood well.

Soon after I started seventh grade in September, 1942 my first nephew, Alan Dean Tuck, Jr. but nicknamed "Butch," was born. He was Evelyn and Dean's first child and my parent's first grandson. Dean was away in the Army but the rest of the family showered the baby with love. I spent as much time as possible with him. Evelyn and Butch lived a couple of miles from us with Dean's parents, close enough for me to walk there several times a week. Within the next year Hazel gave me another nephew, David in April, 1943. Lillian had her first child, Ken, in June and Taylor's wife, Edna, gave birth to Dianne in August, 1943. Our family was growing and I was thrilled.

The first day of school all seventh graders went to the auditorium where we were given our class schedules. There were six periods each day, plus lunch and physical education. I felt very grown up navigating the crowded halls to locate one classroom after another. My math teacher, Mrs. Dixon, was my most memorable teacher. She looked about eighty years old as she was shrunken, wore glasses and had lots of wrinkles. She taught math and had a phobia about decimal points. Anyone who neglected to put a prominent decimal point in the appropriate spot soon learned never to take a paper, still in the notebook, to Mrs. Dixon to ask a question. She had a pencil at least half an inch in diameter and to make her point, your neglected decimal point, she put it in for you and bored a hole all the way through the notebook!

Having spent three years in Camp Fire Girls, in junior high I joined "Girl Reserves," sponsored by the Y.W.C.A. The best part of Girl Reserves included the two camping trips we took each year. Parents drove us to a camp several miles from Atlanta. Two glorious days were spent swimming in a cool creek, playing under waterfalls, hiking and playing games. We slept in tent cabins, the top half canvas and the bottom, wood, six girls to a cabin. We ate our meals in a large rustic dining hall. The entire camp was old and run down but I loved it. At the end of the weekend, we laid our clothes on top of our two blankets and rolled them all up together in a large cumbersome roll. Our bundle had to be carried two miles to the end of a streetcar line that we rode several miles to downtown Atlanta. From there we each transferred to a bus or streetcar that would take us home.

My natural athleticism developed and, as in grade school, I was one of the best in softball, volley ball, and track events.

Elected Athletic Officer, I represented my class at meetings about school athletic events. I also served as a Safety Patrol Officer, monitoring the busy street crossing in front of the school.

A pretty good student without much effort, making mostly A's and B's, with a few C's, I wasn't motivated to work hard to get the best grades. Intimidated by the few kids in my classes who were obviously the smartest, best looking and richest, I had an inferiority complex. They appeared to have confidence in themselves that I didn't have, except for sports, at which I excelled. I was content to remain in the background. No one at home ever asked about my homework or anything else that was going on at school. It was taken for granted that I would do what I was supposed to do and I usually did. I wonder if I was born responsible or learned it at an early age.

The summer of 1944, at thirteen and half and ready for ninth grade, I got my first real job. Mama had recently started working at McCrory's Department Store. During the war all businesses were desperate for workers and would take just about anybody, even a thirteen year old! Much to my embarrassment, the store started me on the lingerie counter where I had to show and sell ladies undergarments!

When school started that fall I felt so good! I spent all of my summer earnings at Rich's, the South's premier department store, on new school clothes. Mama gave me a few dollars and I bought several new sweaters and wool skirts and a pair of "penny" loafers, proud that I'd earned most of the money for my new wardrobe.

In ninth grade English class we had to pick a partner and research and write about the profession or work we'd like to do when we grew up. Another girl and I wanted to be writers. I wrote a letter to Mary Roberts Rinehart who was a well known and prolific writer of mystery stories that I didn't even read! I was disappointed when she didn't answer.

26

In December, 1944 I turned fourteen. Evelyn had rented a house the Tuck's owned near theirs and she gave me a birthday party. I invited several classmates and was surprised and pleased when almost all came. They had to come by bus from various neighborhoods and then walk a mile or so from the end of the line. We played "spin the bottle" and I had my first chaste kiss or two on the cheek. We also had fun with the Ouija Board Evelyn gave me for my birthday.

A new family moved into our neighborhood with a girl my age and a boy a year younger. Betty and I became best friends and I had a crush on David. He asked me out for my first date. We were going to a movie on a Sunday afternoon. Nervous and embarrassed waiting for him I was humiliated when he didn't show up! Betty later told me their mother was mad at everybody that day and wouldn't let David out of the house. A couple of weeks later he took me to a football game. We rode the bus downtown and transferred to another bus to get to the stadium. The weather was very cold and we about froze standing around waiting for buses. Even though we played softball and marbles and other games at home every day, we were shy with each other on a "date" and both of us were tense making conversation.

Many Sunday afternoons Betty and I would dress up in our "Sunday" clothes and take the bus downtown, wobble on our newly acquired "heels" several blocks to one or another of Atlanta's grand old theatres. We had just begun wearing "stockings," held up by elastic "garters." We had to stop in almost every doorway and pull them up. We saved our baby-sitting money for such excursions and saw many of the wonderful musical movies made in the early 1940's – *Meet Me in St. Louis* with Judy Garland and Margaret O'Brien, *The Dolly Sisters* with Betty Grable, John Payne and June Haver, *Anchors Aweigh* with Frank Sinatra and Kathryn Grayson, and, oh,... so many more. Sometimes after the movie we even had enough money left to stop

27

at a drug store soda fountain for a coke.

Near the end of the school year Betty asked me to go to a school dance with her. She attended Sacred Heart Junior High and the boys came from Maris, the Catholic school for boys. She arranged our dates and tried, unsuccessfully, to teach me to dance. While Betty and her date danced and laughed and had a good time, my date and I, both painfully shy, spent the evening sitting silently at the table.

Any weekend I didn't have plans with Betty I spent with Lillian and her boys, one and a half year old Ken, and Billy, who was born in January, 1945 or with Hazel, Jack, Jackie and David or with Evelyn and Butch. I was never one to sit around with nothing to do, was always on the go.

Ninth grade was coming to an end and so was World War II. Victory in Europe was declared on May 8, 1945. My brother, Bill, had just become eligible for the draft; my oldest brother Taylor, was seeing action in the Atlantic aboard a Merchant Marine ship and Dean was back in the U. S. after having been shot through the neck when he stuck his head out of a tank! Elmo, a tail gunner on a B-17, was stationed in England and had been flying missions over Germany. Everyone in my family, in the city, in the entire country was almost overcome with joy and happiness. Our men would be coming home soon. On August 14th the war with Japan ended after the United States had dropped a second atom bomb on Japan. At last it was all over.

Turning into a young woman, I was not comfortable with all that was happening in my head, my heart and my body. Very self-conscious but, having no alternatives, I continued to move on. Soon I would be going to high school.

28

# Chapter Six

## Summer of '45
### 1945

May 8, 1945 had been declared Victory in Europe Day, forever to be known as V-E Day. With victory against the Japanese in the Pacific close at hand, the mood in the United States was one of relief. Everyone looked forward to peaceful, prosperous times ahead.

June brought not only summer in Atlanta but anticipation of seeing our loved ones return from the battlefields. Lillian was making plans to join Elmo, in Lake Charles, Louisiana. Elmo had been transferred there from his wartime duty in England. Lillian wanted to get there as quickly as she could with Ken, just turning two years old and Billy, five months old.

Flying was very expensive and few people could afford it in those days. Since children under three could fly free, Lillian had saved for this, long looked forward to, flight. When she called the airlines to make a reservation, they threw up roadblocks. First, they insisted, because she had two little ones, she would have to pay for a second seat for Ken. No matter how many children one might have less than three years old, only one could travel free. Settling down, after being thrown for a loop, Lillian somehow figured out how to come up with enough money for a second ticket. Calling the airline again to make the reservation brought forth another roadblock! This time the agent said that because she had a baby in arms to take care of, two year old Ken was not old enough to be on his own in the seat she was buying for him! He would need a "travel companion." She would never be able to buy a third ticket. Finally, showing a tiny degree of compassion, the reservations agent gave Lillian the name of the passenger in the third seat in their row.

Lillian called the woman and she agreed to take responsibility for Ken, after hearing Lillian's story that she was trying to reunite with her husband who had just returned from helping win the war in Europe. Lillian called the airline a third time only to run headlong into a new rule! Since the person who had agreed to take responsibility for Ken was not a relative, the airline did not allow that. No one remembers what Lillian told the airline at that point!

In desperation Lillian asked me if I'd like to go to Lake Charles. We'd take the train and I'd help her with Ken and Billy. At fourteen, eager as always, I probably ran from the room to start packing!

From Atlanta, via New Orleans, to Lake Charles, Louisiana was a long journey. Trains were crowded with families on the same sort of journey we were, trying to reunite with loved ones. Many men in uniforms from all the armed services were on board but there were not enough seats for everyone. In those days people were allowed to stand or sit on their suitcases in the aisles. Few trains, if any, had air conditioning and, in July we were forced to have the windows open or suffocate. When the train rounded a bend, coal dust and cinders blew in the windows covering us.

We had a six-hour layover in New Orleans. Travelers Aid had a huge room full of cots available for weary travelers so, for a nominal fee, Lillian obtained a cot and two cribs. Before long Lillian, Ken and Billy were sound asleep. I couldn't stand being in a city I'd never seen, except what I saw from the train window as we approached New Orleans. I just had to go out for a walk. I left the station and walked several blocks into the downtown area, interesting to me simply because I'd never been there before. After a while I decided I'd better get back to the station in case one of the boys woke up while Lillian was still asleep. Forever after, when arriving in a new place, I could hardly wait to go out and walk around and get familiar with it.

Finally we boarded the train to Lake Charles and upon arrival saw Elmo wearing a huge smile as if it were the happiest day of his life. It probably was. He was back with Lillian and his sons again expecting they would all be together from then on.

With great difficulty Elmo had found a place to live, a

bedroom in someone's home with permission to share the kitchen. A small two bedroom house with a living room and moderate sized kitchen and bath, Elmo had rented the largest bedroom and had brought in a cot for Ken and a crib for Billy.

We arrived about sunset at the house that would be our home for the next few weeks. The landlords had not expected me but made a bed for me on the living room sofa. I slept there part of the time and shared Ken's cot part of the time. The landlords were around thirty with two young children so Ken had playmates. Neighbors dropped in frequently and everyone welcomed us.

Elmo wasn't required to spend a lot of time at the Army Air base. He had many hours to lounge around the backyard or the bedroom with Lillian, the boys and me. We played cards a lot; sometimes friends of Elmo's would come over and almost every day Elmo would sing to us. Some of the songs I remember from that time are *Sailboat in the Moonlight, Pennies from Heaven, Smoke Gets in Your Eyes, It Had To Be You, You'll Never Know*, and *Chattanooga Choo-Choo*.

I've never forgotten Elmo's best friend as I had a huge crush on him. Daniel Ford Whitney IV came from Pasadena, California. I already knew, from reading movie magazines, that Pasadena was one of the wealthiest towns in the entire country; not much there in the '40's but the Rose Bowl and magnificent mansions. The first time I met Danny's wife, Hope, was when she showed up on the doorstep one day. Lillian asked her how she'd gotten there as we lived in a semi-rural area, quite a distance from town and there was no public transportation. When Hope, 22 years old and beautiful with long brown hair, said that she had hitch-hiked, I nearly fainted from shock! In the south, girls would never think of hitch-hiking. It was not only "not safe," it was "low class!" Hope had a wonderful sense of humor and kept things lively whenever she was around. We all shared a lot of laughs and they enjoyed Elmo's singing as much as we did. Danny and Hope were very good company.

One day Elmo came in elated. He had rented an apartment near downtown and we could move in immediately. A friend with a car brought him home with the news so we piled in the car with our bags. We were dropped off in front of a large, well-kept, early

20th century house. There were three stories and we had the apartment on the third floor, originally servant's quarters. It wasn't very clean and July in Lake Charles is extremely hot and humid. Air conditioning didn't exist and we didn't even have an electric fan. Nevertheless, drenched in sweat in that attic apartment, we started scrubbing until it met Lillian's approval. We were all so hot we thought we were about to die. We ended on the attached sleeping porch with the windows open hoping for a little breeze.

Elmo got up early the next day and went to the Army Air Base. He and thousands of others spent their time gathering all of their important papers and waiting until their names reached the top of the list so they could be processed and discharged from service. Not long after he left, Lillian and I simply could not stand the heat in our spacious apartment and were worried about Ken and Billy. We spent the day in a nearby park which wasn't much cooler but we had a breeze, at least. When Elmo came home from work, he was disappointed to learn we had to move back to the room we'd vacated the night before because the heat in the apartment was unbearable.

I stayed three weeks, enabling Lillian and Elmo to go out to a movie or a stroll by the lake to have some time alone. Still there when V-J Day (Victory in Japan) was declared on August 14th I babysat while Lillian and Elmo joined the throngs downtown celebrating war's end. The next day Elmo felt he should take me out to celebrate so we went to the lake to swim with a couple of his friends.

A few days later I rode the train alone back to Atlanta. Lucky to have a seat all the way back, it was still a long, hot, tiring trip and I was black with soot when I got home. A few weeks later Lillian, Elmo and the boys returned to Atlanta but didn't stay long. Elmo had a job in Starke, Florida, not far from Gainesville, where he and Lillian had lived near Elmo's father right after they married. I hated to see them leave Atlanta but looked forward to visiting them in Florida. If I'd had a crystal ball I would have seen that the next summer I'd be moving to Florida to live with Lillian and Ken and Billy, without Elmo.

32

*June 1948*

# Chapter Seven

## High School
### 1945 - 1948

In 1945 Atlanta was a rapidly growing city with a population approaching half a million. Prior to World War II the population had been around 300,000 but the war had caused an influx of people from all over the South to work in the many war industries in and near the city. With housing scarce many families with homes rented out rooms to newcomers. Mama and Daddy welcomed our cousins and friends from rural areas around Atlanta so we frequently had someone moving in or out of our house. I enjoyed every minute of it as it kept life interesting and exciting. It may have been those years that planted the seeds of change in my mind that bloomed so profusely the rest of my life.

There were neighborhood elementary schools for kindergarten through sixth grade and several junior high schools for grades seven through nine scattered throughout the city. There were only four high schools - Girls High, Boys High, Tech High for boys and Commercial, for boys and girls wanting a business oriented education.

World War II ended when I was fourteen and I headed off to Girls High for tenth grade with mixed feelings. Insecure and self conscious, I didn't know who I was nor who I wanted to be when I grew up, not that I gave it much thought. I just assumed I'd grow up, fall in love, get married, have a family and live happily ever after. Girls came to Girls High from all over the city so "school friends" remained just that. Seeing each other outside of school would have been difficult. We all rode buses and streetcars from every direction to get to Girls High. Most girls had the same sort of trip I did. I rode a bus five miles downtown then transferred to a streetcar for another four mile ride to Girls High. After getting off the streetcar I walked the last three blocks. The trip took an hour. Girls High was a large beautiful building built in a period of prosperity after World War I. A few years ago while it was being converted into condominiums I visited it and was given a tour. It is still a beautiful building inside and out

Attending school there was a pleasure. The year I was in tenth grade the only sport offered was archery and that didn't interest me. I was there to get my education, not to have fun. That year Grandma Sexton died but she was not a warm, loving hands-on grandmother to me; she had several grandchildren by the time I was born and her death did not disrupt my life. The other significant event was that we had a bus strike that practically shut down the city. Schools were still open, however, and when I couldn't catch a ride with a friend whose parent was driving, I rode my bicycle about ten miles to school.

My life changed in a big way for eleventh grade. In June 1946 Lillian's husband, Elmo, was killed in a plane crash on Daytona Beach. He had been discharged from the Army Air Corps less than a year before and he and Lillian were living in Starke, Florida with Ken, almost three, and Billy, sixteen months old. Elmo had recently qualified for his private pilot's license. He and his best friend flew to Daytona Beach to have lunch with Elmo's boss. After lunch they climbed back into the small plane they had rented to fly home and a short time later crashed on Daytona Beach. Elmo and his friend died in the crash. No one on the ground was hurt. I remember every detail of that day because it was the first time death had so closely touched my life.

Maxine came running down to Chandler Park, near our home, screaming and crying. She was thirteen and the only one home when the call came from Florida. I was at the park with my ten-year-old brother Jimmy and a couple of friends. Loving Elmo very much I couldn't imagine our lives without him and thoughts of Ken and Billy growing up without a daddy seemed more than I could bear. But bear it we had to and when Lillian decided she would stay in Starke and take over management of the Park Theatre, I decided I'd stay with her and help with Ken and Billy.

36

Mama and Daddy were glad that Lillian and the boys wouldn't be alone in Florida.

Starke was a very small town, around 5,000 people. It was easy to get acquainted and starting with the girl next door who was my age, I soon had a lot of friends. We walked all over town, to school, to football and basketball games and to the old USO Building for Friday night dances. We walked to the movies just a few blocks away but parents were generous with their cars so we could drive to one of several lakes for swimming or, with dates, we'd drive to a nearby town for bowling. I loved Starke and thrived in it. I started dating but we always went places in a group as that was more fun. Robert, one of my friends, taught me to drive and at the age of sixteen I logged a lot of miles on rural two-lane highways in central Florida with Ken and Billy in the back seat.

Right after school started I tried out to be a majorette and was accepted. I enjoyed that immensely. We marched with the high school band, not only at football games but also in every holiday parade in town. I was pleasantly surprised when someone put my name up for "Football Queen" and jars with my name and picture were placed in stores. Donations collected benefited the football team and being a new girl in town I had no expectations of winning. There were several candidates and I was pleased when I became first runner-up on the Queen's float at Homecoming. I didn't understand a thing about the game of football but that didn't stop me from yelling myself hoarse at the games.

Fortunate to be taken into a group of girls who were lifelong friends, four of them became my friends and we have stayed close for more than sixty years. Since I was babysitting Ken and Billy we had a lot of fudge making parties at my house, sometimes just girls or other times boys came too. Lillian bought me a phonograph for my sixteenth birthday in December and we'd play records and dance. After Lillian went to work for the government in Green Cove Springs she was home nights so I was free to do things with my friends. I spent many nights with Idell, Vivian, Marian and Minnie Lou and made welcome by their families. Eleventh grade was the best of my high school years.

Gaining more confidence in myself, I became less shy. My friends and I volunteered to be chorus girls in a traveling road show that played in Starke a couple of evenings. Even though I couldn't carry a tune or so I've been told all my life, and wasn't a very good dancer I was accepted and we all had a lot of fun practicing and performing.

The summer of 1947 after eleventh grade was wonderful. Many days several of us road bikes eight miles to a lake where Idell's family had a lake house. We'd spend the day swimming, tanning and just having fun until we'd have to ride back to town. If it sounds idyllic, it was, and so different from life in Atlanta.

By the end of summer Lillian had decided to move back home to Atlanta. Working for the government she was able to transfer and had a good job waiting for her. That left me in a quandary. Mama and Daddy had bought a farm and moved back to their roots away from the city. They did not farm; Daddy commuted to Atlanta for his job as a policeman/detective. I did not want to live in the country so asked Evelyn if I could live with her for my senior year. She lived near our old home so I would be in the right school district. Awaiting orders to join Dean, in Germany, she wasn't sure she'd be there until my graduation but let me move in.

The school system in Atlanta had been totally revamped. The School Board must have spent the war years designing this grand plan to implement when the war was over! All of the junior high schools became high schools so I had to go back to Bass where I'd gone to junior high. I moved in with Evelyn and Butch, age five and Jane, just turning one. Violet, the Tuck family maid for many years lived with us, as did two young women who rented a room from Evelyn. It was a fun household, always something exciting going on. Wanda and Carolyn, the two renters, gave me their cast-off clothes which I appreciated very much.

Senior year was a big letdown after my wonderful junior year. I was back with many kids I'd known all my life from church and school, which was okay, but none of them were close friends. The school itself was learning its way as a high school so there were no traditions to uphold, everything was new to everyone, teachers and students alike, and sometimes the left hand didn't know what the right hand was doing. I tried out for majorette and made the squad. I enjoyed that again but was grieving for Florida and the friends left behind so I didn't get involved in other activities.

Before Christmas Evelyn received the orders she'd been waiting for and she and the children left for Germany. I moved in with Hazel and Jack and Jackie and David and Karen, born in August, 1947 just before school started. They lived a long way from Bass but I didn't want to change schools. I walked a mile to the Decatur streetcar, rode a few miles, walked a couple of blocks and got a bus to Bass. I didn't dare tell anyone at school where I was living because it was out of the district, in another town, actually. Every day I waited for someone to tap me on the shoulder and kick me out of school!

Happy to see the year end I proudly attended graduation ceremonies in the Civic Auditorium in downtown Atlanta. Mama and Daddy were the only family members there. Bass High had kept one part of the old Girl's High tradition. The girls all wore long formal white dresses and carried a large bouquet of red roses.

Not feeling at all like the "grown-up" I was now expected to be, I knew my "real life" was about to begin and it was all up to me.

*1949*

# Chapter Eight

## Single in Atlanta
### 1948 - 1950

*T*he Monday after graduating high school in June 1948 I rode the Decatur streetcar to downtown Atlanta carrying the Sunday Atlanta Journal classifieds with a few ads circled. The first place I went was Liberty Mutual Insurance Company. After telling the receptionist I was looking for a job I was invited in for an interview that ended with my being offered a job as a typist making $30 a week. Hazel had told me that $25 a week would be a good starting salary so I was thrilled to be offered more and accepted the job to start the next day. When I got home and told Hazel the good news she was happy for me and impressed that I would be making $30 a week. She said I could start paying $10 a week room and board and that was fine with me. I expected that because I had been raised knowing that once I finished school I would have to be self-supporting and Hazel and Jack had been generous with me all of my life.

I wished I'd been heading to the University of Georgia in Athens but there was no way that was possible. My parents couldn't afford to pay for college and if there was college counseling available in my senior year I was not aware of it and, to my knowledge, there was no such thing as financial aid. If you went to college you paid for it or Uncle Sam paid for it for returning veterans and they deserved it. Some students worked their way through college but having grown up during the depression and World War II I don't think I knew that was a possibility. So I did what I had to do – got a job.

About a month after I started working Liberty Mutual moved into a new building they'd built about three miles from downtown, across the street from the Biltmore Hotel – the ritziest hotel in

41

Atlanta and maybe in the South. Shortly after we moved there was a company picnic at Chastain Park. A large assortment of food and soft drinks and beer awaited us. We played coed softball and I had a good time. I was only seventeen and did not drink and even if I'd wanted to I thought beer smelled so bad I wouldn't have been able to get it close enough to my nose to drink it. A girl my age in my department drank too much beer and ended up needing to be taken home. A young man who worked in a different department had been paying some attention to both of us that afternoon and he volunteered to take Jeanine home and asked me to go along and assist him, which I did.

His nickname was Tat - the first three letters in his long German name. He was tall, thin, had blonde hair and wore glasses, – very ordinary looking. He was nothing like the boys I'd always liked but he was nice and talked about playing tennis which was something I wanted to learn. He'd gone to Georgia Tech for two years and had been in the Army for a short stint so seemed quite sophisticated to me. Soon after the company picnic Tat left for a vacation in Texas and Mexico. He sent me two or three post cards which surprised me and when he came home he gave me a beautiful gold pin he'd purchased in Mexico. I still have it. He asked to take me to dinner and we began dating. We'd talk on the phone on the nights we didn't go out and I'd keep "My Happiness" playing over and over again on my phonograph until one night my brother-in-law, Jack asked me to please stop! It was driving him crazy!

I'd been raised in a time and place when people married young so the only expectation I had for my life was that I'd get married and have a family. In the meantime I was waiting for that dream man to come and sweep me off my feet. Fantasizing about traveling as much as possible I wanted to see the world but I had no real vision of life after marriage except to live happily ever after.

Tat fit perfectly into that scenario. Early in the fall just before he left Atlanta for Louisville, Kentucky to begin a training course that would enable him to climb the insurance company ladder, he asked me to marry him and I said "Yes!" Hazel was the only one I told as there was no money for an engagement ring which Tat said he'd give me at Christmas time when he came home for the holidays. We would wait and announce it then.

Tat wrote almost daily for a few weeks and called now and then but in November the letters slowed to a trickle and the calls stopped altogether. I sensed something was wrong but preferred to live in denial. When Tat never would tell me the time his train would arrive from Kentucky so I could meet him at the station, I had to face the truth. On the day the trainees returned to the office, he came in with the group, went around greeting everyone and finally came by my desk and said "Hi. I'll call you tonight." He called and then picked me up and gave me an impersonal Christmas present. He said he'd be too busy with family and wouldn't have time to see me again. So there I was, just turned eighteen and my heart was broken.

Bernice, a girl I worked with, and I decided to rent an apartment with Lillian. Ken, six, and Billy, four, were living with Mama and Daddy during the week and spent weekends with Lillian. We found a nice apartment in Kirkwood, not too far from where I'd grown up. Lillian had a large bedroom she shared with Ken and Billy on weekends. Bernice and I shared a small bedroom and I soon tired of her and was glad when she decided to move back home. When I'd been with Liberty Mutual a year and had a week's vacation coming I talked Bernice into going with me to St. Simon's Island, off the southeast coast of Georgia. I'd read about it in the society columns all my life. That was where Atlanta's rich and famous had vacation homes or at least spent time there and I fantasized about rubbing shoulders with them. I didn't.

One week a major airline was interviewing for stewardesses, as they were known then. One lunch hour I went across the street to the Biltmore Hotel, stood in line and was called in for an interview. Being an airline stewardess was at least one dream I'd had since I was very young. The interviewer seemed to like me but I was only eighteen and the airlines had recently raised the required age to twenty-one and preferred girls with college educations. The interviewer told me to get some college and come back when I was twenty-one. I was disappointed but decided I'd start college at night and if I was still single at twenty-one I'd go back and interview again.

After a year or so with Liberty Mutual I knew I could make more money so started reading the want ads again. I got a job with another insurance company, Royal Liverpool Group. I typed letters for executives in the office that they recorded on a Dictaphone cylinder. I had the "player" into which I'd insert the cylinder, put on the earphones, turn it on and type what I heard. I was back in an office in the Healey Building right downtown, just where I'd started from with Liberty Mutual and I liked my new job much better. The office was smaller and I started making some good friends.

I still didn't date much. I was extremely picky about who I'd date and my aspirations were so high I even went so far as to say that if a man liked me, then I probably wouldn't like him! Does that tell you something about my self-esteem?

A few of us in the office hung out together sometimes after work or on weekends. Once a man came from the New York office to work in Atlanta for two weeks. He was very attractive and all of the single girls were trying to get his attention. One night after work several of us went out for a drink. I was still drinking cokes and I was shocked when I discovered his girlfriend was traveling with him! That was something I'd never heard of before! Southern girls didn't do things like that, at least to my knowledge. His girl friend was attractive, vivacious, sophisticated and everything else I wanted to be! Oh, how I envied her! To have the confidence to travel with a man and be totally open about it! Her name was Tucker Lane which I thought was beautiful and I've never forgotten it or the situation. I had a lot to learn about "real life."

A year or so later when the man came back to Atlanta he invited me to dinner. We had a nice dinner but on the way home he kept stopping the car and I had to keep fighting him off. I had a lot of experiences like that; it seemed if a man bought you dinner he felt entitled to something more. It made me feel bad about myself thinking somehow it must be my fault. I tried to screen my dates as well as I could but I didn't have much experience to use in making judgments.

I became friends with two young women in the office. Nita's older sister was a registered nurse in a private mental hospital. One day I was with Nita and we stopped by the hospital. For years I thought I'd like to be a psychiatrist or psychologist so I was interested in seeing the hospital. I began volunteering there on Saturdays and learned a lot about mental illness.

One of the patients was an old man with dementia. I was asked to keep him in his room until his doctor came to visit but it was difficult. Most of the patients had manic-depressive (now called bi-polar) disease and electro convulsive treatment was the primary treatment along with insulin shock. I helped with the ECT. It took four people to hold the patient's arms and legs while the shock was administered so he wouldn't injure himself while convulsing. Mostly I just talked with patients or played games with them or someone would play the piano and we'd sing and I'd try to get patients involved.

When Nita's family moved to Dayton, Ohio, Sue and I drove up with her. We spent the weekend in Dayton and enjoyed an evening out in a Cincinnati hotel nightclub with Nita's brother. I had my first plane ride from Cincinnati to Atlanta – another first crossed off my list.

*Bett ~ 1952*

# Chapter Nine
## An Independent Young Woman
### 1950 - 1952

While working at Royal Liverpool Group I met Doris Williams, still a friend I see once in a while. She was from Mississippi, ambitious and attending the University of Georgia, Atlanta Division, two or three nights a week. I registered and started my college education.

Two other girls working in the office, Betty D. and Bootsie D., became good friends. One night we planned to play bridge at Bootsie's but our fourth player cancelled. Betty prevailed upon her brother, Corwin, (pronounced "Co'hen" in the South) to fill in. He did and we had a real good time. Before the evening was over he asked me if I'd like to go deep-sea fishing in Panama City on an upcoming weekend with some friends of his. Of course I said "Yes." I never turned down a chance to see some place new or do something I'd never done before. Since I worked with his sister I felt he was safe.

Eight of us went to Panama City and Corwin was the only one I'd met before. They were all nice and fun to be with and we had a great time – except for the fishing. The night before we'd partied and Corwin had too much to drink – as a matter of fact he probably was still drunk when we carried him to the fishing boat at 6AM. Commercial fishing boats always leave the dock early for some reason! Corwin was still having fun left over from the night before and kept getting his fishing line tangled with other more serious fishermen and I was afraid somebody was going to throw him overboard. I didn't worry about him very long as by the time we were ten minutes out in the ocean I wasn't feeling very well. I lay down on the engine cover that was large and warm and spent most of the day there. Every time I'd get up, I'd feel sick again so I didn't do any fishing.

Corwin and I continued dating and that summer I talked Bootsie into going to Miami Beach with me for a couple of weeks. Bootsie was from an upper middle class background, went to private schools and lived in an affluent area and she was a bit of a snob. At the train station as we were about to leave Atlanta Bootsie spotted some friends who were traveling first class (we weren't) and she was uptight and afraid of being seen.

After a train ride of sixteen hours, arriving at our hotel on Miami beach we were not disappointed. It was beautiful and our accommodations were spacious and comfortable. Besides the hotel pool and the beach, we explored nearby neighborhoods and I fantasized about owning one of those houses someday. Bootsie knew a couple of girls in Miami who'd moved there from Atlanta and we spent some time with them and boys they knew. We tried new foods and drinks and enjoyed the entire experience. I felt totally grown up and in charge of my life and it was a good feeling!

Corwin talked us into cutting short our vacation in Miami and meeting him in Daytona Beach for three days and he'd drive us home. He was a really nice young man and a hard worker. He owned his own company, a beauty supply business, drove a big new Mercury automobile and liked to go places and do fun things. We had a wonderful time in Daytona Beach enjoying the sand and surf as well as a beachside bar where there was always a fun crowd hanging out. Bootsie really let her hair down and had as much fun as the rest of us.

Corwin and I dated the rest of the summer and into the fall and once he surprised me when he turned to me and said, for no reason that I could see, "You'd be hard to live with." I was so surprised that I didn't think to ask him if was thinking of trying it! Before I was married I heard that same sentiment from a couple of other fellows and I've always wondered what there was about me that gave them that impression. I thought I was easy to get along with! Many years later a southern man in my writing group suggested it was because I was so independent and in 1950 southern men didn't want independent wives. Maybe he's right!

48

That fall I left Royal Liverpool Group for a job making a lot more money as an Executive Secretary for the General Manager of Acme Fast Freight. The first time I'd given notice at Royal Liverpool Group that I was leaving for a better paying job, the big boss called me in and asked how much I'd be making. I told him and he asked if I'd stay if they matched the salary so I stayed. We went through the same scenario the second time but he said they couldn't pay that much so they'd have to let me go.

I had been trying for a couple of years to talk a girl friend, any girl friend, into moving with me to another city – almost any city! I didn't especially want to go to New York City where many girls from Atlanta moved but I would have. I was considering cities such as Richmond, Virginia or New Orleans, Louisiana or Miami. No one would ever go with me and I was not brave enough to strike out alone.

By 1951 Evelyn and Dean had returned from Germany with Butch, Jane and a new addition to the family, two-year-old Mike. Stationed at Fort Campbell, Kentucky, about a six hour drive from Atlanta, various family members drove up to see them and just about every time there was room in the car for me. I kind of liked those handsome 2$^{nd}$ Lieutenants so went as often as I could. One of the Lieutenants invited me to come up for a special dance so I borrowed a formal dress from Betty D. and Mama and I went up on the train. I had a wonderful time and knew I'd like living a military life.

One time Bill and Georgia and I drove to Ft. Campbell for a weekend. We left on Friday directly from work. We were all on tight budgets so Bill didn't stop for dinner. It was around midnight when we got to Evelyn and Dean's quarters on base and the first thing Bill did was go to the kitchen and open the refrigerator. We all heard him say "What the hell?!" He couldn't believe his eyes as there was only a bottle of water and a head of lettuce inside! We all laughed except, possibly Bill, as Evelyn explained that it was the weekend before payday and they were broke so they were eating all their meals at the Officers Club so they could charge them.

By June 1952 I'd been out of high school four years, had held jobs at three different companies, had traveled to several new places and done at least a few things I hadn't done before. Does deep-sea fishing count? The lease on our apartment was up and Lillian rented a smaller apartment so she could live alone for a while except for weekends when Ken and Billy were there. I moved in with Mama and Daddy for the summer so I could save money to buy a car.

Before summer was over I bought my first car. It was a 1950 Plymouth and even though I was 21 years old I needed a cosigner at the bank. I knew Daddy wouldn't sign as he'd been burned by a relative or friend or two during the depression and had told us all "Don't ask." My brother Bill cosigned for the loan and I got the car. I was so proud! Daddy had retired from the police force and was working for the Atlanta Journal. After picking up the car I drove to the newspaper and picked up Daddy and nervously drove us home. I was so happy I'd been able to buy a car on my own never once thinking I wouldn't get to keep it long.

A couple of months later I hitched my wagon to a dream and followed Evelyn and Dean from Ft. Campbell, Kentucky to Albuquerque, New Mexico. It was amazing how many people in Atlanta thought I was moving to a foreign country! As long time readers of New Mexico Magazine know, that's still true today.

*Santa Fe N.M 1952*

# Chapter Ten

## New Mexico
## Land of Enchantment
### 1952 - 1954

Near the end of August 1952 I left my childhood home and family and never looked back. Thrilled and excited to be moving to a state I'd barely heard of and never even thought of visiting, I could hardly contain my joy. Driving from Atlanta to Kentucky alone, my fantasies of my new life danced in my head. Heading west my Plymouth followed close behind Evelyn and Dean's Buick. Butch, Jane and Mike took turns riding with me but it was soon apparent that four-year-old Mike got carsick every time he was in my car! Apparently my car didn't ride as smoothly as their family's Buick. We spent two nights en route, the last night in Amarillo, Texas. I was astounded when I realized the land in southwest Oklahoma and the Texas panhandle was so flat that those lights I'd been seeing for more than two hours were the lights of Amarillo! The West was very different from the South, and that was just the beginning.

Route 66 was the primary east-west highway across the United States. It varied from two lanes to four and even some sections of divided highway. Groupings of four, five or six small red signs with white lettering at the top of a stake, one after the other, stretched out along the highway. Read together they created a jingle:

> *He tried To cross As fast train neared*
> *Death didn't draft him*
> *He Volunteered Burma-Shave*

*The ladies Take one whiff And purr--*
*It's no wonder Men prefer*
*Burma-Shave Lotion.*

There were dozens of these jingles as those signs marched right across the country. There were also signs enticing us to stop and see man-sized jack rabbits, Gila Monsters and other things I'd never heard of. Roadside shops were filled with Indian artifacts, many made in Japan. The further west we got the more different it was from home. Motels of every description lined the highway in small towns. Most were old court-style motels built before the war – individual cabins grouped around a center court, some made of logs, some fake tepees.

Traveling across eastern New Mexico we got our first glimpses of the exotic cultures of the southwest. The fascinating Native American and Spanish cultures we encountered opened up new worlds and presented the adventure of discovery, from old Indian Pueblos to the plazas found in the center of many small towns.

Route 66 wound its way through the Sandia Mountains and Tijeras Canyon east of Albuquerque. When we reached the western end of the canyon I saw the city spread out before me, sparkling like a magnificent jewel in the brilliant sunshine. I could also see miles and miles of empty, flat land to the north, south and west and I was filled with joy and anticipation. Here I was on the precipice of a brand new chapter in my life. I've felt that same joy and excitement with every new place I've visited or lived during the sixty years since. My mind filled with images of adventures and new experiences awaiting me. My enthusiasm was boundless and that flat brown desert was beautiful to my eyes that saw everything in Technicolor.

My first lesson in New Mexico came the next morning at breakfast. I was surprised potatoes were served for breakfast! Who'd ever heard of such a thing? And they'd never heard of grits that people in the South ate for breakfast. Although Denver claims the title, "Mile High City" much of Albuquerque is also a mile high. The change in elevation made us all want to sleep through the first few days that happened to be Labor Day Weekend but I was far too eager to go exploring and that's what we did.

Albuquerque was a medium size city of approximately 100,000 people. The University of New Mexico was located there and a large Hispanic population, descendants of New Mexico's first settlers when it belonged to Mexico. Cultural activities were plentiful, even opera in Santa Fe, as well as Indian reservations in every direction.

I fell in love with Albuquerque at first sight. We went to Old Town and saw real, live Indians for the first time. Some were costumed and doing native dances in the plaza. Indian vendors sold beautifully handcrafted silver and turquoise jewelry, hand-woven rugs with unusual designs, soft leather moccasins and the most beautiful pottery I'd ever seen. For the first time in my life I began noticing, enjoying and appreciating works of art of all kinds. When you live there you soon realize how colorful New Mexico is. What at first might seem to be varying shades of tan, changes mightily as the sun moves from east to west. It became a habit to look east at the Sandia Mountains during the last hour before sunset. Their color changes from moment to moment until you've seen every hue and shade in the entire spectrum of colors. Then if you turn and look west you'll see a spectacular red, orange, pink and gold sunset.

Evelyn and Dean soon found a house to rent and first thing after we moved in I went job-hunting. My first stop was the employment office for Sandia Corporation, a firm that employed hundreds of people on Sandia Base where Dean was stationed. The woman in the employment office seemed to take particular notice of my hat and white gloves and asked where I was from. In the South ladies always wore hats and white gloves when they went downtown or anywhere they were dressed up but I learned that dress in Albuquerque was much more casual. I was disappointed to learn everyone who worked for Sandia Corporation had to have a high-level security clearance called a "Q" (for queen) and it would take sixty to ninety days. I completed the application then headed downtown to look for an interim job. I was hired to start the next day as a clerk typist at an insurance agency, not mentioning I had put in my application at Sandia Corporation.

Salaries were much lower than in Atlanta and I worried about the $150 gasoline credit card bill I knew was coming and due upon receipt. I also needed to pay for my room and board. Deciding I needed a second job I went to the largest department store and inquired about a part time job. They wouldn't need any part-timers until the holiday season, so that was out. As a last resort I took my car, that I'd had less than five months, to a used car lot and sold it for enough to cover the bank balance and the gasoline bill. Fortunately, Albuquerque had an excellent transit bus system.

I'd only worked at the insurance agency a month when I received a call from Sandia Corporation that they had a job for me. Mr. Bray, the owner of the insurance agency, was furious that I was leaving so soon. Within a year I became friends with his son and son's wife, who were my age. I met them through a mutual friend. By that time, Homer Bray (the father) had been killed in a plane crash that had taken off from the Albuquerque airport and crashed into the Sandia Mountains.

Sandia Corporation was affiliated with the Atomic Energy Commission (AEC) and worked closely with Los Alamos, fifty miles northwest, one of the secret places where the atomic bomb was developed. At Sandia Base most of the workers were behind big fences and had to show their ID's as they passed through guarded gates. The job I was called for was in the Employment Division outside the fenced-in areas so I started before my "Q" clearance came through.

As receptionist, I greeted job seekers with appointments with an interviewer, passed out applications to others, answered the phone and typed letters for the interviewers. I thought everyone I met was very friendly when they asked where I was from. Soon it dawned on me that I must have a pronounced southern drawl. Many times after I'd answered the phone there would be a very long pause. Frequently the caller would then say "What part of the South are you from?" By the time I left two years later I had gotten pretty good at identifying what part of the country other people were from by the way they spoke. Sandia invited people, almost all men, with certain job skills from all over the country to come for interviews so I was meeting people from many states every day. I really enjoyed that job.

One thing about the job I didn't like very much was my boss. He reminded me of a little banty rooster. He was small and strutted around and acted as if he were very important. I almost expected him to crow any minute! A vendor drove by our building at the same time every morning and usually one person from our small area would take orders and go outside and buy donuts. Everyone in our area took turns. When the boss started ordering a donut I asked him when he wanted to take his turn. He thought I was kidding but I wasn't! My friend Betty, his secretary, took his turn as well as her own; otherwise when it was my turn I refused to buy him a donut. It was a matter of principle. Years later when I thought about that I was appalled at my behavior and that I had such nerve, especially since I needed the job!

We'd been in Albuquerque about a month when Dean told me his secretary was my age and he'd asked her if she'd like to meet me and maybe introduce me to some of her friends. How could she say "no" to her boss?

Susie was very attractive and engaged to Jim, a handsome young man who was soon getting out of the Army and going to the University of Colorado Dental School. Susie was also sweet and nice. She and Jim came over one evening bringing an Air Force Lieutenant, whose name was Ted. There was a nice civilian club on the base and we went there for dinner and dancing and I really fell for Ted. He was just my type – grew up in Florida, went to the University of Florida at Gainesville where he knew a couple of my Starke friends, then on to MIT where he earned a degree in Naval Architecture. He was tall, nice looking, friendly and an easy conversationalist in any situation. Ted and I started dating regularly and through Susie and Jim met several other people so we always had a fun group to be with. I was falling in love.

# Chapter Eleven

## New Adventures

### 1952 - 1954

*T*ed was an explorer and mountain climber. Growing up in Florida he spent summers in Colorado but had not spent any time in New Mexico. He and I and sometimes others drove as many back roads as we could within a hundred mile radius of Albuquerque. We were fascinated by historic churches and ghost towns that we came across. We went exploring every weekend until the snow got deep enough in the mountains to ski. The first time we went skiing I had no idea what to wear.

The deepest snow I'd ever seen was about one foot in Atlanta so I knew nothing about ski clothes or equipment. Evelyn still had a one-piece turquoise snowsuit she'd had made in Germany so I wore that. Ted didn't say anything but I bet he was embarrassed to be seen with me! I sure did stand out on the bunny slope! A few days later I shopped for clothes and equipment at a local ski shop. I was outfitted!

We went skiing every Saturday and Sunday all winter. We skied at La Madera in the Sandia Mountains overlooking Albuquerque, at Santa Fe, at Taos and several Colorado ski areas including Aspen. Once when we stopped for hot chocolate at the café on the mountain top two famous movie stars, Lana Turner and Lex Barker came in. When we left the café to resume skiing I noticed that Lana Turner rode the chair lift down but Lex Barker was a terrific skier and when I fell right in front of him he stopped and helped me up.

Ted and I once drove all night to Alta, a ski area not far from Salt Lake City. Ted was sleeping and I was driving about 2 AM when we ran out of gas. I could see the gas indicator going down but southeastern Utah in the early 1950's was desolate and we would drive for many miles without passing anything man-made except the highway. We had passed only one gas station after we last filled the tank and it was closed.

When I woke Ted and told him we were out of gas he was so angry he didn't believe me that I'd not passed an open station and on the return trip made a point of stopping at that one station and asking if they'd been open Friday night. Thank goodness they said "No." A truck driver stopped and drove us to the next town. The station there had someone drive us back to the car with a can of gasoline. For trips to Colorado and Utah we'd leave Friday after work, drive all night and get to the ski areas just as they were opening. We'd do a quick change of clothes and hit the slopes. I couldn't get enough of it. I was having more fun than I'd ever had in my life. The two winters I lived in New Mexico we skied from Thanksgiving into May, enjoying May Day races in Santa Fe.

Two or three nights a week I attended classes at the University of New Mexico working towards a degree in psychology. We'd only been in Albuquerque a few months when my brother-in-law, Dean, was transferred to Virginia and the family packed up and moved. I loved my life in New Mexico so I approached the University Housing Office and asked about moving into a dorm. Since I was twenty-two they gave me a room in the graduate dorm and I lived there a few months.

I met Jackie and her handsome boyfriend, Bill, skiing at La Madera. Over dinner Jackie and I started talking. Her parents had bought a travel trailer a few months earlier and taken off for California. She was home alone taking care of things and she'd just received a letter from her mother telling her to get some roommates and start making the mortgage payment for rent because they were having so much fun they didn't know when or if they'd ever be home!

Jackie asked if I'd like to move in with her. It was a nice house, well located, so I jumped at the chance. Her brother was in Korea and we even had his car to drive. Things were great! Bill broke his leg near the end of winter and was on crutches. He was in the Air Force but had no duty except for his doctor's appointments so Bill moved his things from the BOQ (Bachelor

Officers' Quarters) to our house and pretty much lived with us. Jackie and I had the two bedrooms on the main floor and Bill had a room in the finished basement. This was the '50's in every way! Unless we were off doing other things we had a party every Friday and/or Saturday night at our house.

We soon took in a third "official" roommate, Dana, to share my room with twin beds. Dana was beautiful, sophisticated and smart so Jackie and I were afraid she'd take our boyfriends but we needn't have worried. Dana was also nice and had a boyfriend of her own. She ended up becoming a math teacher and marrying a professor at the U of NM. By splitting expenses three ways, or four when Bill was there, we had more spending money. I'm amazed that I was able to go and do as much as I did. Thank goodness there were no credit cards in those days!

Another new experience was camping which we did at the Grand Canyon, at Mesa Verde, Colorado and near the headwaters of the Red River in northern New Mexico. We went to Gallup for the largest Indian Pow Wow and festival in the west. Unable to get motel reservations we camped out there also. When we were at Red River we rented horses and rode for several hours, my first time riding horseback. After we returned the horses we drove to Santa Fe where we had tickets for the biggest rodeo of the year - my first rodeo. By the time we reached the fairgrounds where the rodeo would be held I was so sore I could barely get out of the car, much less walk and then sit down! I had to lean against a post to watch the rodeo as I was too sore to sit, but I had a good time anyway.

Christmas 1953 was approaching. I'd saved my vacation and managed to get two weeks off so I could go "home" for Christmas. It'd been sixteen months since I'd seen my family. I'd missed them and was eager to visit with them all. While in Atlanta I took an overnight train trip to Virginia Beach where Evelyn's family was living. It had been almost a year since I'd seen them so we had a happy reunion and Evelyn took me sightseeing in the area where America began, Jamestown, Yorktown and Williamsburg, Virginia. Flying was costly in 1953 but I managed a one-way ticket to Atlanta. For the return to Albuquerque I arranged to ride with an Air Force friend who drove to South Carolina for Christmas. We

60

met at the bus station in Decatur, an Atlanta suburb near my family home. Miles was right on time and after my brother, Bill, looked him over they stored my bags in the trunk and we headed west.Taking turns driving, we drove straight through to Albuquerque.

As much as I'd enjoyed seeing my family I recognized I'd never live in the South again. Feeling much more at home in the Southwest, I was an outdoor girl and appreciated the active lifestyle I lived there. I liked the climate and felt more joyful and free to be me! People and attitudes seemed more relaxed and less judgmental and rigid than in the Deep South. My dreams and my hope were to continue experiencing other places and bloom where I was planted.

I wasn't dating Ted exclusively but dated several young men, mostly Air Force but a couple of them were engineers from Los Alamos. In those days most dates consisted of dinner and dancing at the Civilian Club on the base or one of the Officers' Clubs or one of the private clubs in the area. There were also a few nightclubs around town that we'd sometimes go to. I drank moderately and never got in trouble with it. Ted was the one in my heart. I knew I cared more for him than he cared for me. I didn't live in denial but accepted the relationship for what it was. Before the end of the second winter he was no longer taking me skiing and the only time we saw each other was by accident. He was dating a Major's daughter who was, by background and education, more in the same "class" as Ted. I always felt I didn't measure up to him. He ended up marrying the Major's daughter the summer of 1954 after he was discharged from the Air Force and they went back to Boston when Ted was accepted to graduate school at Harvard.

Jackie had been in a similar situation with Bill. He had taken Jackie home to meet his affluent family in Larchmont, New York and the visit had not gone well. When Jackie attended the University of New Mexico she had joined the Delta Delta Delta Sorority, (Tri Delts) the same sorority Bill's mother belonged to, so Jackie thought they'd hit it off. After she and Bill returned from New York Bill was discharged from the Air Force and went back to his family home.

Things had cooled a lot between Bill and Jackie but one way or another they worked things out and Jackie started planning their wedding. She knew Bill's parents weren't coming but she and Bill were married that summer of 1954. Dana and I rented a house a couple of blocks from our home with Jackie. Jackie's parents came home, gave Jackie whatever she wanted from the house, sold the rest and put the house on the market for sale. Immediately after the wedding Jackie and Bill left for Royal Oaks, Michigan where Bill had a job as a chemical engineer.

In August 1954 Mama and Daddy and Maxine and Danny stopped to visit me for a few days on their way to California. It was fun showing them some of the places I loved – Old Town in Albuquerque and "The Pink Adobe" in Santa Fe where we always ate after skiing.

The next month, at the age of twenty-three, after exactly two wonderful years in Albuquerque I bid farewell to many friends as I boarded the Santa Fe Chief with my trunk. Sitting in the Club Car watching western New Mexico and Arizona fly by the window I reminisced about friends and good times and wondered what kind of life I'd have in California. Evelyn and Dean met me at the station in Victorville, in the high desert a hundred miles east of Los Angeles. I hadn't found my dream man in New Mexico, how ironic that when I found him in California he was from New Mexico!

# Chapter Twelve

## California, Here I Am!

### 1954 - 1956

Wow! California! Hollywood! Malibu! The Pacific Ocean! The land where oranges and grapefruits grow in your backyard, not in the local grocery store. The land of perpetual sunshine; the land where dreams come true. I'm eager to partake of it all.

Victorville is in the "high desert," not actually in the Mojave Desert but close. Continuing west on Highway 66, over the San Bernardino Mountains and down Cajon Pass, twenty-five miles west of Victorville takes us to the "low desert" small towns of San Bernardino and Riverside with their seemingly unending citrus groves. Another sixty miles west on Highway 66 through Pasadena, home of the Rose Bowl, through Los Angeles and on to Santa Monica where I stepped into the Pacific Ocean.

In the mountains about an hour's drive from Victorville is Lake Arrowhead, a beautiful resort town frequented by movie stars. There are also several ski areas so I'll be able to indulge my passion for skiing. Every weekend Evelyn and Dean and the kids and I go exploring and I rave about the beauty of it all until Dean is sick of hearing it.

Victorville was a very small town of about 7,000 people. We lived in base quarters at George AFB eight miles from town. I started working at the Bank of America as a Teller and making friends with local people. Evelyn and Dean took me to parties at the Officer's Club and I began meeting and dating young Air Force Officers. I met a girl a couple of years younger than me who lived a few blocks from us. Donna's father was manager of the Base Exchange (BX) so they were allowed to live on base. Donna and I became good friends and the family took me with them one weekend to Ventura, a small town on the coast north of Los

Angeles, and Ojai, a spectacularly beautiful community in the low Pacific Coast Range east of Ventura. I never dreamed then that forty years later I'd live a little further north on California's scenic Hwy. 1 on the central coast and would drive through Ventura and Ojai many times.

Two of my best friends at the bank were Candy and Darlene. Candy was a twenty-year-old local girl with beautiful auburn hair and brown eyes. A year after we met she married an Air Force pilot and left for North Africa so I bought her car – a Willys. Darlene's husband was in the Air Force serving a year in Korea. She was happy her husband was gone and she was free at last. She went to Las Vegas and divorced him six weeks before he came home. Darlene had more money than I did plus a car so she and I did a lot of exploring together – Palm Springs, Big Bear, Las Vegas and other places.

Terry, a college student, came to work at the bank for the summer in 1955. Jenny and her husband, Wendy, became good friends. Jenny, Wendy, Terry and I and two or three others who worked at the bank began driving to Los Angeles and Hollywood for dinner and to hear some of the jazz greats. Sarah Vaughn, with her incredible sultry voice was my favorite. Stan Getz, one of the all-time best tenor saxophone players, was always outstanding. We'd leave immediately after work, drive down what we called the "back way" through the mountains and the San Fernando Valley and directly into Hollywood. It was a hundred miles and a two-hour drive but being young that never bothered us. Some of us would get to sleep on the way home.

Taking classes at Victor Valley Community College on the base two or three evenings a week, I soon began taking flying lessons through the base flying club. The flying club had two planes, a Taylorcraft and an Aeronica Chief. My AF Captain instructor gave me lessons in both. I loved flying! It was fantastic up there and I felt as close to being a bird as I ever would. The planes were kept at El Mirage, a privately owned airfield about twenty miles from George AFB. Several people went there to check out in sail planes. We would watch sail planes being towed up and then cut loose – now that is really flying! I never had the opportunity, or didn't look for one, to try that.

64

Another thing we did that was fun was ride in a long go-cart type vehicle with a sail mounted on it. When the wind was blowing, which is most of the time in the desert, we could skim over the dry lakebed at a high rate of speed – scary and thrilling! By the time I had ten or twelve hours of flying instruction and was ready to solo, the flying club went broke and had to sell the planes so that was the end of my flying dream.

My first trip to Las Vegas was in 1955. Darlene and I drove the hundred and fifty miles from Victorville and met two of my friends. Roy and Jim worked in Los Alamos, NM and were in Nevada for underground testing of nuclear bombs. The fellows picked us up at our motel and we set out to see the "Strip." Las Vegas was a tiny town in 1955 with a downtown area embracing a few casinos. The "Strip" was six miles south and development was just beginning. There were about six or eight large beautiful hotels, each set on acreage far back from the road – the *Desert Inn, Sands, Flamingo, Dunes, Royal Nevada* and the *Sahara.*

Roy parked the car and we went into the Flamingo casino – the first I'd ever seen. Seeing the gaming tables and slot machines and bright colored neon lights flashing all around was magical. Best of all were two or three entertainment areas with continuous free shows. We had reservations in the main dining-show room for dinner. A steak dinner was about $15 each and the show was free. There were Hollywood headliners – Frank Sinatra at the Desert Inn and Dean Martin at the Flamingo. Later I saw him at the poker table and said, "Look! There's Dean Martin sitting there by the dealer!"

"He's not sitting down. He's standing," responded Jim. I was surprised at how short Dean Martin was.

At the Flamingo, Roy had good luck with his gambling money and made $200, a lot of money in 1955! For the rest of the evening he'd drive up to the entrance of various hotels and let the attendants park the car. For a few hours we felt like "big shots!" We went from hotel to hotel, doing a little gambling and seeing as many shows as we could. One of the boys said he'd teach me to

65

play Craps so I went to the dice table with him. I didn't understand the game at all. To keep it simple I'd just put a $2 chip down on the "come" or "don't come" line and sometimes the dealer would put chips on top of mine and sometimes he'd rake in my chips. Dice were passed around the table with each person rolling them until they shot craps – seven or eleven. When it was my turn to roll I said "No thank you."

"You roll those dice!" said the large gruff man standing next to me. He scared me so I rolled the dice and I rolled and rolled and rolled and people all around the table were getting excited and a lot of money was on the table and I didn't know what was happening. Finally, I crapped out, the dice moved on and I quickly left that table! I played a little roulette but mostly played nickel slot machines. The evening was fun, exciting and different from anything I'd ever experienced.

Next morning Darlene and I got up ready to head home. It was Sunday, the banks were closed and we didn't have enough money between us to buy gas. Darlene managed to get the home phone number for the manager of the Bank of America in Las Vegas. She called him and explained our predicament mentioning that we worked in the branch in Victorville and were good friends with the manager there. The Las Vegas manager kindly met us downtown and cashed a small check for us. Once we had a few dollars in our hands I was mad! I wanted to go back to those slot machines that took my money and get it back! Foolishly, Darlene agreed and we filled the car with gas then put the rest of our money into the slot machines so couldn't stop for even a little food or drink on the way home.

I'd been in California a year when in September 1955 Dean was transferred to Alaska and the family started packing to move. That meant another new adventure for me. I did not want to go to Alaska with them but I wanted to relocate to a larger city and closer to the beach. Evelyn went with me to look at apartments in

66

Hollywood and Westwood but I soon realized I couldn't afford to live in that area on my bank salary. I rented a little guest house in San Bernardino, just forty-five minutes from Victorville, and transferred to the Bank of America there.

San Bernardino was larger than Victorville but still a small city. The scent of orange blossoms permeated the air as the city was almost surrounded by vast acres of orange groves. The Bank of America was in the center of town so on my lunch hours it was easy to browse and shop. The best thing about it, though, was that it was close enough to Victorville that my friends could easily visit me.

# Part Two

## The Halsey Years

*Chuck - George AFB 1955*

# Chapter Thirteen

## 'The First Time
## Ever I Saw His Face'
### 1955

"*T*hat's my type!" I said to my co-worker, Anita, as the handsome 1st Lieutenant exited the bank where we worked. I usually worked at the downtown branch of the Bank of America in Victorville but occasionally filled in at the branch located on George AFB. It was January 1955 and I had been living in California with my sister Evelyn's family for four months. Every time I worked with Anita she pointed out Air Force men she thought looked perfect for me. My response was always "He's not my type." When Chuck Halsey came into the bank to open an account Anita waited on him. I was not busy with a customer but made myself appear busy and all of the time I was watching this very attractive man with silver wings on his left chest.

The next time I remember seeing Chuck was several months later at a party at the Officer's Club. My date was another pilot in Chuck's squadron, but I didn't know that then. As I was making my way to the ladies room I was about to pass a good-looking man and was surprised when he said "How was your flying today, Betty?" He looked vaguely familiar but I couldn't place him and wondered who he was and how he knew I'd been flying that day. Later I learned that Chuck was flying and towing gliders at El Mirage, a small desert airport where I was learning to fly. He had noticed me but I never remembered seeing him.

A few weeks later, Margaret Canberra, the woman who owned the airfield, came into the bank and got in my line. "Do you know Chuck Halsey?" she asked.

"I think I know who he is but don't really know him," I

responded.

"He wants to ask you out but he's afraid you're not interested."

"Tell him to ask," was my immediate response.

I noticed him immediately when Chuck came into the bank and stood in line at my window. While making a deposit he asked if I played bridge. "Yes, I do."

"Would you like to play with me and another couple Friday night? We'll play at their house in Apple Valley and have dinner there."

"That sounds like fun. What time?"

"I'll pick you up at 6:30. Is that okay?"

"I'll be ready."

So our first date was spent with Chuck's friends, Paul and Marian, having dinner and playing bridge. They were a very interesting couple. They had physically built their charming, small home themselves. We began playing every week alternating between their home and Chuck's place with Chuck preparing dinner.

Chuck drove a red Jaguar roadster with a wide leather belt with a silver buckle across the hood. Our second date he took me to sports car races at Torrey Pines, where the famous golf course is now located. After the races we had dinner at a beautiful, dimly lit restaurant in La Jolla. When we started talking about how many children we each wanted and similar topics, I knew right then I was going to marry this man. On the way home, driving through San Bernardino we were stopped by the CA. Highway Patrol. The officer said we were speeding. Chuck explained that he was just keeping up with traffic because his speedometer wasn't working. The officer was nice but gave him a ticket anyway which didn't dampen our spirits in the least.

By December 1955 we had been dating four months, my sister's family had been transferred to Alaska and I had moved down the mountain pass to live in San Bernardino. To celebrate my

72

twenty-fifth birthday, on the 9<sup>th</sup> of December, Chuck took me skiing at Mammoth Mountain with his brother and sister-in-law, Fryer and Glenna. When we returned we decorated his mobile home by putting lights and greenery around the front window. We bought a blowup Santa on skis but we didn't have a tree so we made one out of newspaper following directions we saw in a magazine. Christmas Day was merry and festive even though it was my first without any of my family. We brought out the Santa on skis every Christmas for the next twenty-five years and he's still part of my family's Christmas..

The day after Christmas we went skiing at Big Bear with Chuck wearing the ski sweater I'd given him. He gave me several small decorative items for the small cottage I rented in San Bernardino. They included a very large brandy snifter and a book for beginning writers. I had shared with him that I'd always wanted to write.

New Year's Eve, 1956 we had dinner at Apple Valley Inn, a popular place near Victorville, and then moved into the lounge for dancing. An Air Force man I knew but hadn't dated stopped by our table to wish us a "Happy New Year." He said he hadn't seen me for a while and heard that I had moved and asked for my new phone number. Feeling awkward I didn't know what to say but mumbled something about dating Chuck. After the lieutenant left it was almost midnight and Chuck and I got up to dance. While dancing he said in my ear "I'd marry you if you'd have me."

Surprised, all I could do was say, "What did you say?" Chuck repeated what he'd said and I kissed him and said "Yes, I'll marry you!"

"You'd better ask me tomorrow if I meant it," he responded with a big smile. The next day I made him confirm in the light of day and cold sober he did want to marry me. He wanted to wait and get married about September after he'd saved some money. I thought that was a good idea as I didn't have any money saved either and owed department stores about $600. His take-home pay as a 1<sup>st</sup> Lieutenant was $430 a month and he had already stated rather emphatically "My wife will never work!"

In early March we learned that Fryer was being transferred to Mississippi. Chuck and I wanted to be together without so much driving up and down Cajon Pass so we set a date of March 17th, St. Patrick's Day, to be married in Las Vegas. I worked in San Bernardino through March 16th. Chuck picked me up and almost delirious with joy the next day we were married. Fryer and Glenna and our bridge-playing friends, Paul and Marian, were with us. The ceremony was held in the "Little Church of the West" and we honeymooned for a couple of days at the Royal Nevada Hotel. For the wedding I wore a light blue sheath style dress overlaid with heavy white cotton lace for the happiest day of my life. I felt beautiful and joyous and very much in love.

Chuck had grown up in the small town of Belen, thirty miles south of Albuquerque. Not long after we married we drove to New Mexico so I could meet his stepfather, Ralph Sale, who had adopted Chuck when he was twelve. I'd met Chuck's mother a few months earlier when she came to California to visit him. While we were in New Mexico I introduced Chuck to a few of my friends in Albuquerque and we went skiing in Santa Fe.

We returned to California eager to begin the "Happily Ever After."

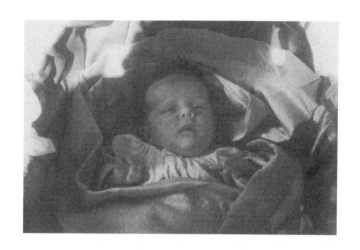

*Chipper - 3 weeks*

# Chapter Fourteen

## Happily Ever After
### 1956

Moving into Chuck's mobile home in a park three miles from George AFB, I believed crossing that threshold led to the fantasy life I'd dreamed of. The mobile home was nice but small, twenty-eight feet in length. I didn't see how I'd get my clothes in the closet with Chuck's but, of course, I did. The park was nicely landscaped, especially for being in the desert. The owners had planted shrubs and flowers for color. We had a small grassy area around our home and eventually we planted a few marigolds.

Not marrying until I was twenty-five I'd already been designated an "old maid" by my family so they were especially happy for me. Having spent time with Evelyn and Dean on various military bases I thought I was well prepared to be a military wife but soon knew I had a lot to learn about military protocol. The Commanding Officer of Chuck's squadron and his wife invited us for coffee and dessert one evening, a mandatory appearance. Mrs. C.O. was not very personable or friendly and was difficult to converse with. After we'd spent the minimum amount of time there Chuck finally said "Tomorrow's a work day so we'd better be leaving."

As we stood to say goodbye Mrs. C.O. pointed to the plant on the coffee table and said "Betty, that's your welcome present." The dusty plant appeared as if it had been sitting on her coffee table for some time but I thanked her, picked it up and we left. That was the only time I ever saw them; they left a short time later for a new assignment. The new C.O., Ed Aune and his wife, Sue, and their family of four lively boys, were a welcome change.

Chuck and I were happy but as in most marriages there were

things we didn't agree on. He had a few strong opinions that I didn't share but I could live with them and did, at least for some time. For one thing he let me know right away that he was not going to be "hen-pecked." He knew men who didn't come to the Officer's Club on Friday nights where many of the squadron's men spent an hour or so drinking, playing dice and "flying" all of their week's missions again, just a general unwinding. True or not everyone thought those who didn't come were "hen-pecked."

The squadron wives changed their monthly meetings from daytime to evening because it was difficult to get babysitters in the daytime. When Chuck came home with my invitation for the first evening meeting he tossed it to me with the words "You're not going." He believed wives had all day every day to do their socializing and didn't need to go out at night when the men were home. That was a typical chauvinist attitude in the 1950's. I had been brainwashed enough by women's magazines that I agreed with him! I didn't like women's clubs, luncheons and meetings then or ever so that gave me a good excuse not to go.

Wives were encouraged to participate in the Officer's Wives Club and in the Squadron Wives Club supposedly to help their husband's career. My feeling about that was Chuck's career was up to him. I was willing to help in any way if he asked me but I never could see how my socializing with other wives made a difference. After my second child was born I didn't hesitate to tell Chuck when I'd decided to go to Bingo at the "O" Club with my friends in the evening or anyplace else. By that time Chuck had begun to change and adjust to who I was so he was glad to see me get out a little bit with my friends, even at night, and anyway, he hated Bingo!

We had a mailbox at the Post Office about a mile away in the crossroads town of Adelanto. One day around lunchtime I walked to the Post Office and picked up the mail from the box. Half way back Chuck's car came up the road, screeched to a halt, made a u-turn and pulled up beside me. Chuck looked grim and I wondered what could be wrong. As I got into the car and greeted him he did not smile. Thinking something might have happened at work I said "What's wrong, Chuck?"

"I expected my wife to be there when I got home" he responded, still unsmiling. I sat quietly while I thought that over but when we got home I wanted to talk about it. We did not have a telephone as we couldn't get one and had to use the park owner's telephone. Chuck's work schedule was different every day depending on whether or not he was flying. Some days he came home for lunch and other days he didn't. I never knew whether he'd be home for lunch or not. When I presented my point of view Chuck agreed it made sense and pretty soon was smiling again. I made it a point to be home around lunchtime most days and I never heard another word about that subject.

The insignificant problems we had were the result of our immaturity, lack of communication skills and each going into marriage with a set of expectations that were different from the other. The worst thing was that we expected each other to be a mind reader and when that didn't happen, either of us would begin to pout for no apparent reason.

Chuck had to go TDY (temporary duty) frequently. I hated it when he was gone as I missed him but wives were never supposed to complain. We were just supposed to support our husbands and not make him feel bad about leaving. After all they were doing a dangerous job (flying) and occasionally there were accidents. A pilot in our squadron was killed the second year we were married. Pilots needed to be able to focus on their job and I surely didn't disagree with that.

A few weeks after we married I began to suspect that I was pregnant. We wanted several children and were thrilled to think maybe we'd have a baby the next January. The happy news was soon confirmed and I resigned from my job at the Bank of America. I had transferred back to Victorville from San Bernardino and even though Chuck didn't want "his wife" to work, I had insisted on working long enough to pay off my department store bills. I worked just that long and we were both happy to have me quit and stay home.

During the next few months we became friends with several couples in the squadron. A few of them were also expecting so we had even more in common. When we were together at small dinner parties or squadron events, it was fun to chat about husbands and babies. The men were across the room "flying" even though they were on the ground. One problem we had was barely having enough money to live on with nothing left for extras. Chuck's take-home pay of $430 a month wasn't much, even in 1956! Fortunately, the only credit cards in those days were American Express and Diner's Club. We had both but used them sparingly as both bills had to be paid in full each month. By necessity we learned early to live on our income.

Evelyn, gave birth to Lisa, her fourth child, in Alaska and I was excited when I received a box of her maternity clothes and glad to save money not having to buy them. The next problem was where we were going to fit a bassinet and baby clothes and everything else a baby needs into our mobile home. Fifty years ago babies didn't "need" nearly as much as they "need" today! Someone in the squadron sold us a bassinet for $8. I bought blue fabric and sewed a shirred lining and a long ruffled skirt. I received many compliments and was proud of how pretty it looked.

Excited and thrilled, but hardly believing it was real, the last couple of months we bought clothes, blankets and diapers for the baby. The ladies in the mobile home park gave me a surprise shower and the Squadron Wives gave me a shower a few weeks before the baby was due so we were ready and waiting. By that time I was attending the wives' monthly meetings even though they were in the evening.

Chuck came home one day in December and said that some of the guys in the squadron were going to Mammoth skiing the next weekend and invited him to go. It was three or four weeks before the baby was due so, not wanting to "hen-peck" him, I agreed he should go. Since this was our first baby we didn't realize that the baby could come at any time and that Chuck should be home with me.

Chuck left Friday after work and Sunday night I was eagerly anticipating his coming home. When I heard a noise outside I opened the door before he knocked and was quite surprised to see Chuck standing there with a cast on his leg and using crutches! The other fellows apologized to me and got out of there as quickly as they could. Chuck's leg was hurting a lot and he kept taking aspirin and drinking Scotch and water. Neither of us got any sleep and at 6AM he let me take him to the emergency room. The cast was too tight and was cut off. He was hospitalized for five or six days and came home just two or three days before Christmas. Christmas Day was a downer, just the two of us and neither of us feeling very well.

The morning of December 26th I started feeling like maybe I was in labor even though it was two weeks before my due date. Thinking I could move things along I went out and walked three miles, a good bit more than I'd been walking every day. Then I came home and ate most of a can of peanuts. Boy, I got such a bad stomachache and didn't know whether it was labor or the peanuts! Another sleepless night for both of us.

Chuck took me to the George AFB Hospital about 6AM on the 27th and after an examination the doctor confirmed I was in labor and admitted me to the hospital. Chuck sat beside my bed with his broken leg resting up on it. We both strongly hoped we'd have a boy and twelve hours later our wish came true. The moment Chipper was born and they laid him on my belly I started crying from happiness. I'd never felt such overwhelming love and joy. I knew that my life was irrevocably changed, that I was a mother and always would be. That was what I'd dreamed of.

Before Chipper was born I read a popular book touting "natural" childbirth, meaning no painkillers of any kind for the birth because of the possibility of adverse effects on the baby. Written by a Dr. Read I was easily convinced and determined my baby would be born the "natural" way. I tried to discuss it with my doctor but he wasn't really interested, just said it was up to me. In the 1950's there was no support system in place for women who chose natural childbirth so there were no training classes for parents as there would be later. Even with Chuck encouraging me I reached a point where I asked for a "spinal" anesthesia before the birth. I was disappointed in myself feeling that I had somehow failed.

I had asked my doctor if Chuck could be in the delivery room when the baby was born but that was not allowed in 1956. About ten years later husbands were allowed in the delivery room and mirrors were installed so that mothers could watch the birth also. When I told my doctor that I planned to nurse the baby I was strongly discouraged. I wanted to nurse my baby but was told that "formula" was much better than mother's milk and the baby would get off to a better start. That also later proved to be untrue. In spite of opposition I did nurse him for a few weeks but I was a nervous wreck wondering if he was getting enough and proper nourishment. I had no one to turn to for advice as everyone I knew gave their babies bottles. Nursing was totally out of style. After a few weeks I switched to bottles and formula, again feeling I'd failed.

The day after Chipper was born Chuck came hopping into the maternity ward on his crutches carrying a pair of little skis about eighteen inches long. He handed them to the first nurse he saw and asked her to take them into the nursery and try them on the baby to see if they'd fit. Everyone had a big laugh, staff and patients alike. His sense of humor was one thing that had attracted me to Chuck. Not only was he good looking with electric green eyes and a beautiful smile, he brought a sense of fun with him wherever he went.

A five day stay in the hospital during which Chuck could only look at the baby through the window into the nursery had me eager to get home. Chuck was not allowed to be there when Chipper was with me so he never had an opportunity to hold him. When Chuck came to the hospital to take me home he was still on crutches so I carried the baby out to the car and held him until we got inside our warm and cozy home. Chuck sat down on the sofa and held out his arms and I put our son into them. Tears rolled down Chuck's cheeks even though he was smiling as he looked at that precious baby boy. He had his "happiest moment."

82

# Chapter Fifteen
## Real Life Begins
### 1957

We named our son Charles Ray Sale Halsey, Jr. which needs an explanation. My husband's name at birth was Charles Ray Halsey. His parents divorced when he was five and his mother remarried when Chuck was twelve. Ralph Sale adopted Chuck and Chuck's name was changed to Charles Ray Sale. While he was growing up Chuck's hero was his brother fourteen years older, a barn-storming pilot and owner of a flight school in the late 1930's and until World War II began. His name, of course, was Halsey and when Chuck was twenty-one he went to Court and changed his name to Charles Ray Sale Halsey. He loved his stepfather and wanted to honor him by keeping "Sale" as well as his own birth name. Even though it was a lot to burden a baby with, we named him for his father. Chipper eventually became Chip and that is what he is still called by almost everyone.

When we weren't holding Chipper we sat and stared at him, watching him sleep, make baby gestures and noises and were fascinated and still found it hard to believe that he was ours to keep. Even though it was winter and cold I made sure to spend some time outside with Chipper every day so that he'd get the recommended amounts of fresh air and sunshine. He was a happy baby except for a couple of hours in the late afternoon every day when he suffered what we were told was "colic." He cried and conveyed his distress and nothing we did soothed him. We almost cried with him.

We soon got into a routine. Chipper awoke every morning about 6AM when Chuck was getting up and ready for work. After being fed he was wide awake and wanted some interaction until after his bath and 10AM feeding. Tired as I was from being up to feed him two or three times during the night I really wanted to go back to bed and sleep for a couple of hours but I didn't get to do that. Chuck started getting up at 6AM with Chipper on weekends and I slept late, grateful because I believed it was really my job to take care of the baby and the house and Chuck's job to be the "provider."

With his dark curly hair and big blue eyes Chuck and I were certain Chipper was the most beautiful baby anyone had ever seen! Even after sleep deprived nights we went through each day grinning at each other. Friends came to see us and agreed our baby was a very special one. Joyce and Mac came over and an innocent remark felt like a dagger in our hearts! Joyce had worked with me at the Bank of America and Mac was in Chuck's squadron. They were dating and soon to be married. Joyce asked the question that caused us to panic. "What's wrong with Chipper's neck?"

Instantly Chuck and I were both staring at the baby's neck. "Joyce, what do you mean, 'What's wrong with Chipper's neck?'"

"Well, to me it looks as if he's holding his head to one side."

Nightmarish thoughts I'd been suppressing rushed up accompanied by images of an older cousin always called "Monk." I hadn't mentioned it to Chuck but ever since Chipper was born I'd been looking at him trying to figure out if something was wrong. Images of Monk, born in the early 1920's, who went through life with his head bent towards one shoulder flooded my mind. Then just about the time I finally decided that Chipper simply had one ear a little lower than the other, and that was no big deal, Joyce asked her question.

First thing next morning, without an appointment, we rushed Chipper to the Air Force Hospital Clinic. When you used military medicine you saw whatever doctor happened to be on duty. That day it was Dr. White, the doctor who'd delivered Chipper. "Dr. White, I'm so glad to see you! Please examine Chipper. It looks as if there might be something wrong with his neck," Chuck blurted.

After examining the baby for a few minutes Dr. White turned to us and said "Chipper had a difficult time coming through the birth canal. He was 'sunny side up,' facing up instead of down, and I had to use high forceps and turn him over. Apparently his neck

84

muscle suffered some damage but it will heal and he'll be just fine. As a matter of fact I was born with a 'wry neck' myself and you can see that I'm fine."

"'Wry neck,' is that what it's called?'" asked Chuck.

"Well, the medical term is 'torticollis' but its commonly called 'wry neck.' It will take several weeks or a few months but he'll be fine. If he's not okay by the time he's a year old we can repair it surgically." With that Dr. White indicated that our time was up and we left his office feeling only slightly better.

Chuck's mother came from New Mexico to visit. She had wanted to come sooner but I asked her to wait a few weeks. Since she was sixty-one and Chuck's two older siblings did not have children Alline was thrilled to have a grandchild at last. She came bearing gifts, beautiful handmade baby clothes and blanket plus a blanket she'd made for Chuck before he was born that we especially treasured.

By mid February Chuck was out of his cast and back at work and one day he came home with news. "Guess what! I have to go to Alaska TDY. I'll be leaving early in March."

"Really? I don't want to hear that! How long will you be gone?" I asked.

"It's a long one, maybe as long as six weeks," he replied.

Both of us were quiet for a few minutes absorbing the news. Then I said "Mmmm, what would you think about Chipper and me going to Atlanta while you're gone? My family is so eager to see us."

I could almost see the wheels in his head turning and after a fairly long pause Chuck said "Well, let's think about this. Maybe this is a good time to sell this 'honeymoon cottage;' we could move all of our things out and give the mobile home to a dealer to sell. I'll talk to Base Housing and see if we can get quarters. When I come back from Alaska I can take leave, catch a hop to Dobbins (an Air Force Base near Atlanta) and drive you two home." We went full steam ahead with the plan even though we both had reservations about me driving coast to coast alone with a baby barely two months old.

As it turned out Gid Terry was going to Alaska with Chuck. Gid and Ann were our best friends. Their baby girl, Debbie, was six weeks older than Chipper. Ann was from Mississippi so it was soon decided that Ann and I and the babies would drive east together while the guys went to Alaska. I'd drop Ann off in Mississippi and continue on to Atlanta. Gid and Ann told us we might be able to sublet quarters in the other end of their four-unit building. The couple who lived there had separated and Roger was on an extended TDY. Chuck contacted Roger and he agreed that the Housing Office could transfer the unit to us. We'd use Roger's furniture indefinitely until we had time to buy our own. Seemed like a good plan and I was excited.

Arrangements were made to store our personal belongings and sell our mobile home. Ann and I were leaving with Debbie and Chipper the day before Chuck and Gid were leaving for Alaska. "You guys know why we want to leave first; you two will have to fit all of the stuff we're taking into the car!" Fortunately, the summer before, Chuck and I had driven his Jaguar and my Willys to Los Angeles and traded them both for a new 1956 Ford Fairlane station wagon. (Just for information that station wagon cost $2,600!) With two babies and all of their paraphernalia plus Ann's suitcases and both cold weather and hot weather clothes for me, it wasn't easy fitting it all in.

Ann and I kissed Gid and Chuck goodbye and they kissed the babies and we started off in high spirits. That station wagon was a big vehicle and it was packed! Hanging on the back of the front bench seat was a car seat, and next to it an "Infantseat" between Ann and me. Immediately behind the front seat was a folding baby travel bed. It fit quite well on the back seat and the babies could take turns sleeping comfortably. Cars did not have seat belts in those days and there was no such thing as "child safety seats." They were simply "car seats" and they were pretty flimsy, a place to contain an infant or toddler while in the car. They weren't designed to keep the baby safe nor, in retrospect, even comfortable!

# Chapter Sixteen
## Highway 66 - It's a Long Road
### 1957

$P$lanning the route was easy because Hwy. 66 was still the primary east-west highway, at least as far as the Texas panhandle where it veered northeast into Oklahoma and beyond. As we got on the highway in Victorville I said to Ann, "I believe we can make Kingman, Arizona before dark We'll stop there tonight and tomorrow we should be able to get to Chuck's parents' home in New Mexico. How does that sound?"

"Sounds good to me. Then how many more days do you think it'll take to get to Mississippi?"

"We'll spend two nights in Belen so Chipper's grandparents can spend a little time with him. Then it will depend on how well the babies do. Texas is mostly flat and straight across so I'd say possibly two more days to Mississippi, but if we have to slow down for any reason, then three at the most."

Traveling with two babies wasn't quite as easy as it sounded! The first day went pretty well. The babies slept a lot; Ann fed each one as needed, changed their diapers and tried to keep them happy. I let Ann drive some but I preferred driving and Ann seemed to prefer that too. We were both pretty tired when we checked into the Holiday Inn ($15 a night) in Kingman, Arizona just as it was getting dark. We lugged in clothes bags for all plus equipment to sterilize baby bottles and supplies to mix formula. By the time all of that was done and I'd fed and played with Chipper, and we'd had a quick dinner, we collapsed in bed. Debbie, at four months old, was sleeping quite well through most of the night but Chipper, not quite two and a half months old, still woke up two or three times a night to be fed.

"Wah! Wah!" Chipper served as our alarm clock. By the time

we were all fed and dressed and we'd loaded everything back into the car and started east again, my excitement about the trip erased any lingering fatigue.

The Arizona desert is quite different from the Mojave Desert in California. Arizona is more colorful with a greater variety of palm trees and cactus as well as more scrub growth. We passed the cut-off to the Grand Canyon, then east of Flagstaff we passed the turnoff to Meteorite Crater. We drove across the Painted Desert and Petrified Forest, all places I'd visited while living in Albuquerque. The most distinctive thing when traveling across eastern Arizona and western New Mexico were the numerous "hogans," ancient Navajo houses, and "hornos," outdoor ovens used for baking.

After crossing the Arizona-New Mexico border soon we were in Gallup, New Mexico. Stopping there for a baby break, feeding and playtime, Ann and I got out of the car and stretched our legs and found a café for lunch. In the 1950's the population of Gallup was mostly Navajo Indians so there were several galleries showing Indian artwork I would have enjoyed visiting, but we didn't take time to browse.

Fifty miles west of Albuquerque I knew a cut-off road that would save us a few miles to Belen, the small town thirty miles south of Albuquerque where Chuck's parents lived. We headed southeast and in the late afternoon pulled into the driveway of Ralph and Alline Sale. They were out the door like a flash of lightening and taking the babies from us. Alline had met Chipper a few weeks before but it was Ralph's first time to meet his grandson. Chipper was their first grandchild and to say they were both happy and excited to see us doesn't really say it all!

Ann and I got a good rest for thirty-six hours while Chipper's grandparents took over a lot of the care for both babies.

When we headed east from Belen, Chipper was wearing a new red wool sweater that his grandmother had knitted for him. The babies had been bathed and fed and were both in a happy mood. Ann and I were relaxed and glad to be on our way again. We wondered how Chuck and Gid were doing. While in New Mexico we learned their flight to Alaska had been delayed two or three days so we didn't know if they were still in California or on their way to Alaska.

After having a nice break in a small town in Texas where we had lunch, fed the babies and played with them for a while, we were back in the car and could see miles ahead of us on the long straight highway. Both babies were awake and in the front seat between Ann and I, one baby in the Infantseat and one in the car seat. Suddenly a flashing light came up behind me catching me by surprise. I looked down and I was going seventy-five miles per hour, faster than I usually drove. After I pulled over a young Texas State Trooper came to the window and I showed him my license and registration.

"Do you know how fast you were driving?"

"After I saw your lights and looked at my speedometer I was surprised to see that I was going seventy-five. I don't usually drive that fast, I try to stay about the speed limit. We're headed to Mississippi and Georgia to show off our babies to our families and I guess I just got a little too eager. Our husbands are in Alaska for a while." After I blurted all of that out the trooper just looked at us a while.

Finally he said, "I'm a new father myself; my son is a month old. I want you to get where you're going safely so please slow down. You have two beautiful babies there." He gave us a big smile and turned and walked away.

"Wow! We were lucky to be stopped by a new father and have both babies in the front seat! That's the only reason he didn't give me a ticket. He's right, we do want to get there safely so if you see that I'm going too fast again please remind me," I said to Ann.

A couple of days later we arrived at Ann's family home in Greenville, Mississippi, to welcoming arms and a delicious home-cooked meal. After an overnight there my next stop was Biloxi, Mississippi where Chuck's brother was stationed at Keesler AFB. It was only a little over two hundred miles so I knew I could get there sometime in the afternoon.

Fryer and Glenna were happy to see us and thrilled to see Chipper, who was their first nephew on the Halsey side of the family. I enjoyed visiting with them a couple of days. They had a speedboat so after finding a trustworthy baby-sitter we went water-skiing. That was my first time to water-ski so it was a learning experience but even though I spent more time in the water than on the skis, I had a good time.

# Chapter Seventeen

## Atlanta, At Last

### 1957

My long coast to coast drive was almost finished.

Leaving Biloxi early I planned to stop in Montgomery, Alabama for the night. Since it was only a five hour drive, I'd be able to relax, make formula and enjoy Chipper for a few hours.

With Chipper sleeping most of the way, the drive to Montgomery was a breeze and once I got there, I decided to keep going. It was early afternoon and Atlanta was just four or five more hours away. Big mistake!

Three hours from Atlanta traffic was much heavier. Rain started, lightly at first and then a good old southern thunderstorm with lightening flashing all around us and thunder claps loud enough to wake sleeping babies. Dusk set in as the storm intensified and I could barely see the car in front of me. Chipper was awake and crying and I was getting more and more nervous. I felt like crying myself!

Finally, pulling off the road I picked up Chipper and plugged the bottle warmer into the dashboard cigarette lighter. The milk warmed and I tried to feed him but he didn't want it. Nothing soothed him. It must be the storm, I thought, or maybe it was that darn colic that I had forgotten about when I decided not to stop in Montgomery!

At that point we were on the southwest outskirts of Atlanta and even though my family lived all the way across the city on the northeastern edges, I felt I had to keep going.

Chipper finally dozed off again and an hour later I was in familiar territory, close to Lillian's house, a few more turns and I'd be there. Going to Lillian's first made sense because since my last visit Mama and Daddy had sold the farm where they'd lived for a few years and bought a house in Tucker. Not sure I'd be able to find it in the dark and rain even though I had directions, going to Lillian's seemed easier. I knew the way there.

After turning off Highway 29 towards Lillian's neighborhood something went wrong and I kept going round and round in a circle and wasn't able to figure out my mistake. It was getting late so I chose a friendly looking house with lights on and a woman framed in the kitchen window.

I rang the doorbell and she answered from the window. Explaining my predicament I asked her to call Lillian. A couple of minutes later she opened the front door and invited me in. She said Lillian lived just a few blocks away and would be right there. I thanked the lady for her help but told her I had a baby in the car so I'd wait there.

I was so glad to see Lillian! I was even happier to see my room set up with a crib for Chipper as I was exhausted! Finally home, I looked forward to seeing Mama and Daddy tomorrow and then the rest of my big family.

More than three years had passed since I'd last been in Atlanta for Christmas 1953. Mama had also borrowed a crib for Chipper so our room was ready. I missed Chuck but was glad I had a few weeks to show off our beautiful son and enjoy a nice long visit with my brothers and sisters and their families plus aunts, uncles and cousins. Many relatives came to Mama's to see us and we spent many days driving around the county visiting extended family and a few old friends. I felt like I'd won the lottery since my last visit! I had a handsome husband and a gorgeous son that I was so proud to show off.

A few days after arriving in Atlanta a telegram and then a phone call came from Chuck wishing me a "Happy Anniversary," our first. His letters started coming almost every day and while we were sad not to be together this was the life Chuck had chosen and I was happy being his wife and a mother.

Still worried about Chipper's head and neck problem and not having much faith in what the Air Force doctor had told us, I wanted to take Chipper for a second opinion about his torticollis

92

(wry neck).

Referred to a pediatric specialist in downtown Atlanta Lillian and I took Chipper there. I was very much afraid of what he might find but desperate to get the best possible treatment for my baby. After examining the baby thoroughly, Dr. Stephens asked me just what the doctor in California had advised and then gave me his opinion.

"I am shocked that any doctor would recommend waiting until Chipper is a year old to do surgery on his neck. By that time he would have definitely developed strabismus, which is a misalignment of the eyes. In general, if torticollis is not corrected before one year of age, facial asymmetry can develop and may become impossible to correct. Surgery involves cutting the sternocleidomastoid muscle that suffered trauma during birth and is now contracted. We have to release the tension. My advice is to have this surgically corrected as soon as possible."

Listening carefully I absorbed everything the doctor said, thought it over for a couple of minutes, then asked,

"Can we wait until we return to California in May
so that my husband will be with us?"

"Since Chipper is barely three months old now you can wait. I certainly understand you'd want your husband with you. How far do you live from Los Angeles?"

"About one hundred miles – it's a two hour drive on the freeways."

"Good. I'll give you a referral to an excellent surgeon associated with Los Angeles Children's Hospital. I'll contact him and I'll give you a full written report to show your husband and also Dr. Williams."

"I feel so much better after your explanation. I'll call and set up an appointment and we'll take Chipper to the doctor at Children's Hospital immediately after we get home. Thank you so much, doctor!"

While Chuck was still in Alaska I drove to North Carolina to spend a few days with Jenny and Wendy, good friends from my single years in California.

Wendy had been discharged from the AF before Chuck and I were married and they moved home to North Carolina. It was great to see them and they were excited to see Chipper. They had been married ten years and wanted children but didn't yet have any.

Wendy had started an interior decorating business and offered to order furniture for Chuck and me at his cost plus shipping to California..

Chuck returned to California from Alaska in early May, spent one night there and the next day a pilot in the squadron flew him to Dobbins AFB, near Atlanta, where we had a joyous reunion. Chuck could hardly believe how much Chipper had grown in two months and carried him around, not wanting to put him down. He also was greatly relieved to learn Chipper would have surgery as soon as we got home. He'd also been worrying about the baby.

After Chuck got to Atlanta we made a quick trip to North Carolina and ordered furniture for our living room, dining room and bedroom at a great price even with shipping costs

I had been so proud introducing Chuck to my family but when it was time to end our visit, I was more than ready. We packed the car and the three of us headed west towards our new home on George AFB near Victorville. After brief family visits in Mississippi and New Mexico we were eager to begin our new life as a family of three in a house instead of the mobile home in which we'd started our marriage.

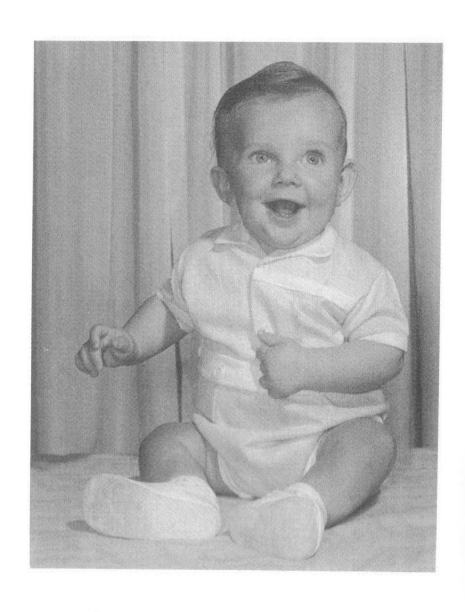

*Chipper ~ 5 months June 1957*

# *Chapter Eighteen*

## *Chipper's Surgery*
### *1957*

*I*t was wonderful being home again. Our mobile home had sold while we were gone and we moved into a spacious two bedroom apartment on the base. The previous tenant allowed us to use his furniture while we waited for the furniture we'd ordered from North Carolina to arrive.

We made an appointment with the doctor we were referred to for Chipper's neck surgery. We were nervous as we drove two hours to his office in Hollywood where he examined Chipper. We liked the doctor very much. He sounded experienced and capable so a date was set for surgery. A week later we drove to Children's Hospital in Los Angeles and checked Chipper in. In 1957 hospitals had strict and limited visiting hours, usually a couple of hours in the afternoon and a couple of hours in the evening. There were no exceptions so we had to leave our precious baby there with only their assurances they'd take good care of him.

Staying in a nearby hotel we were so tense we had a hard time trying to read or watch TV while waiting for visiting hours. When we returned to the hospital that evening Chipper was as happy to see us as we were to see him and it was even harder to leave him again. The next morning we arrived early before they took him to surgery. Restless, we could hardly stand waiting so we went out for a drive around the area. "Stop, Chuck! I want to go in that furniture store." There was a big round pocket watch styled clock in the window that I thought would be perfect with our new Early American furniture. Chuck liked it also so we went in and bought it. We couldn't stand waiting at the hospital but we found we weren't comfortable being away from it either, so headed back

Minutes crawled by for a couple more hours until finally the doctor came and told us the surgery went well. A few days later we took Chipper home but made several of those two hundred mile round trips for checkups and stitches out. Before we were finished with those visits Chipper developed a fear of anyone dressed in white and would immediately start crying if someone in white approached him. It took him quite a while to get over that fear. Chipper's neck healed well and he was able to hold his head straight. At almost six months old his head was already a little asymmetrical. If we'd waited until he was at least a year old before having the surgery, as the Air Force doctor had recommended, it would have been much worse.

The furniture from North Carolina began arriving and it was fun decorating the quarters to our taste. We felt that we were making a comfortable home. We also began accumulating more baby paraphernalia, a full size crib, a feeding table and a playpen. Chipper was growing and thriving and crawling all over the place and we enjoyed every minute of it. Finally, we were able to relax and enjoy the rest of summer, our new home and our incredible son.

# Chapter Nineteen

## More Traveling - Montgomery

### 1957

"Are you ready for another cross-country drive?" Chuck asked the question as he came through the door one afternoon in July, a month after Chipper's surgery.

"What are you talking about? We haven't settled down from the last trip yet, with Chipper's surgery and all the driving back and forth to L. A., I sometimes feel like we live in the car!"

"I'm going to Squadron Officers' School in Montgomery, Alabama. My orders came today. The class lasts four months and begins August 20th. We'll have to leave early in August if we want to stop in New Mexico and Mississippi again."

Giving him a big hug and I said "That's wonderful! I'm proud of you for being selected. I know you've wanted to go. We'll get to see our families again and maybe even spend Thanksgiving and Christmas holidays with them!" Montgomery was only a four-hour drive from Atlanta so I knew some of my family would drive over to see us.

We got advice and information about renting a furnished apartment in Montgomery from friends who had already been to Squadron Officers' School. We quickly decided what the essential things were that we'd need for four months and set them aside for the Air Force to ship.

We were not looking forward to driving back across the country in the August heat as our 1956 Ford station wagon did not have air conditioning. Most cars didn't have air conditioning in those days. It was an expensive extra. Chuck installed a portable air conditioner in a window that kept us fairly comfortable as we crossed the desert from California to New Mexico and then Texas and the Deep South.

Hitting the highway again in early August, two days later we were with family in New Mexico. While grandparents enjoyed playing with Chipper Chuck and I enjoyed our fill of authentic Mexican food at our favorite local restaurant. A few days later we were in Biloxi with Fryer and Glenna again. Leaving Chipper with the trusted babysitter, the four of us drove to New Orleans for an afternoon and evening. New Orleans was different than any city I'd seen and I was fascinated with the architecture in the French Quarter. We browsed through shops, some set behind walls draped in bougainvillea. The French Quarter had a very romantic feel and we immersed ourselves in it. Dinner at "Three Sisters," a restaurant renowned for its food lived up to the hype. While enjoying an after dinner drink, we watched Sally Rand, a famous stripper, perform. As always we had a lot of fun and shared many laughs with Fryer and Glenna.

A few days later we arrived in Montgomery, checked into a Holiday Inn and called the rental agent we'd been referred to. The next day we selected one of the two apartments she showed us. Our shipment of essential items, Chipper's bed, playpen, etc., was delivered within a couple of days so we settled in. Chuck began his classes and spent most evenings studying. During the day, pushing Chipper in his stroller, I explored the city.

Montgomery, the Capitol of Alabama, is a very old southern city filled with beautiful antebellum mansions built prior to the Civil War. Atlanta had many similar forlorn looking mansions and from the time I was a small girl I fantasized about buying and restoring one to its pre-Civil War beauty. I never tired of strolling sidewalks shaded by magnificent old oak and magnolia trees and gazing with envy at the beautiful homes in Montgomery. I visualized Chuck and me and our brood of several happy children enjoying life in a home like these.

After only a few weeks in Montgomery I began having familiar feelings of malaise, sleepiness and nausea at the smell of coffee. Sure enough our second child was letting me know of his presence. Chuck and I were delighted as we'd always planned to have our first two close together. I wrote Ann to tell her the news and she wrote right back that she and Gid were expecting their second baby also! Their daughter, Debbie, was six weeks older than Chipper and our second child was due three weeks before their second so Ann and I still had a lot in common!

Thanksgiving was spent in Atlanta with my family. I wanted to keep my pregnancy a secret from the family and just surprise them when the baby was born. However, while Chuck and I were in Rich's shopping for a maternity dress for his end of the class party, we saw an old friend of Lillian's. She told Lillian not only that she'd seen us, but exactly where, in the maternity department.

There was no dryer in our apartment so I hung laundry on a clothesline just outside the back door. One day when Chipper, 8 months old, was playing contentedly in his playpen I went outside and hung up some laundry. When I came in about five minutes later, he was crawling around the apartment! I could hardly believe my eyes! I knew I'd left him in the playpen but I was equally certain there was no way he could have gotten out. I felt guilty and chastised myself, telling myself to be more careful, to be sure he was in the playpen because obviously I'd made a mistake this time.

A couple of days later while Chipper was in the playpen I was semi-dozing on the sofa. Suddenly, he pulled himself up and over the side and was out of the playpen and crawling around on the floor. From then on he was such an active little boy I had to watch him all of the time as there really wasn't any way to fence him in!

Chuck's end of class party was the middle of December. I indulged myself with my first professional manicure that day and had my hair done. My baby bump was just beginning to show and I wore a beautiful new dress we'd bought at Rich's. I felt very pretty as Chuck introduced me to his classmates. A couple of days later we headed west again for the second time that year. We spent Christmas and Chipper's first birthday in New Mexico where he took his first independent steps. We no longer had a baby, now we had a little boy!

Back home in California we settled down to domestic bliss marred only by an accident involving two squadron planes and the loss of one of the pilots. If I had been blissfully unaware before, the accident made me fully realize that my husband's job was riskier than a 9 – 5 office job but it was also more rewarding for both of us so I never questioned our choices.

On St. Patrick's Day, March 17th, we celebrated our second anniversary. It had been a very busy year in which we'd driven back and forth across the country twice, back and forth from George AFB to Los Angeles many times for Chipper's neck surgery, sold our mobile home and moved into base quarters that we furnished and decorated as our new home. Best of all, we were expecting our second child in two months.

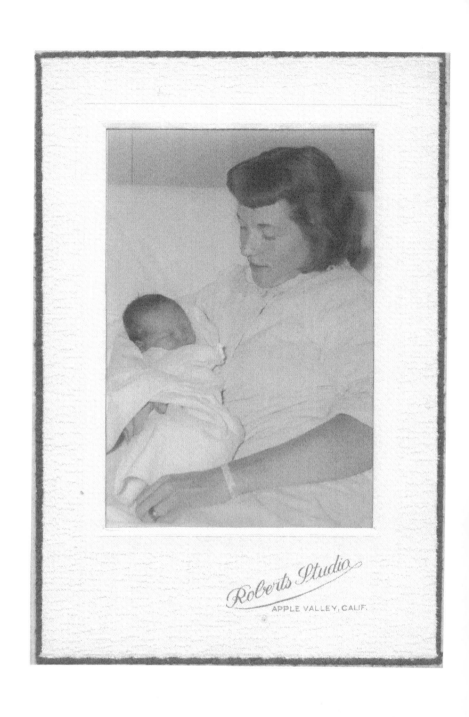

*Bett and Guy ~ May 13, 1958*

# Chapter Twenty

## South America & Another Boy
### 1958

$I$n the spring of 1958 twelve pilots in the 4th Tow Target Squadron were scheduled to deliver six B-26's to Chile's Air Force and six to Peru's Air Force. The trip to Chile was in March and the one to Peru in May. Chuck was originally scheduled to go to Peru but because our second baby was due June 1st one of the other pilots agreed to switch trips so Chuck could go on the March trip. Chuck and five other pilots made the trip to Chile and had a very interesting time. Shortly after they returned the Peru trip was cancelled so Chuck had been lucky to go to Chile.

Captain Dewey Lowe, the senior officer, was in charge and the other five pilots were Chuck, Gid Terry, Bob Danielson, Leon Hull and Lee Collard. They were taken from George AFB on a C-47 to Los Angeles International Airport where they boarded a commercial flight to Washington, DC. After completing applications for passports they flew to Keesler AFB in Biloxi, Mississippi where they picked up six B-26's. No navigators were traveling with them so the six flew formation for the entire trip with Dewey Lowe in the lead plane. For those looking up from the ground it was probably a beautiful sight as most of us thought the B-26 was a pretty plane in flight and six planes in formation is always awesome.

After three days in Miami relaxing and enjoying the hotel pool and beaches the group flew to Guantanamo Bay, Cuba (Gitmo, as the guys called it) and then on to Panama where time was spent lounging around the pool drinking ten cent Cuba Libras. The passports finally came and free as birds they flew to Lima, Peru.

In Lima they bumped into a group of USAF pilots from a different AF base who had delivered B-26's to the Peruvian Air

Force. A member of that group was an avid golfer and he went to the local course where he played golf with a South American man. After the game the American golfer and the South American golfer met the U. S. pilots for a drink and the South American invited the men to go sightseeing. The guys agreed thinking it would be nice to see a bit of Lima.

First stop on the tour was a classy "cat house" and after the men declined that kind of "sightseeing" they continued the tour. The next stop turned out to be a state-run bordello so large it covered an entire block. The South American thought the Americans could not afford the first place so they would enjoy the bordello because it was only twenty-five cents! Some of the men decided to go in just to see what it was like (or so they said)! There were dozens of Dutch doors, each with a girl wearing only a bra and panties, behind the open top door. Beyond each door was a tiny room with a bed in it. Customers lined up outside their chosen door. The guys had a quick "look-see" then told their host they'd had enough "sightseeing!"

After three days in Peru our pilots flew to Santiago, Chile where they were met by Chilean Air Force Generals in full dress uniforms. A champagne brunch was given in honor of the Americans with Chilean AF pilots attending and their visit made the front page of the local papers. They were made honorary Chilean AF pilots and given wings. Captain Dewey Lowe was Chinese-American and while the men were in Santiago there was a riot and negative articles in newspapers because somebody saw Captain Lowe and thought they were getting planes from China!

The men flew home via American Grace Airlines, changed to Bonanza Airlines in L.A. and landed at the tiny Apple Valley airport, twelve miles from home. All of the wives and some of the children were waiting on the tarmac in the hot sun to welcome our husbands/fathers home the minute they started down the stairs from the plane. Ann Terry and I were in the final months of pregnancy and Gid told Anne she looked like a big bouncy ball running across the runway. I probably did too but Chuck was kind enough not to tell me. Some of the men, including Chuck, had grown mustaches while they were away. Ann quickly told Gid he could kiss her after he shaved that hair off his face. Chuck kept his

106

mustache for a few weeks before tiring of it. He grew one periodically through the years but never kept it very long.

One day soon after Chuck returned from Chile he came in with another surprise. "I'm glad you like traveling and seeing new places. Think you'll like El Paso, Texas?"

"What? Are we moving to El Paso? When I lived in Albuquerque I went to Tijuana shopping with friends a couple of times and passed through there but didn't see much of it. I've been hoping your next assignment would be in Europe but after three and half years here I'm even ready for Texas!" The 4$^{th}$ Tow Target Squadron was to be disbanded and everyone would be transferred to the 1$^{st}$ Tow Target Squadron at Biggs AFB in El Paso. The Squadron Commander agreed that Gid Terry and Chuck would be the last two pilots to transfer because of the due dates of our babies.

Several real estate agents from El Paso came to George AFB with pictures and floor plans to try and sell us houses in new developments before we left California. It was exciting to think about buying our own home but we decided to wait and make a decision after we got to Texas. We could buy a house with a VA loan with nothing down and the payments would be no more than our housing allowance of $105 a month so it made sense to buy our first house.

Our baby was due on June 1st but at my regular checkup on May 11th there was a big surprise. "I'm very concerned," my civilian doctor told me. "Your blood pressure is high and your urine is not totally normal. These are symptoms of toxemia which can be dangerous for both you and the baby. Your baby is mature enough so I'd like you to check into Apple Valley Hospital tomorrow and I'll induce delivery."

We called Chuck's mother in New Mexico and she boarded the Santa Fe Chief the next morning to come to California to take care of Chipper while I was in the hospital.

After an overnight labor of twelve hours Stephen Preston Halsey, weighing 6 lbs. 12 oz and measuring 18" long was born just before 8AM on May 13$^{th}$. Another healthy baby boy. Chuck and I were ecstatic! Our little world was getting better all the time.

The baby was such a little guy compared to 16-month old Chipper that we were soon calling him "Guy." "Well, we now have the first two of the six boys we said we wanted," I smiled at Chuck. Cradling his newborn son in his arms and smiling down at him, the proud papa nodded and said "Yep."

"Hon, you carry the little guy in from the car. I'm worried about Chipper. It's the only time I've left him overnight since he was five months old. I want my arms free to scoop him up as soon as I get inside! I know he's missed me!"

Stepping in the front door I saw Chipper across the room. Kneeling and opening my arms, I said, "Chipper, come here! Mama's home!"

He looked at me, looked at his daddy holding a suspicious bundle and threw himself down on the floor screaming at the top of his lungs! His huge temper tantrum was the only way he had to tell me that my leaving him was unacceptable. He was angry and nothing helped. I just had to wait it out. For a few days Chipper didn't like me having anything to do with the little interloper baby either. Thank goodness Chuck's mother was there to distract him and help care for Guy.

Chipper soon got over being mad and let me hug him again. He also started hugging and kissing his brother. Chuck's mother stayed a week or so and we hated to see her leave but she was needed at home.

Immediately after his mother left Chuck had to go to Alaska TDY for a couple of weeks. We hired a young woman as a "mother's helper" for those two weeks and when Chuck returned we were quite happy to be at home with just our little family.

Chuck heard a rumor that the fellows in the squadron who moved to El Paso in the first group were making a lot of money selling their vintage cars several owned for a second car. They were telling the men who were coming to El Paso later to buy an antique car and bring it down; they'd make a lot of money on it! Before long Chuck came home driving a 1928 Ford Model "A."

108

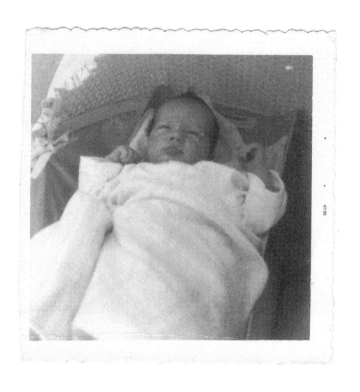

*Guy ~ 1958*

# Chapter Twenty-One
## Move to El Paso
### 1958

Leaving California the latter part of June, with two babies in the car and towing the Model "A" behind our station wagon we were crossing the Mojave Desert in the middle of summer for the third time in a little over a year! Our portable air conditioner kept us fairly comfortable but I worried about the boys, especially Guy who was only a few weeks old.

"Where did that come from?" I yelled. Half way across Arizona suddenly I saw a wheel pass our car headed for an oncoming Cadillac!

"Damn! I don't believe it! We've lost a wheel off the Model "A!" Chuck replied as he pulled the station wagon and the Model "A" onto the shoulder of the road. The wheel hit the Cadillac on the front right side. Thankfully, no one was injured and we exchanged insurance information with the other driver. Chuck unhooked the Model "A" from the station wagon and drove a few miles further to a restaurant.

I settled in a large booth with Chipper and Guy and baby bags with diapers and food and Chuck left, "I'll be back as quickly as I can. Are you going to be okay?"

"Sure. We'll wait right here." Before leaving he called a tow truck from the pay phone and headed back to wait with our "money-maker." Everyone who came into the restaurant looked at me with two babies and a pile of baby stuff as if we might be homeless! The waitresses were quite taken with the boys and when they weren't busy they took turns holding and playing with them. A couple of hours later Chuck returned and we drove to Williams, the next town, and checked into a Holiday Inn with a pool. We needed to relax and unwind.

The Model "A" was repaired and ready to go by noon the next day and we headed east again to Chuck's parents' home. After an uneventful drive we made it in plenty of time for dinner.

"Hello, Aunt Willard! What a nice surprise!" Aunt Willard lived in Kansas. She was Chuck's mother's sister and she wanted to meet the babies she also considered her grandchildren. Chuck's parents divorced when he was five years old; his only siblings were young adults as they were thirteen and fourteen years older than Chuck. While his mother, Alline, was transitioning to single parenthood she left Chuck with her sister, Willard, and husband, Sud, in Wichita, Kansas. Time passed and Chuck had been in Kansas for three years when Sud told Alline she'd better come get Chuck or let them adopt him. Not having children of their own they loved Chuck very much and would like to have kept him. Alline didn't waste time getting to Kansas to pick up her son and take him to New Mexico where she was then living.

Aunt Willard and Alline and Ralph, Chuck's father, offered to take care of the boys for two or three days if we wanted to go on to El Paso and find a place to live. We took them up on the offer and drove to El Paso, about a four hour drive. Within a couple of days we had rented a house so I left Chuck in El Paso with the Model "A" and I drove back to Belen to pick up the boys. Our household goods were delivered and Chuck allowed the moving company to unpack.

Ralph rode with Chipper, Guy and me to El Paso. Never having had children of his own, he'd adopted Chuck and was a great father and thrilled to be a grandfather. A warm, loving man he considered Chuck his son. When I went in the front door of the house we'd rented I could hardly believe my eyes! "What in the world has happened here?" I exclaimed. The house looked much smaller with our furniture in it than when we saw it empty.

"I'm sorry. I've been working and haven't had time to try to organize everything. I wasn't sure where'd you want to put things anyway." Chuck's apologetic expression made me sorry I'd said anything but that was the only time we allowed movers to "unpack" us. It was hard to figure out where to start! Bedroom drawers were full of kitchen items and the kitchen cabinets had

112

linens and clothes, so there was no place to put things and nothing was in the right place. It wasn't easy but within a few days we had things in reasonable order. We didn't plan to live in the house long anyway so we started looking at new houses in two new developments where several of our friends lived.

We quickly decided on the house plan we liked best, a four bedroom, one and half bath brick but had to wait for the house to be built. We picked out a lot and signed a contract after the developer promised the house would be ready in two months. We chose a beige brick with brown trim for the exterior and a cork colored asphalt tile for all of the floors. Our room would be a pale but warm green, Chip's room would be baby blue and Guy's room a sunny yellow. The living room, dining room and kitchen were an off white. There would be a very large covered patio, a carport, a large walled in backyard with a minimum amount of landscaping in front and back. It was exciting to think of being homeowners.

The two month wait for our new home stretched out to seven months but time passed quickly. The boys grew rapidly and thrilled us daily with new accomplishments. We had several houseguests, Ann and Gid Terry and their babies stayed with us a few days after their arrival from California. Mama and Daddy stopped for a brief visit on their way to California and Chuck's parents came from N. M. while they were there so our parents could meet. Evelyn and Dean and their four children stopped to visit on their way to Atlanta and on the way back to California left twelve year old Jane with me for a couple of weeks. I loved having Jane there because she was a huge help with the boys especially since Chuck was TDY in Alaska.

The first night after I put Jane on a train home to California there was a horrendous rain. Flood control channels plugged up and water spilled out into the streets and neighborhoods. By 8AM there was a foot and a half of water inside our house but two good friends, Gid Terry and Bob Danielson, arrived in time to raise rugs and our new piano to higher levels before we walked out in hip deep water carrying the boys wrapped in shower curtains and carrying diapers, baby food, etc. Later that day after the water receded Chuck's Commanding Officer sent an AF truck full of men and cleaning materials and they cleaned my house and put

113

everything back in order, much to the chagrin of Army neighbors on the block who shoveled mud for two weeks! Plus, Chuck was ordered home from Alaska and arrived the next day.

Promoted to Captain, Chuck, together with another promoted officer, hosted a party for the squadron at the Officer's Club where a good time was had by all.

A few of my friends and I attended Bingo once a week at the "O" Club and most of the men usually let off steam and tension at the Friday night "Happy Hour." There were occasional barbeque dinners at one home or another where the primary drink was rum and something or other. In Juarez, just across the Rio Grande from El Paso, we bought Bicardi rum for $4.16 a gallon.

Mrs. Cash, our regular babysitter was a grandmotherly woman that the boys loved so Chuck and I usually made a point to go out to dinner once a week, just the two of us. I attended some of the Officer's Wives Club meetings but only enough to hopefully satisfy the "powers that be" that I was a good helpmate to my husband.

Chuck sold the Model "A" for the same thing he paid for it in California so we learned a lesson. We never made another investment based on "rumor."

*Halsey Family ~ 1960*

# Chapter Twenty-Two

## El Paso Family Life
### 1959 - 1960

We moved into our new home in March, 1959 in time for our third anniversary and were thrilled with the amount of space we had. The house cost $13,500 and our monthly payment was only $93, less than our housing allowance of $105. The furniture bought in North Carolina fit well in the house. We bought a set of bunk beds for Chipper's room and a small chest for his clothes. I put together toy shelves using boards that I painted red resting on concrete blocks. Even though he was less than two and half Chipper was proud of his new "big boy" beds. After Guy was born I'd treated Chipper a lot older than he was. When we were going somewhere I'd say "Chipper, bring the diaper bag and come on to the car."

I'd carry Guy and my purse and little Chipper would say, "Okay, Mommy. I coming" and would start dragging the diaper bag which probably weighed as much as he did! He was such a joy, loved being outside, loved the flowers growing in the yard and was crazy about older kids.

When the boys were two and three we drove a couple of hours up into the closest mountains so they could play in snow. Even though we lived in the desert somehow we came up with sleds to take with us, probably borrowed them, and the four of us had a fun day. We wanted to show the boys the world and everything in it so when we received an unexpected $30 refund we immediately used it to join a nearby swim club. They both loved the water and we took them to the pool frequently during the hot desert summer.

Chuck and I joined a couples bowling league and bowled once a week. I especially enjoyed it as I always liked any physical activity and I'm very competitive.

We had the Baldwin piano we'd bought while still in California just before Guy was born. I took a few lessons but with two such young boys I never could find a convenient time to practice or, at least, that was my excuse. I soon gave up the lessons and one night at a friend's house we saw a chord organ for the first time. It was a Hammond with a full cabinet and was beautiful as well as fairly easy to play and before long we had one just like it in our living room. We all enjoyed the organ and moved it to Japan with us twice during the next several years. I liked being able to sit down, push a few buttons and make it sound like whatever musical instruments I wanted to hear that day. By just playing the melody I could make beautiful music. Chuck had some musical ability; he had played trumpet in his high school band, so he could make that organ come to life!

Life was good and we were very happy. Chuck had to go TDY now and then but that was just a fact of life. I was a strong independent young woman when we married so I became even stronger and more independent as a young mother, always able to take care of things at home. I thought that was what I was supposed to do. When Chuck was TDY I missed him and I'm sure the boys did too but we were all resilient.

Interesting and troubling events were playing in the background of our lives. 1960 was a Presidential election year and a young Senator from Massachusetts was exciting crowds wherever he campaigned. Many thought that if John F. Kennedy was elected President he would restore some luster and respect that America seemed to have lost. Riots in Alabama and Arkansas over desegregation of public schools had deepened the country's divide over civil rights. The Russians appeared to be winning the Cold War. They had launched Sputnik, the first unmanned satellite, and they had tested several hydrogen bombs. Critics claimed Eisenhower had allowed a "missile gap" to open and Nikita Khruschev was boasting that the Soviet Union would "bury" the United States. When an American U-2 spy plane was shot down over Russia Eisenhower denied its existence until the Soviets embarrassed him by parading pilot Francis Gary Powers before the cameras.

In May 1960 Chuck had to go TDY back to George AFB.

118

Since Guy's second birthday was May 13<sup>th</sup>, the boys and I went along. Before Chuck reported in at George AFB the four of us went to Disneyland to celebrate the birthday. Chipper was almost three and a half, old enough to enjoy the kiddie rides. I was thinking that Guy was still too young for the rides and he and I would do other things while Chipper and Daddy went on the rides. The first ride they went on, Guy stood there pointing at them and screaming and trying to get away from me! He wanted to go on the rides also so I started taking him. Many times he had an expression of terror on his face but he was determined – if Chipper was going to ride, he was going to ride also. He set a pattern that day that lasted. If Chipper was doing something, Guy wanted to do it also and he didn't agree that because Chipper was a year and half older Guy should wait a year and a half before he did some things. He was very competitive and very determined, traits that weren't always easy to live with.

Soon after we returned home friends in the squadron began receiving orders. Some were going to North Africa, some to Europe and a few to Japan. I was excited and could hardly wait until Chuck's orders came. He had already served two tours in the Far East so I just knew he'd get orders for Europe. Surely they wouldn't send him to the Far East a third time! I had dreamed for years of touring Europe and the British Isles and fantasized about the traveling I'd do when we got to Europe. In my head I was picturing the boys and me hopping into the car and traveling to Paris or London or Rome, anywhere in Europe, whenever Chuck was away TDY. I was not going to waste any opportunity!

"My orders came today," Chuck said when I met him at the door one afternoon. My first thought was… *I wonder why he didn't call and tell me…* but before I could say anything he said "I know you'll be disappointed and so am I. We're going to Yokota AFB, a couple of hours north of Tokyo." I tried to put on a "good sport" face. After all, this wasn't Chuck's doing any more than it was mine. I'd never had any interest in Japan at all and, other than Tokyo didn't even know if there were other places worth visiting! Never could I have imagined the adventures that awaited us over the next three years.

# Chapter Twenty-Three

## Cherry Blossoms & Culture Shock
### 1961

*Incredible! How lucky I am! That handsome man over there is my husband! Those two tow-headed boys are ours! In a few months, we'll have our third child.*

Lying back in a comfortable lounge chair watching the boys play in Hawaii's warm water made me feel so blessed.

*I have everything I've ever really wanted, my own family!*

On our way to Japan in January 1961 we stopped in Honolulu for a week. We stayed at Ft. DeRussy on Waikiki Beach, a military recreational facility. Hotel rooms were in converted barracks but they were right on the beach and cost very little. On site were eating places and an Officers' Club. Chipper had just turned four and Guy was two and a half. We had fun playing in the sand and water with the boys and exploring the nearby fancy hotels and tourist shops, enjoying the beauty of Hawaii.

Chuck's great-aunt Alice, his grandfather's sister, lived in Honolulu. She and her husband had lived there since 1913 so she was in her eighties when we met her. Aunt Alice knew just about everything there was to know about Hawaii and was an excellent tour guide. She took us all over Oahu including to her lovely Japanese style home, the first house of that style built in Honolulu. She and her husband had it built to their specifications and it looked as stylish in 1961 as it must have in the 1920's when they built it.

While enjoying a day at Aunt Alice's beach club, a waiter approached, "Here you are, 'Mam, enjoy this fresh pineapple," he said as he put the tray on the table. Aunt Alice picked up the knife and expertly opened the pineapple and sliced it. The boys were

120

excited as they had never seen a pineapple before and we all enjoyed the freshest pineapple we'd ever had. (We visited Aunt Alice again in 1969 when we spent Christmas in Honolulu.)

A few hours after departing Honolulu I looked down and saw a very small island all by itself in the middle of the Pacific Ocean. It was Wake Island and I remembered reading about it during World War II. We landed on Wake Island to refuel then proceeded on to Tachikawa AFB, Japan. From Tachi (as we learned to call it) it was a short ride to Yokota AFB where we'd be living for the next three years.

Our squadron "sponsor" had made a reservation for us at the base guest house and had located a house for us to rent. We stayed in the guest house a couple of days while Chuck completed the formalities, picked out furniture from the base furniture warehouse and made arrangements for us to move into our house.

My first impression of Japan was that everything was "gray." Buildings were concrete or dark wood. Both men and women dressed in dark clothes and school children wore dark pants or skirts with matching jacket or sweater and white shirts. When we arrived in January most days were cloudy so even the weather was gray.

Yokota is adjacent to Fussa, a very small town. Off the main two lane highway, few roads were paved. Our house was in the middle of a group of six identical houses surrounded by rice paddies. The living room was large enough to have a dining area at one end. At the other end, just inside the front door, was the oil burning space heater which would heat the entire house. We had three small bedrooms and a small kitchen but the bathroom was large enough to hold a bathinet for the baby due in July.

Most of our shopping was done on base at the well-stocked commissary and the large, modern Base Exchange (BX). Also on base were a bowling center and a movie theatre and swimming pools so while on the base we felt very much at home. Once we exited the gate there was no doubt we were in a foreign land.

There were many bargains in local shops we would take advantage of while there. Some of the best buys were china, lamps, brass candlesticks, beautiful hand-painted silk screens and the latest in electronics, movie cameras, stereo components, turntables, tape decks, speakers and custom built cabinets. I quickly mastered driving on the left (wrong) side of the road and began exploring local shops and nearby towns. Most shops were small and crowded with merchandise. In Hachioji, a city about fifteen minutes away, there were small department stores with an even bigger assortment of many things we didn't even know we wanted.

A critical need right away was milk for me. I was pregnant with our third child and had to make sure I drank plenty of milk for the baby and for my own needs. Milk sold at the commissary was "recombined," meaning it had been dried to powder and then had the water added back and processed for the military. I hated it – it had an "off" taste and I just didn't like it! Friends told me that Navy commissaries at Atsugi and Yokohama sold canned whole milk from the U.S. I decided to make a trip to Atsugi Naval Air Station as it was closer than Yokohama.

With no road maps in English and available Japanese maps very primitive, navigating by other means was necessary. Main highways were two lanes and narrow but paved. Navigation was by odometer and landmarks and directions from friends who'd been there. For example, we'd drive eight miles trying to stay on the main road (*not easy!*) until we came to a certain kind of gas station on the left. There we would turn right and go straight for six and a half miles. If we did not cross railroad tracks within the first mile we knew we were on the wrong road. Railroad tracks were an important navigation tool. Occasionally we might see a sign in English pointing to Tokyo or some other town we knew we had to pass through. With luck and determination we learned our way around a fairly large area between Yokota, Tokyo, Yokohama and beyond.

I set off early one morning with three friends to go to Atsugi. I was driving and they were navigating. After a couple of hours we found the town of Atsugi but no sign of the Naval Air Station. We drove around for a while before pulling into a gas station to ask directions. The attendant had a big smile for us and was *very friendly.* I was asking "Where is the air station?" using English and sign language, waving my arms and pointing to the sky as if I were a bird or an airplane. He didn't appear to understand English until he had put both arms and shoulders and upper body into my car window. With one arm on each side of me he was pointing out the windshield and jabbering in Japanese until suddenly I heard a whisper in my left ear in perfect English "You are so beautiful!" After pushing him out the window and leaving a trail of dust we got out of there and about split our sides laughing. We finally found the air station and bought a couple of cases of canned milk which was drinkable.

We had been in Japan only a few weeks when color burst forth and marked winter's end. First were daffodils and tulips, azaleas and rhododendrons, then the stunningly beautiful pink or white blossoms of cherry trees and the greening of grass. Cherry trees lined both sides of many streets and parts of Japan began to look beautiful. In March were celebrations of the Vernal Equinox, one of the two days in the year when day and night are approximately the same length. Colorful banners hung everywhere, on the front of shops as well as across streets. Big sales in the stores and parades in the streets, women and children dressed in colorful kimonos, and marching bands holding up traffic, the festive mood was infectious and Japan was no longer gray.

The boys adapted well to our new home but Chipper was homesick for quite a while and frequently said "I want to go back to my brown house." Several children lived in our little neighborhood of six houses in the rice paddies so the boys had a lot of playmates. Frankie and Tommy, next door, were almost exactly the same ages as Chipper and Guy. We also had several friends from El Paso with us in Japan so the boys still had those friends too.

As our first Easter approached I got out the Sears catalogue and ordered new Easter outfits for the boys, short white pants, white shirts, navy blazers and red bow ties. They wore their new clothes to Sunday school on base and afterwards there was an Easter egg hunt and brunch at the Officer's Club.

Yugi, our landlord, was a young Japanese man about our age. He dropped by frequently to see how we were doing and if we had any problems with the house. Yugi spoke excellent English and always took a little time to play with the boys, semi-boxing and mild roughhousing. Another unusual treat for children in the neighborhood was entertainers who frequently came to put on a brief show. They would knock on the door and offer to put on a show for a few hundred yen. One hundred yen at that time was worth twenty-eight cents American so if we paid them five hundred yen that was less than a dollar and fifty cents. They would pull costumes from their bicycle baskets and dress up as dragons or wild animals and enact a brief drama dancing and singing in our yard while all of the neighborhood children watched. Just like children all over the world ours were easily entertained.

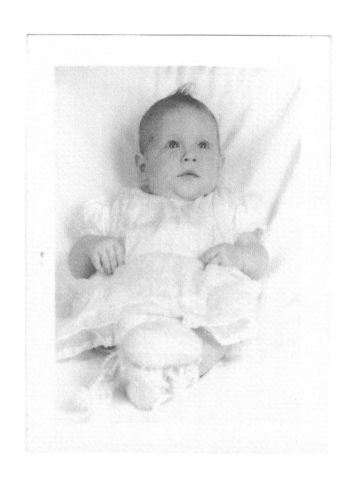

*Heidi 3 months ~ October 1961*

# Chapter Twenty-Four
## A Beautiful Baby Girl
### 1961

Chuck's job the three years we were in Japan was to sit on an "alert pad" in Korea. This meant that flight crews were sent to Korea and while there were on twenty-four hour alert. If the "cold war" became hot – some aggressive action taken against the U. S. by the Russians – our airplanes and crews were instantly ready. The first year we were in Japan Chuck would be gone a week and home a week or ten days. Then the commanders decided to have the flight crews stay in Korea for two weeks at a time. That didn't last long because the men couldn't tolerate two weeks of "alert" duty; it was too intense and they were getting into fights with each other. They cut back to ten days on alert and ten days to two weeks at home and that was tolerable.

On July 25, 1961 Heidi Halsey, a healthy baby girl, was born at Johnson AF Base hospital, about ten miles from Yokota. She weighed eight pounds and one ounce, bigger than both her brothers had been at birth. I denied for a few weeks that her hair was red. Chuck's mother had been a red head when she was young and she always said that when we had a girl she would have red hair. Her daughter, Chuck's sister, was also a redhead and Chuck loved red hair. Heidi's hair turned a beautiful golden copper red that attracted attention throughout her childhood. Japanese people followed us and tried to get close enough to touch Heidi's hair. Having never seen red hair they were fascinated by the color and texture. What more could we ask for, two boys and a girl with red hair, the perfect family.

When the boys were born I would have loved to have them in the same room with me but the policy in those days was to keep babies in the nursery and only take them to their mothers for feeding. Fathers could only see them through the glass windows of the nursery. That policy had just begun to change when Heidi was born and at Johnson Hospital babies were kept in the rooms with their mothers. Since the hospital was in converted barracks buildings with paper-thin walls the poor mothers had a hard time getting any rest all. We could hear all of the babies crying and Heidi added her cries to the din. I literally thought I was going to die from sleep deprivation before they let me go home! After three days Chuck took Heidi and me home where her two brothers were eagerly awaiting the arrival of their baby sister, ready to put her into her new rocking cradle we'd had built especially for her.

Life in Japan became routine as it does wherever one lives, different from life in the U. S. but still it had an established rhythm. Chipper started nursery school, and we took a few trips with and without the children.

We all went to Hakone, a beautiful resort city in the mountains and from there toured the first UNESCO village we'd ever seen. It was a small museum village with houses built in the style of many different countries and we learned a bit about other countries as we toured the houses.

We traveled by bus and cable car to reach a beautiful mountain lake and then took a boat to the opposite end for lunch and sightseeing, new experiences for the boys. Returning late in the afternoon fog closed in on us completely when we were in the cable car, we couldn't see the car in front of us! Then the cable car stopped and the longer we sat there the more frantic I felt because we'd left Heidi, three months old, at the hotel with a sitter. *Oh God, help us! Take care of Heidi. I shouldn't have left her so young! Does anyone even know we're suspended up here in the fog?* After 45 minutes we started moving again and I breathed a sigh of relief.

Leaves turned red and gold and the air frosty. I read about an indoor ski area twenty minutes away. We took Chipper and Guy there and taught them to ski. Not a large area, just man-made snow on a small hill covered with a roof and partial sides, it was fun to be back on skis. Later in the winter we took the boys on the train on a ski trip sponsored by the base recreation department. Chipper

128

had just turned five and Guy was three and a half but they wore backpacks with their clothes and hopped on and off the trains and buses with no trouble. Friends, Rody and Betty Atkinson kept Heidi. That first trip the boys stayed on the bunny slopes and Chuck and I took turns skiing with them. Before we left Japan they were riding the lifts and skiing down the slopes with us.

Chuck and I went to Iwahara for a brief ski trip. On the train a young Japanese woman introduced herself. Her name was Eleanor which was a surprise; I'm sure she had a Japanese name also. Eleanor was married to a European who did not ski so she made a few trips with friends each winter.

The next winter Eleanor planned a ski trip for us and accompanied the boys and Chuck and me to Manza for three days of skiing. On Chip's sixth birthday she arranged a birthday cake for him in the dining room after dinner and everyone helped him celebrate in both Japanese and English. When we moved to Japan again in 1969 Eleanor invited us to her home in Tokyo to have dinner and meet her husband.

In May 1962 after sixteen months of living in the paddies, we moved into base housing, a two story, two and a half bedroom unit that felt luxurious. Downstairs was a large living room, nice size dining room and a kitchen with adequate space for a washer and dryer. Upstairs were two large bedrooms plus the "half" which was designed as a maid's room. Barely large enough for a single bed and small chest it had an adjoining Japanese style bathroom. The toilet was in the floor and one squatted to use it. The bedroom was adequate for Heidi's room and once for about three months we actually had a live-in maid. Wide open space and playgrounds surrounded the buildings so it was great for the kids. On her first birthday a picture shows Heidi pushing her tiny doll buggy up the sidewalk wearing her kimono our maid made for her.

The Japanese tradition "Tango no Sekku" otherwise known as Boys' Day, is celebrated on May 5th. Beautiful multi-colored carp windsocks, one for each son in the family, in descending sizes, are flown from bamboo poles high above the rooftops to wish their sons a good future. Chuck erected a bamboo pole and each May 5th we proudly flew our two carp windsocks.

We spent most summer afternoons at the swimming pool on base. I played bridge occasionally when Chuck was TDY and attended Officers Wives Club luncheons once a month. We had started bowling in El Paso and I really enjoyed the exercise, competition and social time, so we joined a couples league again and I bowled in the Wives Club league. By this time I was quite a good bowler. Silver serving pieces were relatively cheap in Japan so we always gave silver prizes. I came back to the U. S. with a lot of silver, a punch bowl with 24 cups and serving dishes of every size and description. I eventually tired of polishing it all and began giving it away.

Chipper started first grade and the school was just a short block away. Guy was in nursery school and Heidi was approaching a year and a half. Chuck was at home and away and to us, that was normal. Both Christmases we were in Japan we lucked out and Chuck was home with us.

In January 1963 Chuck went to Bangkok, Thailand for two months TDY and from there he went to Saigon, Vietnam for two months. Before he left he was given long shopping lists from friends and acquaintances. Bangkok was a terrific place to shop, especially for bronze flatware, brass candlesticks, jewelry, Thai silk and many other things. Saigon wasn't as good for shopping but he did bring a few things from Vietnam for the children and me.

I'm not sure what Chuck's job was in Bangkok but in Vietnam he was a "Forward Air Controller" advising Vietnamese flight crews who were fighting against the Communists. There was very little in the newspapers available to us about the war in Vietnam but I knew we had military men actually being killed there. I wrote home asking my family and friends if they were even aware there was a war going on in Vietnam and that we had military men there.

Most Americans were unaware in those early years of the war that would grow much bigger and much worse before the 1960's were over. I kept asking "Why are we there?" The only answers I got at that time and later from President Johnson on down had to do with the "domino theory." If Vietnam was lost, the Communists would take over all of Southeast Asia and would then be more of a threat to the U. S. I never understood it then and I still don't

130

understand why the U. S. was involved. In the end besides losing thousands of American lives we lost the war. A united Vietnam is now Communist.

Chuck returned to Japan in May. Before leaving Bangkok he had sent home several boxes of his purchases for other people and for us. The children and I met his flight at Tachikawa AFB. Heidi had been eighteen months old when he left four months before. Chuck picked her up and she pulled back and looked at him for several seconds before smiling and throwing her arms around his neck. It took her a minute or so but Chuck was pleased to see that she remembered him. It was good to have Daddy home again!

In early June Chuck and I flew to Hong Kong for three days of sightseeing and shopping and having fun. Hong Kong in 1963 was, compared to today, not too crowded and not too large to see the highlights and ride the Star Ferry in three days. A few days after we got home we took the children and flew to Okinawa to a military resort on a beautiful beach and had a wonderful time.

The soon-to-be senior class of the Air Force Academy in Colorado Springs arrived at Yokota in June. My oldest nephew, eleven years younger than me, Alan, was a member of the class so we enjoyed some time with him. Alan and I have been close all of our lives with a relationship more like brother-sister than aunt-nephew.

In the fall of 1963 Chipper was in second grade, Guy in kindergarten and Heidi was two years old. They were all growing up. We began to think about where Chuck's next assignment would be and preparing to go home to the States. We applied to go home by ship as we wanted the new adventure. We were turned down and for a couple of reasons and it turned out that we were glad. Chuck received orders to Rome Air Development Center (RADC) at Griffiss AFB in Rome, New York. We would leave Japan on my birthday, December 9th.

On the Sunday morning of November 23rd our telephone rang very early in the morning before we were up. Chuck answered and from his end of the conversation I knew something terrible had happened. He hung up and said "President Kennedy has been assassinated." Just like Americans all over the world and non-

Americans as well, we were shocked and grieved. We didn't have television to watch so had to get our news from the radio and we couldn't just sit and listen to that for long. We had been in the U. S. when John F. Kennedy was elected but had left for Japan before he was sworn in as President so we had lived his entire Presidency outside the U. S.

In early December, a few days before we were scheduled to leave, I started to miscarry our fourth child in the middle of the night. Chuck called for an ambulance to take me to the hospital in Tachikawa. He had to stay with the children so I went alone. It was there I had a "near death experience."

In the middle of the night, those in attendance decided to let nature take its course for a few hours. Someone came to check on me periodically. For a brief period of time I was floating near the ceiling looking down at myself lying in the bed. A nurse came in to check me and said "Oh, My God! Don't go into shock on me." She rushed from the room to summon help and at that time I was thinking *"It would be so easy just to float away – so peaceful."* My next thought was of my three young children and I said to myself *"No! They need me! I can't leave them now."*

The next thing I remembered was waking up in the recovery room after a medical procedure to complete the miscarriage. I recovered rapidly and the next day signed myself out of the hospital and took a taxi home in the robe I'd worn to the hospital. We had already sold our car and Chuck was no longer working but was taking care of the children so it just seemed simpler for me to make my own way home.

A few days later we caught our flight from Tachikawa to the U. S. We encountered a couple of delays before boarding and when we finally were seated on the plane, Heidi started clapping and soon everyone on the flight was applauding. I realized at 2 years and 4 months of age, she was just a few months younger than Guy had been when we moved to Japan. At a re-fueling stop in Seattle before continuing to Los Angeles, I hurried into the terminal and ordered a large glass of milk, my first fresh milk in three years. I had missed it so much! It was delicious and we were all happy to be back in the United States again.

132

*The Halsey Family ~ 1967*

# Chapter Twenty-Five
## Our Last Air Force Assignment
## Rome, New York
### 1964-1967

From the plane's window as we descended in upstate New York I saw a magical kingdom below. Snow covered everything and lights twinkling in the twilight painted a scene much like that in a Christmas story book.

Deeply piled snow on both sides of the runway thrilled us as we knew ski slopes couldn't be far away. Chattering excitedly, we looked forward to living in a place we'd never been and to exploring the northeastern states and eastern Canada during school holidays. It had been a month's journey and we'd finally reached our destination, the place in which we would make our new home, Rome, New York.

Leaving Japan in early December 1963, at two-and-a-half Heidi was quite a talker. When we entered the terminal in Los Angeles Heidi said to the first gray haired woman she saw "Are you my grandmother?" After a few days in warm and sunny southern California to visit Evelyn's family in Riverside, we went on to sunny but cold New Mexico to celebrate Christmas with Chuck's family. New Year's was spent in Atlanta with my family. It was wonderful to see all of our warm loving relatives. They were equally happy to see us after three years and finally meet Heidi.

We arrived in Rome in January 1964. Winter coats bought for a more moderate climate let us know we would have to shop for new winter wear immediately.

Our first day in New York was spent shopping. An officer Chuck would be working with was our assigned sponsor and he drove us to look at new cars. We bought a new Ford station wagon then took the kids shopping for warm winter clothes, snow jackets, pants, boots, mittens and sleds. A day or two later we moved into the four bedroom tri-level house awaiting us in base housing and a couple of days after that the boys started school. In spite of deep snow neighborhood kids walked through the woods to the elementary school half a mile away and Chipper and Guy walked with them. Heidi and I began getting the house organized and meeting our neighbors who were all welcoming.

Chuck planned to retire from the Air Force in June 1967 when he would have twenty years of active duty and would only be thirty-seven years old. Griffiss AFB would be his last assignment. Retiring while he was under forty he expected to have more employment opportunities because in the 1960's there was definitely age discrimination and forty was the age at which a job-seeker was considered "old." That was especially true for pilots and age thirty-five was the maximum for many flying jobs. Chuck had been flying since he was fourteen; it was his passion and he definitely wanted to find a civilian flying job.

The assignment to Rome Air Development Center at Griffiss AFB was a golden opportunity. Chuck would be flying C-135's, the same plane as the Boeing 707, flown by many airlines. The C-135's Chuck flew were filled with high tech equipment which was used to test ground navigational aids all over the world. While in Rome he would be able to prepare for and take the examination for an Air Transport Rating, necessary to fly larger, multi-engine planes such as airliners.

Shortly before we left Japan Chipper's second grade teacher called me to come in. "I've noticed Chipper appears to hold his head to one side. Is there something wrong with him?" Her words frightened me and I explained that Chipper had a birth injury that had been corrected when he was five months old.

"We'll take him to a doctor as soon as we get to New York."

Shortly after we arrived in Rome we took Chipper to an orthopedic specialist. He determined that Chipper had scar tissue from the first surgery and it was pulling his head to the side again. He needed surgery again to release the scar tissue.

Chipper had the operation in a civilian hospital in Utica, New

136

York and spent a week there recuperating with me visiting every day and Chuck in the evenings. He received so many packages and cards from family and friends that when he came home with all of his gifts Guy and Heidi wished they could spend a week in the hospital too!

Our house and the house next door faced each other and shared a large double driveway. At the end of the driveway was a small hill on a level with our front doors which were reached by stairs from the driveway. The boys quickly turned that hill into a sledding hill. They piled snow high and dug tunnels through it for the sleds and spent hours every day playing outside in the snow. Every winter Chuck and the boys packed down the snow in our back yard and every night Chuck sprayed it with water and we had an ice skating rink. Chipper and Guy learned to ice skate and shared fun with many neighborhood kids.

The first spring we lived in New York we saw our neighbor's small travel trailer. It was the first recreational type vehicle we had looked at and we were intrigued. They had four girls and they could all cook, eat and sleep in it.

We soon bought a sixteen foot travel trailer with a double bed in a cab-over. With a sofa bed and a dining booth that made out into a bed, it accommodated all of us.

We tested it on a weekend trip to a lake a couple of hours from home to get used to driving it. We had a good time fishing and hiking and toasting marshmallows over the campfire. That summer when my parents visited we went to the Thousand Islands in the St. Lawrence River in Canada and later when my sister Hazel and her husband Jack and son Dennis came we went to London, Ontario for sightseeing. It was a little crowded with houseguests but we managed because the boys slept in the back of the station wagon. One funny family story was when we were packing the trailer for our first weekend trip I discovered that Chipper had packed almost everything he owned in the trailer! I assured him we were coming home in a couple of days as I insisted he take most of it back inside the house.

The three and a half years we lived in New York we had many wonderful trips towing that little travel trailer behind our station

137

wagon. An early trip was to Niagara Falls, two hundred miles west of Rome. After admiring the grandeur and magnificence of the falls we crossed a bridge and toured a little bit of Canada.

During our first summer there Chuck took leave and we toured eastern Canada and New England. We headed northeast into New York's Adirondack Mountains which were only an hour from our home. Our first stop was Lake Placid, New York, a town made famous in 1932 when it hosted the Winter Olympics and Sonja Henie won her third consecutive Gold Medal for ice skating. Lake Placid is also famous for its bobsled and luge runs. In 1964 it was not much of a summer tourist attraction and we were free to roam over the ski hills and down the toboggan run. Chipper found an old rusty cowbell which we took home and Chuck cleaned and polished and coated it with urethane and we still treasure it.

Going north into Canada we toured Montreal and Quebec City - beautiful and interesting cities with French culture, language and architecture. Traveling across northern Quebec we re-entered the U. S. in northern Maine. Maine is a beautiful heavily forested state and we passed many rivers filled with logs from side to side. When we reached the coast the highlight was Acadia National Park on Mt. Desert Island and Bar Harbor. Acadia is one of the most visited national parks in the U.S. and it was easy to see why. Views are spectacular, the landscape pristine and wildlife plentiful and protected. Bar Harbor is a village on Mt. Desert Island in one of the most picturesque locations in the country. It has been famous for decades, not only because of its beautiful natural surroundings but also because of the genetic research facilities located there and a population of summer residents from many of America's wealthiest families.

After crossing New Hampshire and Vermont we stopped for our last night in a park on the shores of Lake Champlain, the border between New York State and Vermont, where the biggest and hungriest mosquitoes I've ever encountered feasted on us. Throughout our trip the countryside was beautiful and parks with good camping facilities were plentiful..

138

# Chapter Twenty-Six
## More Exploring

The summer of 1965 was the last summer of the New York World's Fair. Heidi was turning four and the boys were seven and eight so we knew we had to go. Not being bold enough to tow the travel trailer through New York City and into crowded areas of Long Island, we stayed at a camping park in New Jersey across the Hudson River and drove to Flushing Meadows in Queens where the fair was held. We spent three days visiting the fair and saw many interesting things from the past and inventions forecasting the future.

Later that summer my sister Lillian and her husband, Larry, came to visit. They arrived at our house after visiting Niagara Falls and Lillian told us all about their time there. From then on, when Heidi was talking to Lillian Heidi kept saying "When you were at "Youragra Falls......."

While they were with us we all went to Cape Cod. We stayed at a park about midway out the cape from which it was easy to explore the area from the Kennedy compound in Hyannis Port to Provincetown on the far eastern tip of the cape.

Our last summer in New York we drove north and west into Canada and drove around the Great Lakes – Ontario, Erie, Huron and Michigan. We didn't go around Lake Superior but when we crossed the bridge at Sault Ste. Marie, Ontario into Michigan, we crossed the edge of Lake Superior. We then drove down the west side of Lake Michigan through Wisconsin and into Illinois, stopping in Chicago for sightseeing. We rendezvoused at a large park on Lake Erie in a campground right on the beach with old friends of mine from Albuquerque days. They now lived in Ohio. After three days of swimming and boating in their boat, we got back on the freeway and headed home.

Two memories from that trip stand out. In Canada we stopped at a ranch where the children rode ponies out in a large pasture. Watching from outside the fence Chuck and I had the scare of our lives when five year old Heidi's pony ran away with her! It looked like it was going fifty miles an hour. Heidi's feet came out of the stirrups, her hair was flying straight behind her and she was holding on for dear life while bouncing up and down in the saddle. One of the workers jumped on a horse and took off after her; just like you see in the movies when he got along side he reached out and grabbed Heidi off that pony. Chuck and I went running across the field to comfort her but when we tried to take her out of the pasture she said "No! I haven't finished my ride yet!"

The second incident involved Heidi also. We were at the beach on Lake Erie with our friends and suddenly I couldn't see Heidi. We all jumped up and started looking and not finding her in the water's edge I headed back toward our camping spot. Just on the other side of it was a large marsh and the children had been there the night before looking for frogs. She wasn't in sight there either and I was almost overcome with fear for what had happened to her. We were all frantically searching when a block or more down the road I spotted Heidi walking towards us holding a woman's hand.

I ran to meet them and the woman said she lived in the permanent mobile home park on the opposite side of the marsh, actually quite a walk away for a five year old. The woman's husband saw Heidi walking around their area, knew she didn't belong and tried to talk to her but Heidi ignored him and kept going. He called for his wife to come out and Heidi talked to her so the woman brought her over to the beach area assuming someone was searching for her. Before we parted she said "Your little girl is well trained. She wouldn't speak to my husband but she didn't hesitate to tell me she was lost."

Winters we skied frequently. Woods Valley was a small ski area less than thirty minutes from home. That was where Heidi learned to ski but a large part of the time she preferred drinking hot chocolate in the warm lodge and watching out the window for us to come skiing down the hill. A larger ski area was an hour or so from us; we went there a few times but not very often.

140

Chuck and I bowled in a couples bowling league and I bowled in the Officer's Wives League. By this time I was a very good bowler and always liked to be the anchor man on our team because I was good under pressure. Frequently if I needed a strike or two in the tenth frame I was able to come through and win the game. Since the Oneida Silver Company was about fifteen miles from Rome, again our bowling trophies were silver serving pieces and we left Rome with our share. My team won our league championship and then the Rome City Championship our last year in New York.

One winter Chuck and I joined our friends from Ohio for a week of skiing in Vermont. We had a warm, motherly middle-age baby sitter who stayed with the children. The morning we were to leave it was snowing heavily so Chuck shoveled the driveway. The snow was coming down so thick and fast he realized the boys would be unable to keep the driveway clear so he hired a teenage neighbor boy to help them with the job. We left with our friends heading east on the New York Thruway while those large, lacy white flakes were piling up.

After a tension-filled five hour drive we made it safely to the lodge at Mt. Snow. Very soon after we arrived we heard an announcement on the loudspeakers set up throughout the village – no one could leave the area because all roads were closed. We later learned that the New York Thruway had been closing right behind us throughout our drive. We had warm accommodations in a comfortable lodge that served delicious food in the dining room. The ski area was open, all lifts were operating, the weather was good and the four of us had a fantastic five days of skiing. We knew the children were well taken care of so none of us thought it necessary to call home.

The following Saturday as we were driving west we noticed the snow piled on the sides of the NY Thruway was getting higher and higher. After we left the Thruway to drive on a state highway the last twenty miles to Rome, it was apparent the region had received massive amounts of snow while we were away. As we got into Rome the snow on each side of all the roads was as high as a house. It was like driving through a tunnel and we became more and more nervous. When we finally reached our street one lane had been plowed down the middle and when we reached home the boys had cleared enough snow from the driveway that we could pull in.

Rushing inside we found everyone warm and safe. They'd been worried about us because they'd heard about the NY Thruway closing stranding thousands of travelers. They tried to call our lodge to find out if we'd made it there but telephone lines were down throughout the northeast so they were unable to get through. They called the State Highway Patrol who were so busy with accidents and stranded travelers that they couldn't learn if we were among them. School was out the entire week so the kids and baby-sitter had a fun-filled vacation. A neighbor stopped by in the middle of the week pulling a big sled. He was walking to the base commissary and stopped to see if our kids needed anything. When we got the entire story we learned that the snow-belt east of Lake Ontario where Rome was located had received the most snow from one storm, twelve feet, that it had received in many years.

We'd been in New York a year when a new family moved in across the street. Stan worked with Chuck and Ruth was a great mother and homemaker. Their four children were close in age to ours so we soon became good friends. Ruth was a very good cook and taught me to make a few of her specialties. She also enjoyed and was good at various crafts. She talked me into making a few things, mostly household decorations, but I was never good nor very interested and soon declined those activities.

Chuck and I bought a side of beef for our new freezer - the first and last time. We discovered two things. We had cuts of meat we'd never bought before and I didn't know what to do with them and we had too many picky eaters in our family who wouldn't eat some of the things I cooked. We needed something else to fill the freezer. The area around us was prime apple-growing country so Ruth and I visited an apple orchard and bought a bushel of apples and spent a few days baking apple pies. We'd no sooner finished than Stan got orders to Vietnam. In 1966 the war was heating up and many of our friends went to Vietnam. The Kibbe's left quickly so the neighbors enjoyed Ruth's pies.

Chuck narrowly missed going to Vietnam again. Shortly after

Stan and Ruth left Chuck was in a group of officers who were "extended" by orders from Air Force Headquarters. This meant Chuck would not be able to retire in June 1967 as planned. We were terribly upset, me especially. A few months before, Chuck would almost routinely have been promoted to Major, but at the time the promotion board met Chuck had less than two years of active duty remaining until he retired. Therefore, he was not considered for promotion.

Being "extended" meant he would be in the Air Force indefinitely and also likely to get orders for Vietnam soon. The men in the "extended" group felt they should be considered for promotion retroactively. They started protesting through official channels asking for reconsideration. I started writing letters to editors of big city newspapers, especially the New York Times and the Washington Post. It took several weeks but just when I thought I was going to have to go on a hunger strike to gain some attention to this grossly unfair situation the order was rescinded and we could turn our attention to planning and preparing for retirement.

Our last year in New York we investigated a variety of job opportunities, both civilian and government. Chuck was the job-seeker while I was the executive secretary. We prepared a resume and filled out multiple applications. The two of us went to New York City for a few days where Chuck had two interviews and I shopped. We also had time for sightseeing and had two dinners in restaurants I'd read about in Playboy. "Mama's Kitchen" was behind a grocery store and we had a great Italian dinner. "Peter's Backyard" was in Greenwich Village so we went early enough to browse the streets and shops before dinner. I bought a dress to wear to our farewell party. It was navy with a 4" white border around the neckline and at the bottom and I received many compliments when I wore it. Again, dinner was delicious and "Peter's Backyard" was a lively place with good music.

Chuck sent an application to The Boeing Company in Seattle, Washington. He was called to come for an interview where he was offered a job in the Flight Test Division to start the middle of July. Chuck accepted the job offer and arranged a thirty-day leave so we left New York in early June, 1967 as soon as school was out. After twenty years and one day in the Air Force, at the age of thirty-seven, Chuck's retirement date and promotion to Major was June 30' 1967. We celebrated in California with my sister Evelyn and her husband, Dean.

I was exhilarated imagining the new life awaiting us in Seattle as we left New York headed south towing our little trailer behind us. After visiting my family in Atlanta we then headed west towards New Mexico. It was summer and hot so we always stopped at RV parks with swimming pools where we could work off energy after driving several hours. We stopped in Memphis to visit Gid and Ann Terry and Debbie and Lisa, good friends in California and Texas and Japan, whom we had not seen since 1962. Next stop was Wichita, Kansas to visit Chuck's Aunt Willard as we hadn't seen her for several years and Chuck was very close to her.

We visited Chuck's mother and sister in New Mexico and indulged ourselves with our favorite Mexican food, then pointed the car towards California. After visiting the Tuck's in Riverside, CA we started up the west coast to go further north than we'd ever been before. In Sunnyvale, we celebrated the 4$^{th}$ of July with the Dooley's who had lived next door to us in New York and had introduced us to travel trailers.

I was especially looking forward to seeing Oregon. When I was in fifth grade, Donna, a good friend and classmate, was bedridden for a year with a heart condition. I visited her two or three times a week, always trying to take something to interest her, a new book or puzzle or game. Donna's relatives in Oregon sent her a View Master 3-D viewer into which she inserted a round disk with about ten pictures on it. When I looked into the viewer scenes of Mt. Hood, Crater Lake, thick forests of evergreens and the rocky Pacific coast came to life. Oregon was the prettiest place I'd ever seen and now I was going to live next door to it in Washington.

After the holiday we began the last leg of our long journey to Seattle looking forward to a new way of life and adventures. When I realized that Seattle was on approximately the same latitude as Quebec, Canada and much further north than Rome, New York, I was afraid that we'd be so far from our friends and family that no one would ever come to visit us. Again, I was very wrong!

144

# Chapter Twenty-Seven
## Mercer Island - Home To Stay
### 1967-1968

Northern California, Oregon and Washington were as green and beautiful as any place I'd ever seen. The mountains were higher and some still had snow on them. The evergreens were huge and majestic and the sky was bluer and bluer as we drove north. By the time we reached Kent, a few miles south of Seattle, my Technicolor eyes were working overtime and I was already in love.

We parked the travel trailer in Kent in a mobile home park with a pool and a recreation room for kids to play in. After finding a Realtor we started looking at houses. We were shown beautiful houses in Bellevue, Lake Sammamish and Issaquah but to people used to living five minutes from Chuck's work they seemed way too far from Boeing Field. Finally we were taken to Mercer Island and I knew instantly that was "it" for me. Mercer Island was in Lake Washington, a thirty-two mile long lake bordering Seattle's east side. The island was six miles long and one mile wide. We could reach downtown Seattle in fifteen minutes by crossing over a floating bridge and going through a tunnel under a small mountain. Chuck could reach Boeing Field in about fifteen minutes as well.

We looked at several houses in our price range from one end of the island to the other. We decided we'd like to live in Mercer Island Country Club Estates, a development of new homes near the south end of the island where there was still a lot of open space and a rural feel. The house we liked best was right across the street from the club with its swimming pool and tennis courts and we loved the location. Unfortunately, it had sold the day before so our Realtor took us to the offices of Swanson & Dean, the builders, who agreed to build us a similar house a block away. They also agreed to rent us one of their new, unsold houses nearby. A few days later we moved into the rental and early on the first morning as I walked into the kitchen, I saw a very large dog crossing our back yard. I was startled when I realized it was a deer!

Before we left New York Chuck had ordered a Mercury Cougar, a popular new model automobile that year, as we knew we'd need two cars. We picked it up at the Mercury dealer in Burien and Chuck started to work at Boeing Field. After he was fully checked out in Boeing planes his job was to check out the pilots of airlines around the world who bought Boeing's airplanes, at that time 707's and 727's. He would fly home with them to their country in Europe or the Middle East and fly their routes with them until everyone was comfortable with the airplane. The 747 was being built and we were taken on a bus to Everett to see the first one when it was finished. It was all very exciting to me.

Living just a block away it was easy to keep watch over construction of our new home, the one I expected to live in for a long, long time. We caught several errors during construction early enough to have them corrected and almost always they were due to the workers not paying attention to the architectural plans for the house. We had started with one of Swanson & Dean's plans but we'd made a few changes and the actual builders would just do things as they always had. When I pointed out to an electrician that he was putting an outside light in a location where there wasn't supposed to be one, irritated, he said to me "This is where we always put the light on Swanson & Dean houses!"

"Do you have a copy of the plans for this house?" I asked.

"They're in the truck," was the gruff reply.

"I suggest you look at them. You'll see that there will not be a light there on this Swanson and Dean house!"   And so it went – day after day. I learned a lot about building a house and in the end we were very happy with it. Swanson & Dean were a pleasure to work with and they finished the house in the four months they'd promised so we moved in before Thanksgiving. We had five bedrooms, three baths, three fireplaces, family room and recreation room plus living room, dining room and kitchen. All we had to do now was furnish it, cover the many large windows and landscape, all to be accomplished slowly as we could afford it. We settled in and felt fortunate that Chuck had such a good job and we could afford such a nice house. For the interest of those reading this many years later, I'll give you some numbers. Chuck's Air Force retired pay was four hundred and fifty dollars a month. His salary at Boeing was $18,000 a year and in 1967 that was a pretty good income. The house cost $40,000, nothing down on a VA loan, closing costs maybe $2,000 and monthly payments including insurance and taxes less than $300.

Immediately after moving into the rental house the kids started asking "When do we get our dog? What kind are we going to get?" For years whenever they'd ask for a pet we put them off by telling them

"When Daddy retires and we're living in our permanent home, that's when we'll get a dog. We can't get a pet as long as we're moving every three years." I think they almost expected their dog to be waiting on the doorstep and wagging its tail when we got to Washington.

We went to the library and borrowed several books about dogs with pictures of the different breeds and traits and characteristics of each. We studied books for several days and when we read about Norwegian Elkhounds they sounded like the perfect dog for us. The book said they were excellent family dogs, gentle with children but good watch dogs as well. We decided on that breed and started calling around. I located a breeder in what is now Federal Way; they had puppies that were just four weeks old and they would not show or sell them until they were eight weeks old so we'd have to wait. Once we were that close to getting a dog it was like waiting for a baby to be born; we were eager and impatient.

Finally, the evening came when Chuck drove us to Federal Way after he came home from work. When we arrived at the breeder's kennel and home, she invited us into the house. She had a litter of eight puppies and seven of them were in the backyard and one was in the kitchen. Even though she had a barrier two or three feet high from the kitchen to the backyard to keep the puppies out, one of the puppies was able to get over it and was in the kitchen. She picked it up and we all went into the back yard.

The puppies had fur so thick they looked like bear cubs. They were all cute and cuddly and we sat on the grass and played with them. The kitchen puppy was the smallest, the runt of the litter, and she had a slight sideways gait but she was the one the kids chose to take home. I had lined a box with newspapers and held the puppy in my lap in the box for the drive home. After a couple of days we decided to name her "Princess Elke" because she definitely acted like a princess and "Elke" because it sounded Norwegian. Heidi insisted on adding the name "Fireball" because she was also that, constantly jumping up on six year old Heidi and sending her jumping up on chairs or tables or running from the room with Elke on her heels. And so our puppy became "Fireball Princess Elke" and brought us great joy and comfort for sixteen years.

When school started in September Heidi was in first grade. Guy, who now wanted to be called Steve, was in fourth grade and Chipper, from now on known as Chip, was in sixth grade. It was about a mile to their schools but there was a bus and because it was dark when they left in the early winter mornings they usually rode the bus. When spring came the boys started playing Little League baseball and taking tennis lessons. In the summer all three were on swim teams at the swim/tennis club. The family across the street had three boys around the ages of Chip and Steve and a girl Heidi's age so with school friends close by they had a lot of friends. We settled into an average every-day life. Elke was a happy dog with a nice fenced yard to run in but when the kids weren't home she would frequently manage to get out. Her two favorite spots were the pond a quarter of a mile from our house or the horse ring a block and a half in the other direction. No matter which one she chose she always came home wet and stinking and I would have to give her a bath. Invariably I ended up soaked also!

We had our first houseguest about a month after we arrived in Washington, my nephew Ken. He had recently graduated college and was spending the summer driving around the country. Ken and the kids and I left early one morning and drove one hundred miles to Vancouver, Canada, a stunningly beautiful city between the mountains and the sea. In the few hours we had there, we drove through downtown and Stanley Park. This was a tour I learned well gradually adding more of the sites around Vancouver to show people. The two years we lived in Washington we had a steady stream of visitors, both friends and family. Since 1967 I have seen many cities around the world and Vancouver still tops my list of beautiful cities. The mountains, the water and the city right there; stunning views wherever you look.

We'd been in Washington a year when Mama and Daddy came to visit us, Daddy's first commercial flight. Mama had flown on trips with her seniors club but Daddy always said "If the Lord wanted me to fly he'd have given me wings." At least he said that until a few years before when my brother-in-law, Danny, had bought a small plane. Not long before they came to Washington Danny had finally persuaded Daddy to go up with him and I had a conversation with Daddy about that.

"Daddy, after refusing to fly in an airplane for so many years when you finally decided you'd do it, the least you could have done was to choose a professional pilot!"

"I prayed about it and the Lord told me that if I trusted the pilot I would be safe and I trusted Danny."

I used that as leverage to get Mama and Daddy to fly to Washington to visit us. Towing our travel trailer we showed them and ourselves a good bit of western Washington. We camped in a state park on Whidbey Island and took a ferry through the San Juan Islands. The ferry system is incredible and such a fun way to travel! We went to Ocean Shores for clamming and Mama cooked us a big pot of clam chowder. We all had our first visit to a rain forest after driving north on Hwy. 101 from Ocean Shores. We had taken them into Mexico when they visited us in El Paso and into Ontario, Canada when they came to see us in New York so now, of course, we had to take them to Vancouver, British Columbia. They agreed with me about its beauty. Who wouldn't?

While Mama and Daddy were visiting, Chuck and I took a trip. We drove to Port Angeles, on the Olympic Peninsula, and took the ferry to Victoria, B. C. where we stayed in a picturesque English cottage style hotel. Buchart Gardens was a picturesque treat and gave us some ideas for additions to our landscaping. Victoria is a very interesting old city and we enjoyed our three day stay there. We took the ferry from Victoria to Vancouver and after sightseeing there we drove east to Kelowna and Penticton then south on Hwy. 97 into Washington and back through central Washington. Chuck and I always grabbed every chance we had to get away alone for a few days. Of course he had always traveled a lot in his work but he recognized that I needed a break now and then from my regular routine.

Chuck was training Egyptian Airlines pilots and said he'd like to have them for dinner. I tried to figure out what to feed them as I knew their religion forbade most meats and various other things. We decided we'd serve salmon. I had never cooked salmon but studied my recipes and Chuck planned to grill it on the hibachi we'd brought from Japan. After greeting our guests and serving hors d'oeuvres I excused myself and went to the kitchen to prepare the salmon for the grill. I had pre-ordered fresh salmon from the butcher a few blocks away and had picked up the package that afternoon. What I had in mind was salmon fillets but when I opened it and saw that large fish eye staring up at me I was horrified and panicked! I called Chuck to the kitchen and told him to keep the conversation going while I dashed to the butcher's to see if I could get some salmon fillets. Chuck tried to slow me down but I wouldn't listen and was out the back door like a flash. When I returned with a package of fillets Chuck and the guests were in the kitchen filleting the fish that had panicked me so. Terribly embarrassed I apologized and we all had a good laugh and later an excellent dinner. From that point on we served salmon whenever we could.    Chuck and I joined a bowling league and made many new friends. We also played in a couple's bridge club and I belonged to the Newcomer's Club so we were settling in, making friends and making Mercer Island our home.

# Chapter Twenty-Eight

## Big Changes
### 1968-1969

Air Force friends from our California and El Paso days moved to Washington. Dave Robinson left the Air Force and was flying for United Airlines. He asked to be transferred to Seattle and he and Jan stayed with us when they came up to search for a home. They found a place on Lake Morton in Kent and soon were back to sign the closing papers and leave a couple of their kids with us for a few days while they went back to California to complete arrangements for moving. We loved Dave and Jan and were happy to have them close enough to visit.

Robinson's invited the kids and me to Kent to share Thanksgiving dinner with them since Chuck was away working. Though missing Chuck we enjoyed the day with our friends. I watched Jan prepare her turkey and put it into a brown paper bag that she rubbed with cooking oil. The turkey came out of the oven a beautiful golden brown and was the best I'd ever tasted. She gave me the directions for preparing the turkey and the bag and for many years we cooked our Thanksgiving turkey in a brown paper bag. It was always delicious but we always had the same problem. Somehow we'd manage to poke a hole in the bag, spill the juices onto the oven floor and start a fire! After the first few times we just laughed and said it wouldn't be Thanksgiving without a fire in the oven!

We hadn't yet bought much furniture, making do with what we had. When we moved into our new home we bought Heidi's first real bedroom furniture. I had fallen in love with it when I first saw it and when I showed it to Heidi she liked it also. The furniture was made by Stanley and was kind of Mexican style, heavy, distressed and painted antique yellow with rose and green trim. We only bought one twin bed and a dresser and mirror as that was all we could afford. We intended to add more pieces later.

For the boys' rooms we bought unfinished furniture, a chest of drawers and a desk for each room. They each had one of the bunk beds we'd purchased in New York. We painted Chipper's furniture a rich, full blue and Steve's a medium shade of red and finished each piece with a distressed look. All of the kids were happy to have their own rooms plus we had an extra bedroom that I used for an office until we could afford to furnish it for a guest bedroom. Meanwhile, Chuck and I slept on the sofa bed in the family room whenever we had guests.

"Chip, what is that you're carrying?" He'd asked a couple of hours before if he could go to the pet store with the family across the street. Now he was cradling in his arms a precious orange and white stripped young kitty.

"It's just a small kitty cat. I only paid a dollar for him."

"Oh, Chip! You know I've never liked cats." I looked at the tiny kitty and at the look of love on Chip's face and what could I say? "He is cute and small. I guess I won't be afraid of him. He just better not brush up against my legs though. I hate that!"

Elke and Tiger became the best of friends, chasing each other around the house and yard and we frequently found Elke snoozing on the deck with Tiger curled up closely against her. Tiger quickly learned that I did not like him to brush against my legs and he didn't do that. He wanted to please me because even though it wasn't my job I was the one who most often fed him. Frequently in the late evenings I'd get out of bed where I'd been reading and go in to find Chuck in the family room with both Elke and Tiger snuggled in his lap.

We had our usual good Christmas in 1968 with a big tree in front of the living room windows. We shared Christmas cheer with our neighbors across the street and took in the kids' school pageants.

A few days after Christmas our world and my visions of our future exploded. The kids and I were leaving to go to Sears, near Boeing Field, when Chuck called and said he'd meet us in the

152

parking lot. The instant I saw his face it was obvious something had happened. "Honey, what's wrong? You look terrible! Are you sick?"

"I've been fired!"

"I don't believe it! Don't kid me!"

"I'm not kidding! Several of us in Flight Test have been fired. They didn't give us much of an explanation but, apparently, Boeing hasn't sold enough airplanes so they don't need all of us."

"Oh, my gosh! What are we going to do?" Looking at the shocked expression on Chuck's face, I added, "Try not to worry. We'll figure it out." Inside I was feeling very scared.

First thing when we got home I put pencil to paper to figure out how we were going to make ends meet until Chuck found a new job. I quickly wrote a letter to Chuck's brother for Chuck to sign and asked if he could please repay us money he'd borrowed when we first got to Washington. He owed us about eight hundred dollars and we needed it now but we didn't get it.

The next thing I did was something that has bothered my conscience ever since. Chipper was in seventh grade and we had allowed him to sign up for a weekly ski trip to Snoqualmie sponsored by the school. We had recently paid the $150 it cost and I called the school and explained that we'd be moving soon and needed to cancel Chipper's participation and asked for a refund. They reluctantly agreed to send it. I felt I had no choice. We did not know how quickly we might have to sell the house and move and since we were cutting down on all non-essential expenses it didn't seem fair to the other kids to allow Chipper to go skiing every week. I still wonder if that was the right decision.

There was no way we could live on Chuck's Air Force retirement pay and we had put all of our savings into our new house. I checked his life insurance policies and saw that we had cash value available that we could borrow so I knew we'd be able to stay afloat for a few months.

Chuck and I began updating his resume and the list of potential employers and he began contacting those that seemed the most promising. It was then we began to learn that the civilian aviation industry is an unstable one, suffering highs and lows in an unpredictable cycle.

In spite of the knot of fear I was carrying around - some days it seemed to be in my chest and other days in my stomach - we carried on our lives as well as we could. I felt guilty about spending money for Chuck and I to continue in our bowling league and asked our partners to try to find someone to take our place. We told them we might have to move before the league ended and thought it would be more fair to them and to the replacement couple to have them start as quickly as possible. Before a replacement was found though, we had to quit anyway.

One night while bowling I reached out with one hand and picked up my ball from the rack. Chuck had always told me to use both hands to pick up the ball. When I picked it up I felt a small sensation in my lower back, so small it felt like a rubber band breaking. Instantly I knew I wouldn't be able to roll that ball. I didn't say anything, however, and prepared to roll the ball but I had to stop. My back was beginning to hurt and I just couldn't do it.

The next morning it was as if I was paralyzed. I couldn't move a finger without excruciating pain in my back. After getting the children off to school Chuck carried me to the car and loaded me in. Since it was the closest place Chuck took me to the Public Health Hospital not far past the floating bridge and tunnel leading to Seattle. X-rays were taken and evaluated before the doctor sat down with us. "You have a ruptured disk. It's a pretty bad rupture and it's going to take a while to heal. You can stay here in the hospital in traction, but, how old are your children?"

"The boys are 12 and 10 and Heidi is 7."

"Due to the ages of your children, I know you'd rather be home. I can give you a prescription for muscle relaxants and pain killers and you can go home. You'll have to stay in bed, but I know you won't be moving around anyway. This is going to take a while to resolve itself."

As I lay in bed in horrible pain needing assistance for everything, it almost seemed a blessing that Chuck was out of work and at home taking care of the kids and house and me, all

154

while looking for a new job.

After a month when I was no better at all I studied the telephone book. I wanted some kind of active intervention for my back. I felt as if I could lie in bed forever and nothing would change. I had always heard that chiropractors were "quacks" and I was afraid to go to one. I knew that osteopaths did some muscular manipulation and that they had more medical training. Desperate for help I called an osteopathic physician and made an appointment. Chuck still had to practically carry me to the car and put me in and help me hobble into the doctor's office.

The doctor was a miracle worker. First he gave me heat treatments on my back and then the most gentle massage I'd ever had from the top of my head to the bottom of my feet. I was lying there thinking this was a waste of time and money! But, you know what? I was able to get off the massage table and stand up straighter than I had since I'd picked up that bowling ball, then walked out to the car on my own. After a second treatment I was well on the road to recovery and that was just in time.

Chuck had scheduled an interview in Burlingame CA with a company called IASCO, International Air Service Company. IASCO supplied commercial pilots to airlines around the world. By the time he left I was able to drop him off at the airport and drive the car home and then pick him up a few days later. Chuck had been offered a job flying as a Captain for Japan Air Lines. It was now the middle of March and Chuck would leave the middle of April to go to Japan for Ground School training. When that was completed in July he would return to Moses Lake WA for JAL's flight training.

My heart and mind were full of mixed feelings. Very relieved that Chuck had found a flying job that paid well, I was disappointed that we'd have to move back to Japan. I hadn't liked it the first time we'd lived there and now, six years after returning to the States, I had a tough decision to make. I was excited about the generous number of free and ninety per cent discount tickets allotted us and knew we could travel every time the kids were out of school. For me that was the redeeming factor that helped me say "Yes, Chuck, if that's what you want to do, we will move back to

Japan."

Chuck left the middle of April shortly after we'd put the house on the market for sale. It wasn't a very good time to sell because thousands of Boeing employees had been let go and homes were for sale all over the Seattle area. There was even a big billboard along I-5 that said "Would the last person leaving Seattle please turn off the lights." Our house sold for $47,500, an amount that after sales costs and money we'd spent on the house for window treatments, landscaping, etc., allowed us to just about break even. We could stay in it until school was out.

By early June besides the house, I'd sold two cars, most of our furniture and sorted out fifteen hundred pounds of personal effects for JAL to ship to Japan for us. Another few hundred pounds went to storage. We spent one night in a hotel close to the airport where, at 9PM, the buyer picked up the Ford station wagon we'd bought when we moved to Rome, New York in 1964. Early the next morning Chip, Steve, Heidi, Elke and Tiger and I boarded a flight to Atlanta where we'd spend a month with our extended family before heading back to Japan.

# Chapter Twenty-Nine

## Summer of 1969

Lillian and Larry graciously opened their home as well as their arms to us when we arrived to spend a few weeks in Atlanta. They would keep Tiger and send Elke to us in Japan as soon as we had a house.. Our only definite plans were for Heidi to go to camp in July with my brother, Jimmy's daughters, Selina and Dee Anne. We'd spend our time visiting Mama and Daddy and my brothers and sisters and their families and I hoped to see some of my aunts, uncles and cousins that I hadn't seen for a long time.

I was full of energy and enthusiasm for whatever was in front of us. We had embarked on another adventure unable to even imagine what our life would be like living in Japan again. This time we would live in Yokohama, a very large city, totally different from the rural area two hours north of Tokyo where we'd lived before. After recovering from my ruptured disk in Washington I had gone on a strict diet to lose the extra pounds I'd accumulated the weeks I'd spent in bed. I had my weight down to 107 lbs. and wore sizes six and seven, the smallest I'd been since before Chuck and I had married thirteen years before. I had all new clothes and relished looking good. I was happy and excited!

"You're too skinny!"

"Your wrinkles are starting to show!" (I was thirty-eight years old!)

"You need to gain some weight!"

All words I'd never heard before and honestly never expected to hear in my life. These remarks greeted me over and over in Atlanta. Most of my family ranged from just the right size to maybe a little pleasingly plump but I can't think of one blood relative who was ever called "skinny." Nothing they said could burst my balloon of happiness. I was going to have a whole new life and I was looking forward to it, mentally planning trips all over the world that I'd be taking with free and ninety per cent discount tickets.

We filled our time visiting family and keeping busy with whatever activities came along. Lillian and I decided to take the kids to the beach in Florida. We drove to Starke, a full day's drive from Atlanta, and stayed there a few days reminiscing with old friends, most we hadn't seen since we'd left Florida in 1947. That was where I'd lived with Lillian and Ken and Billy for a year after Elmo was killed in a plane crash in 1946. From Starke we went to Cocoa Beach where we had a reservation at a hotel right on the beach. Vivian, one of my best friends from the year of high school I went to in Starke, lived in nearby Merritt Island and we spent a fun day with her and her children. The kids could hardly believe how warm the Atlantic Ocean is compared to the Pacific and we all really enjoyed the wide white sandy beach.

Chuck and I kept the Post Office busy with letters going back and forth between us. I had much to write about. He'd left the middle of April and I'd handled all of the business of selling the house, cars, furniture, and arranging the move.

While going through training Chuck was living in Bayside Court, the Navy Guest Hotel in Yokohama. The Officer's Club was next door and he ate most of his meals there. About one hundred IASCO-JAL crews (pilots and navigators) lived in the Yokohama area so Chuck met and spent time with several of them as well as the group of pilots he was going through training with. Everyone shared information about houses, the best areas to live in, schools, both military and international, and shopping. There were a lot of retired military pilots and some of the ones who were already settled into their own homes invited the "temporary bachelors" living at Bayside Courts to a home cooked meal now and then which the men greatly appreciated.

Chuck's letters were filled with details of his days spent in DC-8 Ground School and simulator training. He wrote several letters each week and they all began: *Dear Ones,*

*... ...We have to take a cab from here to the Yokohama train*

158

*station, then catch a bus to the Haneda Air Terminal, then a JAL shuttle bus to the other side of the airport for ground school. The commute takes about an hour and a half. I had a personal interview with the Vice President of JAL who, along with the Assistant Chief Pilot and the Director of Training, decides who is OK to be hired by JAL.*

Chuck might not have been hired had they seen the tattoo he had on his left forearm. In Japan tattoos are associated with criminals. Before he left Washington he had begun surgery to remove it but since it was done in small increments he wasn't finished with it and kept a skin colored bandage over it. He rued the day the drunken nineteen year old Air Force man that he was went along with his buddies to get a tattoo. Chuck's was a heart with a flag across it with his name "Chuck" on the flag. Guess he was lucky he didn't have a girlfriend at the time!

His letters were long, six or eight pages, as he had a lot to tell us, not only about his training but what kinds of things were available to buy in the Base Exchanges, furniture, appliances, etc. He also always asked a lot of questions:

*…..Do you have your passports yet? Any interest in the house yet? Things keep getting delayed here so I'm not sure when I'll be in Moses Lake. If the house is sold what will you do – go to Atlanta?* Every letter was full of potential schedules – both his and ours.

Chuck was already looking at houses; he'd write about houses some of the men had rented and houses he'd looked at for us, telling us in detail where they were and why they might or might not be good for us.

*…..Dave Holdsworth got a big house down south near the ocean but he has a commuting problem. He is flying 727's,* meaning shorter routes and more flying days per month. *But he said the DC-8 guys can live practically anywhere because we will only be flying four or five trips a month. Dave has seven bedrooms and five baths for $300 per month. He said there are a lot of western style houses in his area and the kids can get to the international school pretty easy.*

Pretty soon Chuck bought a used Toyota for $250 with a

guarantee the dealer would buy it back at the end of his ground school training. Three or four friends rode with him each day and shared the cost of gas and tolls. The commute was cut in half to forty-five minutes.

Chuck was missing us all and looking forward to getting his family back together again. He recognized the huge job I'd been left with and appreciated that I was up to the challenge and

*... ...I'm hoping you're getting some rest and relaxation.*

The kids and I were enjoying our summer vacation but we were also eager for it to end so we could begin our regular life again in Yokohama – whatever kind of life that would be.

We'd been in Atlanta a month or so when Chuck finally knew the date he'd be in Moses Lake. After a lot of writing back and forth about plans and dates I received an envelope full of tickets. My ticket was from Atlanta to Seattle to Moses Lake where I'd spend a week with Chuck while he had flight training in the DC-8. Chip, Steve and Heidi had tickets to Riverside, CA where they'd stay with my sister Evelyn's family until I joined them there after a week in Moses Lake. Later we'd all meet Chuck in San Francisco to travel to Japan together. He'd send those tickets later.

I was happy to be on my way back to Washington and to Chuck. When I picked up my bags at SeaTac I was missing my small cosmetic bag. When I reported it to the airline they said to fill out a lost bag report and if and when it turned up they'd send it to me. I insisted that would not do! I had medications in that bag that I must have (a lie) – "Won't you please send someone out to the plane for another look?" I was actually surprised when they did that but a few minutes later someone showed up carrying my bag and I headed to Boeing Field for my flight to Ephrata.

Ephrata was the closest commercial airport to Moses Lake in 1969 and the flight from Seattle took just under two hours. Chuck had said he'd meet me but if he was flying he'd have someone else meet me or, if necessary, I should rent a car and drive to Moses Lake as it was not too far.

The flight arrived at 9:05PM but since it was the middle of July it was still light outside. Just two or three of us got off the plane at Ephrata and everyone quickly left the small airport. No one else was around and after I waited a few minutes I spoke to the only airport worker still there. I asked him about getting a taxi to Moses Lake and he told me taxi service wasn't available. He helped me find the number for the Travelodge because he was closing the airport for the night.

I called and Chuck was nervously waiting to hear from me. When he learned there was apparently no way for me to get to Moses Lake on my own he borrowed the motel manager's car and said he'd be there as quickly as he could. By the time Chuck arrived it was almost dark and I was totally alone and trying to hide in the shadows so as not to attract attention if the bogey man happened by. After about thirty minutes Chuck drove up and the minute I recognized him I was running towards the car and he was out of it and running towards me. It had been three months since we'd parted the middle of April and we had a joyous reunion.

Thankfully, Chuck was not scheduled to fly the next day. He was eager to see my new slimmed down self in my new swimsuit so after breakfast we headed for the pool. Chuck began introducing me to some of his classmates and a few of their family members. Dave Lindig was there with his wife Dianne. Dave became a good friend and he visited me after Chuck's death and I was living in southern California. I also met Fernando Serra and his wife Mavis and their five year old auburn haired daughter, Sharon. We became good friends with the Serra's and spent much time together in Japan and later in Anchorage. Fernando was from Chile and Mavis from Northern Ireland but Sharon was American, having been born in San Francisco. Through the Serra's I began to learn about the international airline pilots' community. Fernando had worked for several different international airlines and knew some of the JAL pilots when he went to work for JAL. I learned it is a large, fluid community that moves around the world wherever the jobs are. While in Japan we made many good friends from European countries and Australia. The people were always interesting to me because their lives had been so different from mine.

I'd been in Moses Lake a couple of days when on July 20, 1969 the United States achieved the first manned landing on Earth's Moon as part of the Apollo 11 mission. Commanded by Neil Armstrong who was accompanied by Buzz Aldrin they landed

161

the lunar module "Eagle" on the surface of the moon. Chuck and I were part of the five hundred million people worldwide who, through the magic of television, were watching the historic event. Armstrong said the famous words "Houston, Tranquility Base here. The Eagle has landed." Six and half hours later, by now July 21st, Armstrong made his descent to the Moon's surface and spoke his famous line "That's one small step for man, one giant leap for mankind." We were both thrilled and excited to be witnessing history.

One day we rented a car and with the Serra's drove to Grand Coulee Dam and to the lake near Moses Lake. We just wanted to see a little of central Washington.

My week with Chuck ended too soon and I had to tell him good-bye again. Good-byes had been a constant in our marriage but each time I knew the next "hello" reunion would again be sweet. I flew to Riverside to reclaim my children who'd been with Evelyn and Dean for several days and playing with their cousins Lisa and Ross. Evelyn and I took them all to Laguna Beach for a few days of California sun and fun. Before long Chip, Steve, Heidi and I flew to San Francisco for a reunion with Chuck whom the children had not seen in more than three months. After a couple of days in San Francisco the family boarded a Japan Air Lines DC-8 and all flew together to Japan for the next chapter in our nomadic-seeming life.

*Isogo, Japan ~ 1969*

# Chapter Thirty

## Japan Air Lines Yokohama 1969

In late July, 1969 we landed at Tokyo's Haneda Airport. Chuck had recently completed JAL flight training and now the family was going to live in Yokohama. Chip was twelve, Steve eleven and Heidi had just had her eighth birthday. Excited about the opportunities we'd have to travel with free and ninety per cent discount tickets I still had mixed emotions about living in Japan again. I felt like I'd been there and done that and once was enough!

Seeing the drab gray buildings, throngs of Japanese people and inhaling the familiar smells I was almost overcome with shock and sadness. It was all I could do to get through immigration without bursting into tears. I didn't want to do that to Chuck and the children so gritted my teeth and walked ahead of them so they couldn't see my face. We climbed into a limousine with our bags and headed for Yokohama.

A city with more than a million inhabitants, Yokohama supplied an endless variety of things to do and see. An international seaport for a hundred years it was home to businesses from Europe and Asia as well as the United States. A large international community attracted residents from around the world and we would soon become a part of it.

Our temporary home was Bayside Court, the U. S. Navy Guest Hotel in Yokohama. The hotel was located in a group of old two story barracks buildings. Within the compound was a coffee shop where we had breakfast, beauty and barber shops, a library and various other facilities. We had two rooms on the second floor of one of the buildings. The rooms were quite large and each room had twin beds, a table, a desk and a refrigerator. They added a third bed for Heidi in the boys' room. There was a community kitchen down the hall and men's and women's showers and rest rooms, the kind of place we wouldn't have considered staying in if we were in the U. S. but we weren't and under the circumstances we were glad to have the accommodations. The price was right – about $10 a night for both rooms.

Located on the bluff above the hotel complex was the Navy Officers' Club where we ate dinner every night. Even after we moved into a house we continued to eat there several nights a week. Our many non-American friends could only go the "O" Club as guests of members. Since living on the Japanese economy was extremely expensive our friends saved a lot of money by eating there. We enjoyed the camaraderie and soon had a group of five or six families that we regularly shared dinners with. Every Sunday before dinner the Club had a floor show especially for children – magicians, acrobats, comedians, etc. Monday night was Mongolian BBQ night and for three years we rarely missed a Monday night. Tuesday night was steak and movie night, usually a fairly current movie. Every night had its theme but those were our favorites.

School would be starting soon. We had a choice of U. S. Navy schools or international schools and decided to register the kids at the Navy schools. Since Chuck was not active duty military we had to pay tuition but it was reimbursed by Japan Air Lines. Chip went into eighth grade at Niles C. Kinnick High School, Steve went into sixth grade and Heidi into third grade at the Navy elementary school. School buses picked them up at the hotel.

Chuck had looked at a number of houses for rent before the family got to Japan but had not found one he liked so we started searching for a place together. With such a large foreign colony in Yokohama there was a lot of competition for houses. Many foreign companies owned houses for their employees but Japan Air Lines did not. We were on our own to find a place with our housing allowance of $500 a month. Compared to our house payment in Mercer Island of $325 a month that sounded generous. However, when we began looking at houses for rent, naturally we found that almost every place we looked at rented for $500 or more a month.

The Bluff area of Yokohama was a desirable place to live. Homes dated back to early in the twentieth century and most were quite large and were British or European in design. Only those

166

homes that had been seriously renovated met American standards for comfort, especially in the kitchen, bathroom and closet areas. We looked at several houses on the bluff but I was always dragging my feet and by the time I decided a house was acceptable someone else had already signed a contract! Unbeknownst to me I acquired a reputation for being hard to please and real estate agents didn't want to waste time even though they knew we had to have a place to live. Once they had showed a customer three places they believed a decision should be made!

Eventually I found a house in Isogo – a suburb three or four miles south towards Yokosuka. The house had a lot of potential. Large and imposing, it sat on top of a hill. At street level 8' iron gates were immediately adjacent to the road. Our parking space was right on the other side of the gates which meant we had to stop our car in traffic, get out and open the gates and then maneuver into our spot. This procedure was reversed every time we left. From the parking space stairs traversed the hill from side to side up to the house. Renting a house with a parking space was essential because you were not allowed to buy or register a car until you had a legal parking place. The police actually came out and inspected before you got your registration. Until we bought a car we used taxis to get around and, fortunately, they were very inexpensive. The yard was mostly fenced and we only had to add one small section before we sent for Elke to come to us from Atlanta.

We had left Elke, our Norwegian Elkhound in Atlanta with Lillian and Larry. Larry loved dogs more than anyone I've ever known. He always had his own constant canine companion. In early September we had a letter from Lillian telling us that Larry said we'd better send for Elke soon or he'd have a problem letting her go. By the time we received the letter we had rented the house in Isogo but had not yet moved in. We were still living in Bayside Court but Elke had been in Atlanta going on three months and we knew we had to send for her.

It was a long, long way from Atlanta to Tokyo and when we met Elke at the airport cargo area I don't know who was more excited, Elke or our family. The minute they opened her kennel she bounded out and was all over us. Rain earlier that day had left puddles on the pavement so after greeting us Elke found a deep

167

puddle and drank it dry. Clearly she had not been given enough water en route but was okay and she was with us again. Bayside Court didn't allow pets but we couldn't stand the thought of taking Elke to the Navy Base kennel so we parked the car near the back entrance to our building and led Elke up the back stairs to our rooms. We got away with keeping her with us until we moved into our house a few days later.

Once we moved into the Isogo house we really enjoyed it. It was sunny and spacious. The entry hall was quite wide and ran past the living room on the right, then a tatami room and ended at the dining room. On the left side of the entry hall was a toilet, just that, no sink. Then came stairs leading up to three bedrooms. Past the stairs was a large library style cabinet along the wall; it was quite attractive with glass doors and we used it to store books and knick-knacks. Our telephone sat on top of the cabinet. Behind that wall was a bedroom which became Chip's room. Past Chip's room was a full western style bath and then a huge Japanese style bath, a large fully tiled room with a family sized soaking tub. We rarely used the Japanese bath because it took more than a full tank of hot water to put just a few inches of water into the tub. There was another older hot water tank especially for that bath but it was so old we were afraid to use it.

The dining room, made bright and cheerful with a full wall of windows, was my favorite. I also loved the tatami room. On the floor were tatami mats (made of straw) and shoji screens closed it off from the entry hall. From a back corner of the dining room you entered a poor excuse for a kitchen. There was an ancient sink, a kitchen cabinet similar to the one in my family kitchen in the 1930's and a stove from the same era. Upstairs were three bedrooms and a full bath. Steve's and Heidi's rooms opened onto a balcony which gave me some comfort knowing that in case of fire they could quickly exit to the balcony and drop one story to the grass. The house was old, probably built in the 1920's, and fires did happen. Acquaintances lost a little girl Heidi's age and a baby when their house burned down so the threat of fire was always a concern.

Before we moved in we had the entire house painted inside and purchased new rugs, one of which we designed and had made.

168

I sewed drapes for all the windows. We bought a new stove and refrigerator and had a cabinet built for the kitchen but managed to get along with the rest. The yard was large and fenced so it was perfect for Elke. There were many shrubs and flowers and a waterfall in one corner and a gardener came with the house.

Soon we had a "milkman" that we called and asked for a designated number of quarts. Each quart represented one thousand dollars and he would soon deliver a bag of Japanese "yen." For example we usually ordered from three to five quarts at a time, depending on the current exchange rate. If the milkman's rate was good, and it was always better than the bank rate, we'd order five quarts; if it was lower than we liked we'd order one or two quarts. We knew this was an illegal transaction but everyone we knew bought their yen from the milkman so we did also. Fortunately no one was arrested while we were there. Even riskier, and today I can't explain how I had the nerve, I made at least one trip alone to Hong Kong to buy $5,000 worth of yen because the rate in Hong Kong was much better than the milkman's! It was illegal to take it into Japan but I got away with it.

The kids had to walk down the steep hill beside our house to "D" Street, the main north-south thoroughfare through Yokohama and on south to Yokosuka and Atamai. On "D" Street their school buses picked them up and dropped them off. Chip was going to junior high and left early, around 8 AM. Steve and Heidi were still in elementary school and they were on the second shift so they didn't have to leave until around 11AM. We learned to enjoy sleeping late and getting up to do homework in the morning when everyone was rested. At first I got up early with Chip and tried to fix breakfast for him but he was adamant and insisted he could fix his own breakfast and liked to get up and out of the house alone. It didn't take much to persuade me to stay in bed! Early in the school year Chip broke his arm in gym class. The next morning when I got up early to help him with breakfast he said "Mom, go back to bed! I don't need any help; I can get my breakfast with one hand!"

# Chapter Thirty-One

## Yokohama - Isogo
### 1969

$O$ur family's life soon settled into a routine. We joined the Yokohama Country and Athletic Club, a club started by British expatriates around 1890. Now it was an international club with members from many different countries. Athletics available were bowling, tennis, cricket and, most important, darts. In summer there was also swimming.

There was always a dart game being played in the bar and sometimes we joined in. Chuck started playing tennis on his days off and I wanted to play also. Even though all of my life I had gone to a tennis court and hit balls, I'd only had a few lessons in Mercer Island and I wasn't yet a good player. The tennis pro at YCAC was much in demand and I had a hard time lining up lessons with him. Eventually I learned to play well enough to play with other beginners but I never took it seriously as I would ten years later.

Much of our social life revolved around the YCAC and the JAL friends we'd made. We had frequent lunch and dinners at the YCAC and once in a while played Bingo. Kids could play Bingo also and Heidi won a tansu chest – a style of Japanese antique chests. Hers was painted yellow with black wrought iron drawer pulls and she used it for several years. At the YCAC we made many new friends working for international companies and I especially enjoyed that. An English friend, Mavis, and I decided we'd like to learn yoga so I connected with a yoga teacher who started coming to my house once a week to teach the two of us. As word spread among our friends we had so many ladies who wanted to join our group that we outgrew my tatami room so we moved it to the YCAC. That worked out great because when I tired of it or was away traveling I didn't have to feel guilty about the other ladies or the teacher as he kept the group going.

When Chuck was home we frequently went to the YCAC for lunch and played tennis or darts while the kids were at school. When Chuck was on a trip I explored various areas of Yokohama and occasionally ventured into Tokyo. I enjoyed being able to afford to have my hair done every week and regular manicures as well. I had a lot of free time because at home I had a maid that I loved.

Suziko was quite a bit older than me but I never could guess her age. She had been educated in private schools and spoke English perfectly and when she was younger her family had been members of the YCAC. I felt so bad for her because it was apparent that she had grown up in an affluent family but after her husband died she had to support herself as a maid. Her daughter was well educated and worked on the Navy Base. Mariko's husband was in the British Navy and came home once in a while. Suziko's granddaughter, Barbara, was the same age as Heidi and they became friends. Suziko came to see us at our hotel when we visited Japan a few years after we'd moved to Alaska and we stayed in touch until her death.

Motomachi Street was my favorite browsing street. Shops were beautiful, full of designer clothes, beautiful works of art, the latest designs in lamps and accessories for the home. I never bought much there but loved to window shop. I would buy a small loaf of cheese bread just out of the oven and stroll down the street eating it. Aaahh, such pleasure! Issesakicho Street was a favorite for actually shopping. There were four and five story department stores and, compared to U. S. prices, many bargains to be had. We bought dining room furniture there and occasionally I'd find clothes for Heidi or me. We also purchased several expanding suitcases that we made good use of.

My nephew, Alan, who had visited us in Japan in 1963 while a cadet at the Air Force Academy, was now on active duty and stationed at Yokota AFB. Yokota was a two hour drive from Yokohama and we drove there once in a while to see Alan's family. They had two small boys and were expecting a third child who turned out to be another son. Shortly after moving into their house in American Village, just outside the gates of Yokota AFB, Alan discovered they were living next door to good friends of ours. Ez and Marie Aberle had been at Yokota with us from 1961-1963 and were again based there. So when we went to Yokota we were able to get together with them as well. Sometimes the Tuck's and/or the Aberle's visited us in Yokohama or we'd meet in Tokyo for dinner.

While living in Bayside Court I attended the University of Maryland, on base, a couple of nights a week. I was learning to speak, read and write Japanese, Katakana, which is Japanese phonetically spelled in English. Living in Japan for the second time I wanted to be able to talk to Japanese people in words I knew they'd understand! And if you think that has a double meaning, it does! I became proficient enough that I could read Japanese road signs and signs in the train stations. This led to a funny incident on the way home from Yokota one Sunday evening.

Our car suddenly filled with mist and fog while we were on the Chuo Freeway. Chuck pulled into the emergency lane and said that a radiator hose had burst and we'd need water as well as a new hose. Just ahead of us was an emergency call box so after taking a few minutes figuring how to say what I needed to say in Japanese, I made the call. While waiting for the aid truck to arrive I burst out laughing. "What's so funny?" Chuck and the kids started asking.

"I just realized that instead of saying 'my car needs water' I said 'my train needs water!'" The operator hadn't said a word but I'm sure when he hung up they must have had a laugh in the office about the "gaiijin" (means foreigner) on the Chuo Freeway needing water for her train! When the truck arrived they had both a radiator hose and water so I was proud of myself.

Our first Christmas in Japan, 1969, Chuck was scheduled to be in Hawaii. The kids and I were going with him so we pretended it was Christmas a couple of days early, opened our presents, had our Christmas dinner and then took down our Christmas tree. During the night before we were to leave Chuck received a telegram and then a phone call, his schedule was being changed! Chuck took a flight to New York and Chip, Steve, Heidi and I went to Honolulu.

172

When Chuck returned to Japan he arranged to take a few days off and joined us in Hawaii for a brief vacation. Our good friends, the Kibbe's, whom we hadn't seen since 1966 when Stan left New York for Vietnam and Ruth and the children went to California, were now living in Honolulu so we enjoyed a happy reunion and one of Ruth's delicious dinners. That was the first but not the last time we rearranged Christmas!.

# Chapter Thirty-Two

## Hong Kong, India, Greece
### 1970

Living in Japan was an educational and cultural experience for the entire family and in spite my mixed feelings about moving back to Japan I settled in to enjoy my life as long as we were there. Of course the icing on the cake was being able to travel extensively.

Spring break in 1970 I took the kids to Hong Kong. I'd been there with Chuck in 1963 and remembered it fairly well. I sent the kids on a half-day sightseeing tour while I shopped. That afternoon while we were all walking down a street I heard "Betty – hi! What are you doing here?" It was Margaret Johnson with her son. Her husband had been in Chuck's Air Force squadron in Rome, New York and we were all surprised to see each other walking down a street in Hong Kong. They were living on an Air Force base in the Philippines and were also in Hong Kong for spring break.

I had been planning our summer of 1970 travel almost since we'd arrived in Japan the summer before. In June 1970 Steve, just turned twelve, and Heidi, not quite nine, flew from Tokyo to New York City via Pan American Airlines. In New York City they were escorted to their Delta flight to Atlanta where they were met by Lillian and Larry and other family members. Chip and I would be joining them there in about three weeks but, first, Chip, thirteen, and I were going around the world!

We flew from Tokyo on a nonstop flight to New Delhi, India. As soon as we got to our hotel I hired a car for the next morning to drive us to Agra to see the Taj Mahal. I'd been fascinated by the story of the Taj Mahal and pictures of it since I'd learned about it in fourth grade. Not surprising that was at the top of my travel list

174

once we'd moved back to Japan. After making plans for the next day Chip and I walked a couple of blocks on filthy sidewalks trying not to see the many beggars, among them crippled people as well as elderly and children. Amidst throngs of people we entered a large, crowded marketplace and found a moneychanger the hotel desk clerk had recommended. We changed some U. S. dollars for enough Indian money to last us a couple of days, then browsed the marketplace for a little while. Having been warned about pickpockets and worse we didn't stay long.

The drive to Agra from New Delhi wasn't measured in kilometers but in hours. Our driver was a handsome man around thirty and obviously experienced driving the narrow roads that sometimes seemed as small as a cattle trail. Narrow, full of potholes and many animals, it was slow going. In India cows are sacred and they always had the right of way on the roads and they knew it! They wandered leisurely across the road and then maybe back again. Sometimes there was only one and other times there were several. We passed a shepherd with his flock of goats and another with sheep. We were going slowly enough that packs of dogs would chase the car and could easily get ahead of it.

Passing through tiny villages or simply groups of dwellings that appeared to be hundreds of years old we had a close-up look at daily life for the masses of India. We'd see them eating, doing laundry, cleaning up the area or cooking; everyone was always busy and it was obvious that India was a very poor country.

Once we got to Agra, the village was much cleaner, at least the tourist area where we were. We were not disappointed – the Taj Mahal is magnificent to behold and, easily one of the most beautiful structures in the world. While the white domed marble and tile mausoleum is most familiar, Taj Mahal is an integrated symmetric complex of structures that was completed around 1648. It combines elements from Persian, Turkish, Indian and Islamic architectural styles. In 1983, the Taj Mahal became a UNESCO World Heritage Site and was cited as "the jewel of Muslim art in India and one of the universally admired masterpieces of the world's heritage." The Taj Mahal is a mausoleum built by Mughal Emperor Shah Jahan in memory of his favorite wife, Mumtaz Mahal. We spent a few hours strolling around admiring the

175

structures from every angle. As the sun transited overhead the light on the Taj Mahal changed and the marble itself seemed to change colors.

We visited a few shops in the area and I bought a small marble box with a design on top of colorful inlaid marble chips, which I treasure to this day. We could have enjoyed more time there but we had reservations the next day to fly to Athens, Greece to see the Acropolis and the Parthenon and we had the drive back to New Delhi. A nice memory of the drive back is when we spotted a wedding taking place in the courtyard of an ancient house. I asked the driver to stop and let us watch and he did. Everyone was dressed in their best and most colorful clothes and we enjoyed watching for a while.

Leaving New Delhi and India Chip and I were excited to be on our way to Athens, Greece. During the flight we read the meager tourist brochures I'd gotten from The American Express office in Tokyo. The first place I wanted to see was the Acropolis and the Parthenon. Booked into a mid-price range hotel I was happy to see it was comfortable and well located. A five minute walk took us to a U. S. Armed Forces Exchange and restaurant. Since Chuck was retired from the Air Force we still had military ID cards so could use the facilities in most countries. We enjoyed some good old American food although we ate in Greek restaurants most of the time we were in Greece.

After climbing the many steps up the hill to visit the Acropolis we were at the entrance to the Parthenon. Long considered one of the greatest of all archaeological sites it is important because it is considered the most perfect building by the world's most advanced civilizations at the time it was completed. Although the site has been studied for centuries no one has yet figured out how they accomplished it. Even in its deteriorated condition it is easy to see the magnificence of the structure. The Parthenon and other main buildings on the Acropolis were built by Pericles in the fifth century BC as a monument to the cultural and political achievements of the inhabitants of Athens. The term *acropolis* means upper city and many of the city states of ancient Greece were built around an acropolis where the inhabitants can go as a place of refuge in times of invasion. For this reason the most

176

sacred buildings are usually on the acropolis and it is the safest most secure place in town.

We enjoyed visiting the National Archaeological Museum of Athens, the oldest and most important museum there. It contains one of the richest collections of ancient Greek art in the world and is representative of all the cultures that flourished in Greece. We also enjoyed a city tour that took us all over Athens and some outlying areas.

The most fun day was a cruise to three Greek islands. Many different bus tours going to various places in Greece all left from a central plaza in downtown Athens. The area was crowded with buses and tourists trying to find the right bus for their tour and tour operators trying to locate all of their passengers. By the time we signed up for the Island Cruise and were directed to our bus which would take us to the port of Piraeus to board our ship it was time for the bus to leave. We ran for it but we didn't make it. A tour operator put us in a taxi and directed the driver to take us to Piraeus and to our ship. We made it to the ship and boarded on time.

The scenery was spectacular. The waters of the Aegean Sea are very blue, as is the sky and the sunshine was brilliant. There are scores of islands off the coast of the mainland and the three we visited were beautiful. The most interesting was Mykonos, a small fishing village with many tourist shops. The buildings were all white and most homes had flower boxes overflowing with bright colored blossoms. We browsed the shops and strolled the residential lanes and enjoyed a snack and cold drinks overlooking the harbor.

The second stop island was similar to the first, a small fishing village and tourist resorts. On the ship's last stop at another island there was a beach club located on a beautiful white sand beach. Chip and I changed to our swim suits and enjoyed swimming in the very warm blue water of the Aegean. There was much more of interest to see in Athens but we had to save the rest for a later trip.

# Chapter Thirty-Three

## Italy to Paris
### 1970

Flying from Athens to Rome Chip and I were eager for our reunion with Chuck. From Fiumicino Airport we took a taxi to the hotel where Japan Air Lines crews stayed. Chuck was waiting for us and the three of us were happy to be together again. We spent three days touring the most well known attractions in Rome including a tour of the Vatican complex, the highlight of which was the Sistine Chapel and Michelangelo's masterpieces. I loved Italian food and much to my delight no matter what was ordered it came with a side dish of pasta. Rome was crowded and we were eager to leave the congestion and see some of the countryside.

We rented a car and, armed with nothing but a map written in Italian, we drove north as close to the coast as we could. The rocky coastline of the Mediterranean was on our left as we traveled through green valleys of vineyards and cultivated fields with high hills east of us. Passing through many small towns we glimpsed average Italian people going about their daily lives. Castles topped several of the hills looking like fortresses which they probably were when they were built. We stopped at the Leaning Tower of Pisa and it really does lean.

We drove west on a peninsula until we reached a charming fishing village. Asking around we were referred to a small hotel on a hillside above the harbor. After checking in the manager directed us to a beautiful restaurant overlooking the harbor where we enjoyed a delicious dinner of fresh seafood and pasta. Before retiring for the night we enjoyed strolling through the village in the pleasant evening air.

Chuck, Chip and I continued our drive up Italy's west coast

stopping in Livorno for lunch at a seaside restaurant, after which we swam in the warm waters of the Mediterranean Sea. Continuing north we spent the night in a small hotel near Genoa. We always traveled with the "Europe on $5-$10 Per Day" travel guide which was very popular with tourists at that time. We were usually satisfied with budget hotels or bed and breakfast accommodations we selected.

We left Genoa the next morning and quickly began a long uphill climb through northern Italy's Alps. The mountain peaks and lakes were as beautiful as any paintings I'd seen. We drove through mountain villages and small towns until we eventually crossed the border into Switzerland. Very soon we were crossing the Alps by way of the St. Bernard pass, one of Europe's highest mountain passes, and it's most ancient. About two miles of the pass, along the side of a very steep mountain, was covered by a snow shed, creating a tunnel. Before we actually entered the tunnel when the road twisted in a u-turn we could see the snow shed appearing to hang on the mountainside. Having a good look at it before we actually entered the tunnel, didn't quiet my pounding heart!

I was happy when we started the descent as I knew we'd soon be traveling through some of Switzerland's verdant valleys. As we drove I felt I'd seen it all before, and I had. Switzerland looked exactly as it did in one of my favorite childhood movies, "Heidi," which starred Shirley Temple. Starting at the age of three or four, she was a huge star in the 1930's, an entertaining singer and dancer, very talented and beautiful with a head full of curls. She easily won the hearts of all who saw her perform. I kept watching for her climbing the green hills up to the crotchety grandpa's cottage.

We spent a night near Montreux and took a self-directed sightseeing tour, viewing an ancient castle on the edge of Lake Geneva. Lausane, also near Lake Geneva was a pristine city, and we continued through postcard vistas until we reached Basel, near the border with France.

Leaving the mountains out the back window eventually we entered France. Two lane highways took us through the hearts of small towns and cities on our route to Paris. The leisurely pace enabled us enjoy the trip and feel as if we had seen the real life of the parts of each country we passed through. It was easy to stop at a small market and buy bread and cheese and a small bottle of local wine for a picnic lunch or to stop and visit a small bistro where we were the only "outsiders."

After a leisurely drive from Rome our stay in Paris presented us with a few challenges. The first was actually getting into Paris as the roads were jammed with traffic making the last couple of hours of the drive tense and frustrating. We had planned on arriving in Paris midday as we did not have hotel reservations but by the time we got there it was late afternoon. I knew there was a USO* close to the Eiffel Tower where we could get help finding a hotel. When we finally got into the city, somehow found a parking place and made our way to the USO, we learned we had arrived on Bastille Day** France's most important holiday! No wonder it looked like all of France's population was on the Champs-Elyse, often called the most beautiful avenue in the world.

A clerk at the USO made many calls trying to find us a hotel in the city and finally found a room a few blocks away. It took a while to get back to the car, find the hotel and get checked in with our bags. Eventually, I learned to travel with far fewer bags than I carried in those days! After checking in Chuck left to return the rental car to the agency. Chip and I looked around the room. It was large and had two beds so our minimum needs were met. It was old, dreary and did not feel clean to me. I decided rather quickly that first thing the next day we'd go back to the USO and ask for help again at finding a hotel I'd be more comfortable in. Most of the time I'm a pretty easy traveler but I just did not want to stay in that place.

When Chuck returned we started walking towards the Champs-Elysees. It was still crowded but not as bad as it had been a few hours earlier. Sitting down at one of the many sidewalk cafes we ordered drinks and dinner. Still hardly believing I was actually in Paris I continued to try to take it all in. The conversations in French that I couldn't understand, the well dressed people strolling the boulevard in the pleasant evening air combined to make me feel a bit of a country bumpkin. A very happy one!

180

After a Continental breakfast of fruit juice, cheese, croissants and butter and coffee, next morning we returned to the USO and asked for help in finding another hotel. They found us one a couple of blocks from the Arc de Triomphe, at the head of the Champs-Elysees. We had two small rooms in a charming small hotel and it was clean! We had four days in Paris before Chuck had to leave to go back to Japan and work. While he was with us we saw the highlights of Paris – the Paris Opera House, Notre Dame Cathedral and Louvre Museum, where we saw the famed *Mona Lisa*. We went to the Eiffel Tower intending to go to the top. However, once we got there the line was hours long and we decided we'd let that wait for a later trip and instead took a boat trip on the River Seine.

A half-day trip to the Palace of Versailles gave us a glimpse of the lifestyle of French nobility. The Palace is famous around the world for its lavish interiors and formal gardens. Built by Louis the XIV, designed to awe with its opulence, it does that. The almost one thousand foot long Hall of Mirrors is particularly impressive with its seventeen huge mirrors and stucco work showing the monarch in various guises. The beautiful formal gardens are almost as impressive as the palace itself. Marble and bronze statues adorned the many terraces. Vast gardens highlighted by a spectacular water show accompanied by the music of one of the composers from the Court of Louis XIV, was particularly delightful. I couldn't stop thinking how incredible it was for me to be in Paris!

One night we made reservations at a famous restaurant I'd read about in society columns. We arrived at the restaurant at 6:30 PM and discovered we were the only patrons! We had a delicious dinner but we didn't see Art Buchwald or any of the other celebrities I'd read were regulars. The reason was that Parisians and most other Europeans do not have dinner until much later in the evening. Another night we went to the famed Moulin Rouge and saw a wonderful show.

When Chuck left for Japan Chip and I flew to Frankfurt, Germany where we visited my nephew, David and his wife, Pat, and their 13 month old daughter, Amanda. David is my oldest sister, Hazel's son and he was in the Air Force at the time. After a couple of days of local sightseeing and some good American as well as German food, Chip and I flew to London.

*USO - United Service Organizations started just before World War II to support our servicemen away from home.

**Bastille Day is much like our Independence Day, 4th of July. The Bastille was a prison in France where kings and queens locked up citizens who did not agree with their decisions. On July 14, 1789 the people of Paris stormed the Bastille and freed the prisoners, thus, the start of the French Revolution..

*Elke*

# Chapter Thirty-Four
## England and Elke
### 1970

Chip and I landed at Heathrow Airport and took one of London's famed large black cabs into the city. The Hotel Jerome was across the street and down half a block from Buckingham Palace. It was small, built in the early 1900's with ornate Victorian architecture, charming but needing a facelift. From there we easily walked all around central London.

As usual, the first thing we did was take a city tour which oriented us and helped us make a list of those places we wanted to be sure to visit. We enjoyed watching the "Changing of the Guard" ceremony at Buckingham Palace, the official residence of Her Majesty, Queen Elizabeth II. There is a formal ceremony every morning at 11AM during the summer months when the Queen is not in residence. At the Tower of London we stood in line to see the dazzling Crown Jewels. The Tower is nearly a thousand years old and has been the seat of government as well as living quarters of monarchs and a prison for traitors or members of the court who fell out of favor with the monarch.

Our tour took us to the Houses of Parliament, St. Paul's Cathedral, Westminster Abbey and the British Museum. On our own we enjoyed Harrods Department Store where we bought a few things to take home. My English friend, Mavis, told me that Oxford Street, with its many department stores, was for serious clothes shopping and I made a few purchases there. The expandable suitcases bought in Japan were maxed out by the time we got home.

Theatre tickets in London were relatively inexpensive in 1970 so I got tickets to see Agatha Christie's famous play "The Mousetrap," which had been playing in London for twenty-two

185

years. When Chip, age 13, realized he was going to have to wear a sport coat and tie, he decided he didn't want to go! I insisted and Chip has been a theatre lover every since. At the first intermission he moved to an empty seat he'd spotted in the second row to get as close to the action as possible. The next morning when I asked him what he'd like to do that day Chip said "Maybe we can go to the theatre again." That night we saw "Fiddler On The Roof," a magnificent production that we both enjoyed tremendously.

We toured Windsor Castle, the largest continuously occupied castle in the world, with almost half a million square feet. Many Royals and people in favor have apartments there. The castle is a thousand year old fortress transformed into a royal palace. While not as opulent as Versailles, which we'd just toured in France, it was impressive.

While we were in England in late July the weather was cool with a few showers but also with some warm sunny days, much like the weather in the northwestern United States. Chip and I walked miles every day through St. James Park, Green Park, Hyde Park and Regents Park, one or the other always on our route to somewhere else. We loved the different areas of London, Piccadilly Circus and the theatre district, along Knightsbridge Road to Harrods and the Mayfair district with its five star hotels and embassies. We left London feeling eager to return and see more of London and more of the British Isles.

From London we flew to Atlanta, via New York to join up with Steve and Heidi and visit family. We were also eager to get home to Yokohama, our starting point on this round-the-world trip, because not only was Chuck there but we'd learned our beloved Norwegian Elkhound, Elke, was missing.

What would we do with Elke? That was a major concern as we planned our summer of 1970 travel. What about Elke? I worried about her as if she were a child, old enough to miss us but unable to understand my reassurances that we would return. Suziko, our maid, came to the rescue and agreed to stay all summer with Elke.

Chuck was working so he was in and out of the house every few days. Things went well for Elke until Chuck took vacation to

186

meet Chip and me in Europe for a couple of weeks. When he returned home to Yokohama, Elke had taken a little vacation of her own! She had jumped over our six foot fence, was missing, and Suziko was frantic! The day after Chuck got home he received a phone call from someone who had found Elke. Our name and phone number were on her collar. Chuck picked her up, then rigged a line in the back yard and attached her leash to the line. Elke accepted the situation for a few days until Chuck left again, then over the fence she went again and resumed her summer travel, leaving her collar dangling at the end of her leash hanging from the line. Now she was without ID.

The children and I were in Atlanta when we got the bad news so we were anxious to get home. When we got there Elke had been gone for three weeks and we set out to find her. Japan has a very strict leash law that says dogs are to be confined within a fenced yard and chained to a central point so you seldom see dogs running free. However, many people allowed their dogs loose to roam at dawn and very late at night. Their custom became our custom. The kids and I went out soon after dawn every morning calling for Elke. I had flyers printed with Elke's picture and all information written in Japanese. Every neighborhood in Yokohama has its own "police box" - a one or two man station serving a relatively small area. I delivered flyers to the Yokohama police station headquarters and to many "police boxes" within five miles of our house. I also posted flyers on telephone poles and in shop windows.

Soon we began getting calls from people who'd seen Elke. They remembered because she was an unusual dog in Japan, plus she had that endearing sideways gait that people noticed. One early call was from a police box about three miles from us. The caller spoke to Suziko and told her he knew where Elke was. Excitedly, I jumped in the car with Suziko in tow to show me where to go. When we got to the police box, the policeman motioned for me to follow him. Thinking we were going close by to retrieve Elke, I left Suziko at the station and followed the policeman. We walked and walked and walked, up and up and around until we arrived at a house near the top of a small mountain. If he'd indicated how far it was I would have driven us! When we got there the policeman had a long, long discussion with the woman of the house then summed up the conversation to me with a few words, "She's not here."

Disappointed, I followed him back down the mountain to the police box where Suziko got the details for me. The story was that Elke had come into their yard a few days before, looking tired and bedraggled. The homeowner prepared Elke a bowl of rice and some water. Elke drank the water but refused the rice. They tried other typical Japanese food but Elke would have none of it. Finally, they gave her meat and she gobbled it right down. The man told his wife "You take this dog to police box! She only eats meat. She rich man's dog!" Obediently, next day the wife, carrying her small child, and with a rope around Elke's neck, made her way down the steep hillside. She reported the "lost dog" to the police box. The police had not yet received my flyers so they told the woman to take the dog home. A day or two later when the policemen saw the flyers, one called me but it was too late. Elke had escaped from the woman as she led her back up the hill.

The next call came from a restaurant owner where Elke had eaten for a few days. Suziko and I searched the neighborhood passing out flyers and many people remembered seeing Elke hanging around the restaurant but none knew where she was. There were a couple of other false alarms before calls stopped and we were devastated.

Shortly after the kids left for school one morning the phone rang. Roy Begerson, a JAL navigator, said "Nina and Bente just saw Elke! A Japanese man was walking her! You come! Elsa and I will go out now and look for her!" The girls had just called Roy. While walking a few blocks to catch a bus to school, they had not only seen Elke, they had stopped and petted her!

"Is this your dog?" the Japanese man said in English to the girls.

"No, but she belongs to our good friends," Nina replied. Hearing that, the man walked on and Nina stopped at the first pay phone she saw and called her Dad. When Roy called me I dropped the load of clothes I was carrying to the washing machine, grabbed a stack of flyers, got in the car and drove to the Sankien neighborhood. Passing out flyers to everyone on the streets I asked

188

"Inu O imaska?" (Have you seen my dog?). Pretty soon several people joined me, climbing trees to look over fences and at one point six young Japanese women had me follow them to a house they knew where many stray dogs lived. They took me to the house but Elke wasn't there.

When it was time for the kids to get home from school, I drove home. As I walked in the door, the phone was ringing. "I have your dog! You gave me picture this morning and few minutes later I saw dog running down street with rope around neck. I work for BX laundry so I put dog in my truck. I call you all day!"

"Where are you? Stop! Stay right there! I'll be there in fifteen minutes." The kids and I raced to the car. Elke was as glad to see us as we were to see her! She'd always been an outside dog but for a week she refused to leave the house unless someone went outside with her. From then on, she was a house dog.

Elke was left with psychic scars from her solitary summer vacation. Whenever she heard fireworks or a car backfiring she would hide and tremble with fear. That told us all of her adventures had not been as pleasant as ours

# Chapter Thirty-Five

## Yokohama Life & Travels
### 1970-1971

After our summer travels and then hunting for our lost dog and finally bringing her home, we settled into our normal everyday life. Chuck was flying to various cities in Southeast Asia as well as Honolulu, Los Angeles and New York. The boys joined bowling leagues and baseball teams and Heidi joined a dance class at the YCAC. She also traveled to Tokyo with a few members of her class to make a TV commercial which, unfortunately, we never saw.

We'd been in Japan a year when Steve went into seventh grade in junior high so he was taking the early bus with Chip. We enrolled Heidi at Yokohama International School because most of her friends went there and it was an excellent school. She went to fourth and fifth grades at Y.I.S. For a few days I traveled with Heidi to school each day. We took a taxi about a mile to the Isogo train station, rode the commuter train for two stops, got off, walked down the hill and crossed "D" Street, a very wide boulevard always congested with traffic. We boarded a bus going up the hill to the bluffs area and rode about a mile to the school. Heidi was only nine years old but after a few days I trusted her to make the trip alone! It was a different world then but, even so, looking back I can't believe I let her do that! After a couple of weeks Heidi decided she would rather just walk down our hill and get on a bus on "D" Street and ride it four or five miles to the intersection where she changed buses to get to school.

Even though we'd been living in Isogo for more than a year I'd never stopped searching for a house closer to the kids' schools. One day driving through Sankei-dai a neighborhood of very nice Japanese style houses built on the hill above Sankien Gardens I

190

saw a brand new house with a real estate sign on it. I immediately called and asked to see it. Built on the side of a hill the bottom level was a garage and a huge unfinished area. Up one flight of stairs was a large tiled patio leading to the front door. The house was two stories with an entry hall, living room, tatami room, dining room, kitchen and powder room on the main floor and four bedrooms and a bathroom upstairs. There were beautiful hardwood floors and a very large tiled terrace off the living and tatami rooms. The kitchen was modern with built in cabinets and sink. The best thing though was it had central heat, propane powered small wall radiators downstairs and up. The rent was $500 per month with six months rent in advance and six months rent for a deposit called key money. It would take $6,000 to move in and I said "We'll take it."

When Chuck saw the house he liked it, especially the location. It was just a mile from the Navy base, schools, shopping, etc. Much closer to Heidi's school, her long bus ride was cut in half and closer to the YCAC and all of our friends' homes, it was perfect!

When Christmas 1970 approached Chuck was scheduled on a trip that would bring him home the day after Christmas, the 26th. Since the kids were out of school a week before Christmas we decided to go skiing in the Japanese Alps. The JAL family that rented our house in Isogo asked if Camille (the wife/mother) and their ten year old son, Marcel, could go with us. We said they could so they joined us for the train trip. We were all wearing backpacks and carrying our skis, poles, boots, etc. so it was a little frantic making sure the six of us were all on the train with all of our stuff. Japanese trains never stay in a station very long, just a couple of minutes most of the time. Steve kept lagging behind and whenever I'd turn around to check on him I usually found that he had some nice Japanese person helping him with his gear! Heidi and I struggled on without help!

We had arranged to meet our Air Force friends who lived near Yokota AFB, the Aberle's, at the ski area. They were going with a school group. Ez and Marie were good friends from the first time we lived in Japan and Dan and Dianne were the ages of Chip and Steve so they had been friends earlier as well. We ended up part of a large, congenial group. The snow was excellent, deep powder,

191

the sun was shining and it wasn't too cold so we all had a marvelous time.

The kids and I got back to Yokohama on the 24<sup>th</sup> of December, pretended the 25<sup>th</sup> was Christmas Eve and prepared to celebrate Christmas the 26<sup>th</sup> as Chuck would arrive home about 10 AM. He came in as scheduled and we opened our presents and feasted on our usual Christmas dinner of standing rib roast and all the trimmings.

For the school spring break in 1971, Chuck took vacation and the five of us went to Bangkok. Chuck showed us "Johnny's Gems," the store where he'd done a lot of shopping for us and many of our friends when he was there for two months in 1963. He also took us to his favorite restaurant, Nick's Steak House, for dinner.

In the past Bangkok was known as the "Venice of the East" because of its many rivers and canals, called "Klongs." The most important means of transportation for centuries and today, even though Bangkok has become a modern city, the Chao Phraya River, as well as the klongs, are an important part of life there. A cruise on one of the klongs is an essential part of any visit to Bangkok. The river and its banks teemed with people going about their daily lives. Floating homes and markets lined their banks. We saw families bathing in the klong, others brushing their teeth and others washing dishes or clothes.

Bangkok has many beautiful temples and we visited a few of them. We also visited a wildlife park a few kilometers north of the city where we rode an elephant. I'll tell you, sitting in a basket high atop an elephant while it walks along and the basket is swaying from side to side, is not really my idea of fun! However, I'm never willing to miss anything so I did it once. We all had a good time in Thailand and when we returned to Japan and work and school, I started planning our summer of 1971 travel.

Since I was so late planning our trip I could not get a hotel reservation in Amsterdam at all. I remembered that my niece, Jackie, a school teacher, had taken a year's sabbatical with a friend and toured Europe. They had stayed in a bed and breakfast in Amsterdam. Later when Jackie's brother, David, and his wife and

192

baby were living in Germany, while touring in Holland they stayed with the same people. Still later, Jackie's parents, my oldest sister, Hazel, and her husband, Jack, had also stayed there, so by this time, they were almost family! I called Jackie and got the name and address and wrote asking if we could make a reservation. I had an immediate reply that they would be expecting us and would meet us at the airport.

When summer came the whole family flew to Atlanta. After a few days, leaving Chip and Heidi there, Chuck and Steve and I flew to Amsterdam.

The bed and breakfast was a two bedroom apartment with living-dining room, kitchen and bath. When we arrived one of the bedrooms was occupied, so Chuck, Steve and I shared the second bedroom. Mr. & Mrs. Dorland, the owners, and a visiting sister, all slept in the living-dining room. The Dorland's had two daughters living in California and had visited the U.S. several times. They all spoke excellent English and we soon felt as if we were visiting family. The man who was occupying the other bedroom left the next day so we took that room also and were more comfortable.

While in Amsterdam I was sad visiting the house where Ann Frank was hidden with her family during World War II. Again, I felt thankful all of my family had survived that terrible time. We took in a circus, a canal tour and a sightseeing tour of the city, which is beautiful. I especially loved the architecture. Mr. Dorland got us up very early one morning to take us to the flower market which opens at 6AM. Buyers from around the world were there bidding on "lots" of flowers. The acres and acres of flowers were stunning and the auction was interesting but it was all happening so fast it was hard to keep up with the action! After we left the flower market, we stopped for breakfast and then Mr. Dorland drove us all over Holland, filling us in on the history as we went along. We stopped at the only working windmill still in Holland and since Mr. Dorland was friends with the owner we got to climb to the top and come down on a rope.

The Netherlands, also called Holland, is a geographically low-lying country, bordered on the west by the North Sea. About twenty-seven percent of its area and sixty percent of its population are located below sea level. Significant land areas have been gained through land reclamation and preserved through an elaborate system of dikes. The country is beautiful and the people are warm-hearted and friendly and love Americans.

From Amsterdam we flew to Bergen, on Norway's northwest coast. It is a beautiful, old seaport in a mountainous area where the mountains meet the sea. We took a cruise up a fjord and enjoyed the spectacular scenery. After a couple of days in Bergen we flew to Oslo where our Norwegian friends who lived near us in Yokohama, met us for lunch. Else directed us to a wonderful store where we all bought gorgeous hand knit ski sweaters. Oslo is a beautiful city and we enjoyed touring it.

At the Oslo Viking Museum we saw the Viking ships but I was most interested in Kon-Tiki, the raft used by Norwegian explorer and writer, Thor Heyerdahl. I'd read his book about his 1947 expedition across the Pacific Ocean from South America to the Polynesian Islands. He believed that people from South America could have settled Polynesia in pre-Columbian times and his aim in mounting the *Kon Tiki* expedition, using only materials and technologies available to those people at that time, was to show that there were no technical reasons to prevent them from having done so. Having read the book, I was thrilled to see the actual raft.

Our last day of sightseeing in Norway took us to Holmenkollen, site of the 1952 winter Olympics, where we saw the largest ski jump in the world. Even though it was summer it was easy to visualize skiers flying off that high, long jump and I imagined myself one of them.

From Oslo we flew to Stockholm, one of my favorite European cities. The oldest parts of the city have been restored and I loved the cobblestone streets and the small shops that look as if they've been there for centuries. Stockholm has many islands within the city so a boat tour of the area is essential. In Stockholm we splurged and stayed in a very expensive hotel because it was magnificent and well located and because I just felt like we deserved a break from the $5 - $10 a day book!

We ended our summer tour in Denmark. Copenhagen is a

modern and cosmopolitan city and pristine clean. Shops were filled with classic Danish designed pieces, everything from kitchen utensils to furniture for the entire house. I loved the Danish designed ladies wear and bought a few good traveling pieces. One of the most famous sights of Denmark is The Little Mermaid, a bronze statue on a granite stone by the sea. The reason for its popularity is its association with the world famous and much loved Danish fairy tale writer, Hans Christian Anderson, who published the story, "The Little Mermaid" in 1837. We visited world famous Tivioli Gardens, the first known amusement park and pleasure gardens, which opened in 1843. It is the oldest known amusement park to have survived intact to the present. Food in Denmark was always excellent and beautifully served.

We flew to Frankfurt, Germany where we were to catch a JAL flight back to New York. Early in the morning at our hotel Chuck received a call from Japan Air Lines. The plane we were scheduled to fly on had crashed in India so they had made reservations for us on Pan American World Airways to New York, leaving later that day. We left Frankfurt on a somber note, praying none of the JAL people we knew were on the India flight. They weren't, we later learned. When we got to New York, Chuck continued on to Japan. Steve and I went to Atlanta to pick up Chip and Heidi and then headed home to our lives in Japan. We didn't know it then but we only had a few more months to live in Japan. In March of 1972 we were thrilled when we got word that we were moving to Anchorage, Alaska..

# Chapter Thirty-Six

## Leaving Japan

In March, 1972 our lives suddenly turned upside down. JAL friends were finding notices from the Japanese government tacked to their front door stating they owed many, many thousands of dollars to Japan for taxes, and all of the property they had in Japan was subject to confiscation.

All flight crews were working in Japan under a contract with JAL that they would pay Japan a flat rate of twenty-per cent of their pay each year in income taxes. That amount was deducted from gross pay and paid directly to the government by JAL. The contract between the Japanese government and Japan Air Lines, regarding the amount of taxes the foreign crew members would have to pay, had expired. As you can imagine, that is when the feathers hit the fan!

Crew members were immediately transferred on paper to a new crew base in Anchorage and told to move their families as soon as possible. For those families with children in school, "possible" wasn't until after the first of May. JAL started shipping household goods and asked all family members to leave Japan, even if only for a few hours, so we could turn in our "resident" visas and return simply as tourists until May.

"I haven't seen Singapore yet!" I decided to make one last shopping trip around Southeast Asia before we left. Chuck was okay with the idea and I planned to go when he would be home. He took me to the airport and gave me last minute instructions as if I were twelve years old, and saw me off alone to shop in Hong Kong, Bangkok, Singapore and Taipei.

I'd been to Hong Kong several times so I knew my way around and was perfectly comfortable alone there for two days. Among other things, I bought my first fur coat. Fortunately, I'm not the mink type of woman so was happy with a very pretty fur coat with red fox trim. I also bought a full length leather coat that I enjoyed for many years..

A couple of nights in Bangkok was next. The driver of the hired car I'd negotiated for at the airport, offered to come back the next morning and take me on my shopping trip. He also offered to come back that evening and take me dancing but I declined that offer. He picked me up the next morning and as we drove through very crowded streets in parts of Bangkok I didn't remember seeing on my previous trips there, I began feeling vulnerable. *I could just disappear forever and no one would ever know what happened to me.* I looked appraisingly at the driver and decided, *He's no bigger than I am. If I have to fight him, I think I can hold my own!* Needless to say, I never had to fight him. After a full day of shopping for gifts for family, brass trays, large brass candlesticks and bronze flatware, and I don't remember what else, I was delivered safely back to my hotel.

Singapore felt different. I had read how strict the government was and felt that I was in a "police state." Flying into the airport, all of the window shades had to be down. We were not allowed to look out. We'd experienced the same thing in Taipei in 1963. You could be arrested for things we'd never dream of in the U. S. Chewing gum was not allowed in Singapore; it was easier to keep the streets and sidewalks clean. I spent a couple of days sightseeing and Singapore had a lot of natural beauty. It was still early in their renovation and building projects but the areas that had already received attention were beautiful

My last stop was Taipei where I bought a big rattan "Papa-san" chair and ottoman plus a tall "Princess" chair, both perfect for the family room we'd have in our new house. I also bought two big, heavy, carved wood screens, each of the four panels depicted a season of the year in China. One was for my sister, Evelyn. I ordered a zabuton table, an end table built to hold zabuton pillows which are used to sit on the floor. Fortunately, everything I bought was shipped to Yokohama immediately and arrived in time to be shipped to Alaska with our household goods.

I had thoroughly enjoyed my trip alone and when I got home

was glad I'd taken it. The next few weeks would be busy and hectic, sorting, packing and moving into Bayside Court, the Navy Guest Hotel. We'd stayed there for two months when we arrived in Japan in 1969. Also, Chuck wanted me to go to Anchorage with him to look at houses.

Pam Sundeen, one of our English friends, was with me and as we landed in Anchorage the first of April, 1972 we could see snow still covered the landscape. I was excited to be having a first look at the place that would become my new home. The sun was shining and the light reflecting off the snow was so brilliant it almost made my eyes hurt! As we were driven about fifteen minutes to the crew hotel downtown, I was surprised that the trees weren't very large. I had expected them to be much bigger and more dense, as they are in Washington. I would learn that the depth of the permafrost limited the size of the trees. I saw mountains nearby and was reminded of Washington because, again, I would be living between the mountains and the sea, both of which I love.

I'd worn my new fur coat and brought several suitcases of clothes to be stored at the hotel until we moved to Anchorage. I was a little concerned about having to pay customs on my new purchases but, after a cursory inspection I was waved through.

Chuck and I spent several days looking at houses for sale and didn't find anything either of us liked. We had looked at houses in a beautiful subdivision ten minutes from downtown and just behind the junior and senior high schools. We liked the neighborhood but didn't like any of the three houses that were for sale. We met with a builder who lived there and he still had a couple of lots so Chuck and I chose a lot and a house plan, picked out colors for the inside and outside of the house, went to the bank to apply for a mortgage, then wrote a check for the deposit. We crossed our fingers and trusted to luck that the house would be finished before school started, as promised. We also reserved a two-bedroom furnished apartment for the first of May. We could get by with two bedrooms because the kids and I would only be living there a couple of weeks before we left for the summer.

After my house-hunting trip, once I got back to Japan, I started packing in earnest. The moving company would soon be coming to

198

pick up our things for shipment to Anchorage. We sold most of the furniture, keeping only special pieces. On his last trip before we moved into Bayside Court, Chuck took Elke to Anchorage and put her in a kennel that friends recommended. He visited her whenever he was in Alaska until we were all there.

Settling into Bayside Court again, surrounded by friends in the same situation, life seemed a little surreal but we still had our ordinary lives to live. The kids were in school and bowling in their leagues which would end in May. They were all good students so missing the last few weeks of school wouldn't really hurt them. Japan Air Lines was anxious for us to get rid of our resident visas and convert to tourist status so I decided to get that done.

The kids and I got up very early one morning and took a taxi to the airport. When we arrived I laid four tickets on the counter at the check-in desk and said "We're going to Seoul for a few hours. We'll be coming back tonight." After a long pause and a questioning look at me, the agent said,

"But, Mrs., this ticket is for New York."

"What? Let me see that! Oh, my gosh! I don't believe it!" Staring at the kids for a moment, I said, "You kids go without me! Take a taxi to the big new shopping center in Seoul. Spend a couple of hours there and take a taxi back to the airport." Chip was fifteen, Steve, thirteen and Heidi ten.

"No way!"

"I'm not going if you aren't going!"

I think I might have persuaded the boys but Heidi wasn't having any part of it. I had brought the wrong ticket for me. We all had tickets to New York that we planned to use later and, in my haste, I had picked up one wrong ticket. Feeling embarrassed, stupid, frustrated and ready to scream, back out of the airport we went, and into a taxi. When we reached Bayside Court, about 9:30 AM, I hopped out, closed the door and said to the driver, "Take the kids to school. They'll show you where to go." Amid cries of

"No, Mom. It's too late!"

"Why can't we just stay here?"

I looked at the driver and repeated, more forcefully, "Take

these kids to school!" I went to my room and lay down with a damp towel on my forehead, thinking, "I've finally done it. I've finally flipped my lid, gone off the deep end, acted like a crazy woman. Will our lives ever be normal again?"

A couple of hours later I heard yelling and looked out my window. Bob and Alice Huey were on the sidewalk yelling at each other! That was a shocker because Alice was the calmest, most easy going and laid back person I'd ever known. I knew that the tension of the past couple of months had also gotten to her. For some reason, that made me feel better.

In early May, Chip, Steve, Heidi and I were finally at the Japan Air Lines check-in counter at Haneda Airport. I gave the agent our tickets to Anchorage and told the boys to start loading our ten huge pieces of luggage onto the scales. We also had several smaller bags we intended to carry on the flight with us. Since mid-March when Japan Air Lines ordered us to pack our household goods and ship them off to Anchorage and prepare to move as soon as possible, our lives had been frantic, as we responded to one unexpected turn of events after another. By the time we were checking in at JAL and the ticket agent started telling me that we couldn't take that many pieces of luggage, I'd reached my breaking point. "Japan Air Lines is moving us to Anchorage. They made us vacate our home weeks ago and live in a hotel! The children had to stay in school until May lst to get credit for the school year. We had to pack up our household goods and ship them on very short notice! This is what we had left to live with for two months! *Start putting tags on those bags!"*

200

# Part Three Alaska

## The Best & The Worst

*JAL 747 Captain*

# Chapter Thirty Seven
## The Beginning
### 1972

*T*he snow-capped mountains east of the city sparkled in brilliant sunshine when we landed in Anchorage, Alaska in May, 1972, to begin a new chapter of Halsey family life. We were all excited to be back in the United States after three years of living in Yokohama. Several friends were on the flight with us - Pam and Sheryl Sundeen and Barbara Dolan and her daughters, Kathy, Carolyn and Susan. Kathy, soon to be a junior in high school, cried most of the way because she had left her boyfriend in Japan.

Bill Sundeen was at the airport to meet Pam and Sheryl and Tom Dolan was there to meet his family. Chuck was waiting with the vehicle he'd purchased a few days before, a huge four-wheel drive International Harvester station wagon. After loading our mountain of luggage in the back we still had plenty of room so the boys loaded a lot of Sundeen's bags in as well. Bill had bought a small car and all of their luggage wouldn't fit inside. The five of us piled in the I-H and drove to the apartment we'd rented. After getting all of our bags inside, the apartment looked pretty small but the kids and I would be leaving for the summer in a couple of weeks.

The first thing we wanted to do was see our new house. It was framed but nothing much to see yet. Next we wanted to go get Elke. Driving to the kennel, Chip, Steve and Heidi got their first look at the city. The population in 1972 was 100,000. The city was bordered by Cook Inlet on the west and spread from downtown about ten miles east, to climb the foothills of the mountains. The population was swelled by Elmendorf AFB located northeast of town and an Army post, Fort Richardson, in the far northeast. The actual downtown area was hardly a mile long and just a few blocks wide, so it was rather compact. There were three large hotels and a few smaller ones; one independent department store, Northern Commercial, plus Penney's and Sears. A couple of furniture stores and several small shops, many catering to tourists, provided everything we'd need and I expected we'd be happy here.

When we got to the kennel and reunited with Elke, our family felt complete again. "That dog is fat! You are going to kill her!" The kennel owner was yelling, "And this is how much you should feed her," holding out a meager handful of kibbles. "You must see that she gets a lot of exercise. She is a beautiful dog and you want to keep her that way. I've had her on a diet and you keep her on it!" We were happy to take our slimmer pet home, already feeling guilty knowing we'd be bringing her back in a couple of weeks.

We drove our huge International Harvester for ten days and I did not like sitting at eye level with big truck drivers. We were only getting about seven miles to the gallon and gas was expensive in Alaska. As we passed a new car dealer one day, I said "Let's stop and look." When we came out we'd traded in the I-H, at the same price Chuck had paid for it, and drove away in a new four wheel drive Jeep Wagoner.

We'd been in Anchorage a few weeks when Chip and Steve flew to Atlanta to visit our family. My sister, Hazel, was in charge of recreation at a large park in southwest Atlanta. She helped Chip get a summer job as a lifeguard at the pool so he stayed with Hazel and Jack. He had gotten the required Red Cross certifications in Japan. Steve stayed with his grandparents and other family members.

Chuck, Heidi and I flew to Frankfurt, Germany. We rented a car and, following their directions very well, we drove to the home of the Bergersen's. Roy, Else, Nina and Bente were our Norwegian friends in Japan and Nina and Bente were the girls responsible for us finally finding Elke when she was lost the summer before. Roy had left Japan Air Lines the previous December and was now flying for Nairobi Airlines. They had a comfortable home in Germany and were happy to be living in Europe again. We had a delicious lunch and a most enjoyable reunion visit.

Waving good-bye to the Bergersen's, we headed to the

204

Autobahn, which we'd drive seventy miles south to Wiesbaden. There is no speed limit on most of Germany's famed super highway and German cars are built to handle high speeds well. I was nervous as Porsches and BMW's raced ahead in the fast lanes and was relieved when I saw the exit sign for Wiesbaden. I doubt that Chuck was nervous; after all he was used to "driving" 747's. My nephew, Mike, my sister Evelyn's son, was in the Army stationed in Wiesbaden. Mike and Rosemary welcomed us and spent a couple of days acting as tour guides. Heidi especially enjoyed seeing Heidelberg Castle, which dates back to the twelfth century. Friends of Mike's took Heidi back to the castle after dark, as legend had it that Hobbits and Trolls could be seen in the woods around the castle at night. Heidi had read some of J. R. Tolkien's books about Hobbits so she was disappointed when she didn't see any.

From Weisbaden we drove through Switzerland, stopping in Basel where Chuck bought me a beautiful Girard-Perreaux watch. We took a train to a small town where we boarded a funicular that took us to the top of a very high mountain in the Swiss Alps. The view of the Alps and a couple of large lakes was spectacular. A funicular is also called an incline railway. In the U. S. I'm familiar with one on Pike's Peak in Colorado. Cables are used to pull the railway car up a very steep mountainside. It is balanced by another car coming down the mountainside at the same time. Next, we went to Zurich, one of Switzerland's most beautiful cities. While in Zurich we cruised on a nearby lake from which we viewed magnificent homes and estates.

Leaving Switzerland we drove across the very small country of Liechtenstein into Austria. We had only been in Austria a few minutes when we arrived in the small town of Feldkirch. A celebration was underway in the town square. There were many picnic tables, a band playing in the bandstand and several carnival-like games and food booths. We were hungry for lunch so we parked the car and went to see what it was all about. The celebration was a "Wine Festival." Chuck and I sat down at one of the tables where we could keep an eye on Heidi, who went to play some of the games. She was almost eleven and still had her beautiful coppery red hair, which drew attention no matter what country we were in. Chuck got us a glass of wine and we relaxed and enjoyed the lively music coming from the bandstand.

Soon, an older couple sat at the other end of our table. For a few minutes we didn't speak to each other but I smiled whenever I'd catch their eyes. After a while, the woman looked rather shyly at me and said something I didn't understand. Her husband then smiled at us, reached for his wife's hand and said "They speak English." Looking at us again he said, "She understands English but is shy about speaking it." They introduced themselves as Kurt and Ingrid Linser. Kurt spoke excellent English so we started chatting with them, with Kurt doing most of the talking for both. After we'd been there an hour or so, Ingrid invited us to go home with them for cake and coffee. She said they lived nearby and would drive us there and later bring us back to get our car. We agreed. They seemed to be nice, friendly people who liked Americans. We could see an Austrian home and learn more about the people, a good lesson for all of us, especially Heidi. Later, as we were preparing to leave the festival, a look of horror suddenly was on Ingrid's face. She began to speak rapidly to Kurt, who burst out laughing. "She just remembered, we didn't drive here! We walked."

Laughing, Chuck said "That's no problem, we'll drive you home." The five us of soon located our car and squeezed in. It was only about a mile to their house, a very nice red brick house set on an acre or two. There was a detached garage and before they took us into the house Ingrid insisted we have a look in the garage so we could see they really did have a car.

Inside the house we were introduced to the Linser's twenty-one year old daughter and a teenager, a visiting nephew. Both of the young people spoke excellent English. We enjoyed delicious homemade apple cake, an Austrian specialty, with coffee for us and hot chocolate for Heidi. We visited for an hour or so, asking questions about their jobs and schools and answering their questions about the U.S., especially Alaska. We exchanged addresses before saying goodbye. When we got to Atlanta, I sent them some lovely placemats depicting beautiful scenes from around the state of Georgia. For many years we exchanged Christmas cards, always with a lovely note from them about their year. Feldkirch was a highlight of our entire trip and one we've talked about many times through the years.

From Feldkirch we drove east to Innsbruck, capitol of the Tyrol region of Austria. Innsbruck is a medieval town, gilded in baroque, dripping in rococo, bordered by the Inn River and almost surrounded by snow covered peaks, even in summer. It has long been famous for its ski areas. We found a small hotel down one of the cobblestone lanes in the Altstad (old town) region. We loved soaking up the atmosphere in the old town while enjoying a delicious dinner of Beef Burgundy. Next morning, in a small café, we were served a scrumptious breakfast of flavorful Austrian sausages and very thin pancakes, served with a variety of fruit. The aroma of hearty Austrian coffee permeated the air.

We toured the local highlights of the city, including a museum, to learn a little local history. Maximillian the First was widely considered too extravagant for his own good, and his "Goldernes Dachl" is an example. He ordered that all 2,600 copper shingles on the royal balcony should be covered in gold as a "gift" to the people of Innsbruck. This stretched the royal household's finances so much that the emperor was forced to take out a loan! The balcony was used by the royal family to watch theatrical productions and other forms of court entertainment.

Next day we left Innsbruck and continued to drive east, arriving in Salzburg in time for lunch. Salzburg is located on the Salzach River and is on the northern edge of the Alps. The city is hundreds of years old and is well-known as the birthplace of Wolfgang Amadeus Mozart, still regarded by many as the ultimate musical genius. He was a serious classical composer, yet he also penned catchy tunes and was pampered as some of our Hollywood stars are today. We toured his residence, now a museum. After touring the city and enjoying a lunch featuring a variety of Austrian sausages and cheeses, we headed east again towards Vienna.

We detoured out of our way to cross the German border to turn in our rental car. Since we rented the car in Germany it would have been much more expensive to return it in Austria. The scenery in both Austria and Germany, was exceptional, mountain vistas, lakes and thick forests. We spent a night in a hotel in a small city near the Austrian border and next morning returned the rental car. The automobile agency arranged for us to pick up another car across the border in Austria and return it when we reached Vienna. They drove us across the border to pick it up.

Arriving in Vienna in late afternoon we located our small hotel. The building, a short bus ride from downtown, appeared to be hundreds of years old but our room, though plain, was large and comfortable. We were disappointed to learn that the famous Lipizzaner performing horses were out of the city touring. We had been looking forward to seeing them.

As was our custom, we took a city tour to make sure we saw the most interesting things around the city. Then we went a few miles outside the city to visit Schonbrunn Palace, the summer palace of the Hapsburg royal family and the home of Emperor Franz Josef for most of this life. Schonbrunn Palace was as magnificent as other European palaces we had seen and the grounds and gardens may have been the most beautiful. An elevator took us to the top of Danube Tower to see expansive views of Vienna and the Danube River. A ferris wheel, built by Goodyear, was reputed to be the world's largest, so of course we had to ride it. I'm afraid of heights and dislike ferris wheels but I also don't like to miss anything!

Chuck flew home to Anchorage to go back to work and to check on the progress of our house which was still under construction. Heidi and I flew to Atlanta to visit my family for a few days before leaving with Chip and Steve for California to spend some time at the beach with Evelyn's family. Chuck was going to try to meet us there. As things turned out his schedule didn't permit his joining us in California so the kids and I flew home to get ready for school.

# Chapter Thirty-Eight

## Settling In
### 1972

The climate in Alaska's interior runs the gamut between extremely high and extremely low temperatures. Summer temperatures in Fairbanks and the interior reach 100 degrees F.; in winter sixty or seventy degrees below zero is not unusual.

Anchorage, however, is located in the so-called "banana belt." The south coastal climate, moderated by the influence of Japanese currents and the Gulf of Alaska, has a much milder climate, milder even than the northern states in the lower 48. Although winter temperatures might fall to twenty or thirty degrees below zero for a few days, typically winters have two or three weeks of very cold weather when the thermometer never registers above zero. Except when snowing, days are bright and sunny with temperatures usually in the twenties. The shortest winter day has six to seven hours of daylight. People rarely zip or button up coats unless walking more than a few blocks. Hoarfrosts are common; trees coated with ice crystals sparkling in the bright sunlight. Mother Nature shows us, once again, her artistic ability. Northern lights create a spectacular show, lighting up the sky, as colors of the rainbow chase each other across the northern horizon.

In August, 1972 our family reunited in Anchorage and prepared to move into our new house. After five months of transition, upheaval and travel we were all happy to be "home." Alaska would be another adventure.

What were we thinking when we went over house plans with a builder, left for the summer and expected the house to be just the way we wanted it? Many things were not as specified, including exterior color and roof. Several mistakes were made inside as well but, eager to get settled, we accepted the house as it was.

Retrieving Elke from the kennel we happily moved into our new house and began unpacking boxes shipped four months earlier plus other boxes stored since June, 1969 when we left Mercer Island to live in Japan. Finally, all of our family and all of our "stuff" were together again and we were excited to be in Alaska and starting a new chapter of our lives.

One of the first things we had to do was shop for furniture because we didn't have any. Anchorage was a small city and shopping was limited because everything was shipped in from "outside," as everywhere outside Alaska was called. We took the easy way out and made selections from what was on hand whether we found things we liked or not. Either that or "special order" and wait months for it to come in, hopefully undamaged.

All five of us bought new clothes suitable for the climate, which meant down coats with fur trimmed hoods, warm shoes, boots, gloves, etc. In anticipation I had bought a fur coat in Hong that kept me warm on the coldest days for all of my winters in Alaska. The kids bought "waffle stompers" for everyday wear because they were warm, durable and kept their feet dry walking through snow. It took me a while to figure out why they called them "waffle stompers" – the soles made a waffle pattern in the snow.

Heidi started sixth grade at Northern Lights Elementary a mile away. Steve went to ninth grade at Romig Junior High and Chip entered the junior class at West High. Both Romig and West High were a few blocks from our house and even though there was bus service the boys walked to school most of the time.

Chuck flew to Tokyo, Los Angeles, New York and various European cities. Most trips were four to six days, then he'd have at least a week at home. Furnishing and decorating the house kept me busy for a while but I already had personal plans of my own.

Thinking I might learn something useful I began a tax preparation class given by H&R Block. I'd always done our taxes but after Chuck went to work for Japan Air Lines we used a CPA because figuring foreign tax credits and taxes we paid to Japan was complicated. At the same time I started a real estate licensing class.

Having taken Economics classes in college, I was fascinated

by compounding interest and ways to make money work for us instead of spending it all. Long interested in real estate investments, while living in Mercer Island from 1967–1969 I toured many income properties. With no money to invest, a free education began when I learned we could buy rental properties and tenants would pay for them while we enjoyed tax benefits. My sister, Evelyn, came to visit us in Mercer Island and she and I spent a lot time touring new real estate developments, analyzing their good and bad points. I convinced Evelyn to get her real estate license. While I was tied to Yokohama for three years Evelyn was selling real estate in southern California, enjoying it tremendously and making lots of money. Now I was eager to get started making my own fortune!

Hired by AREA Realtors, the largest real estate firm in Anchorage and the only one with separate departments, Land, Residential and Income Commercial, I began my career. AREA allowed agents to specialize so my plan was to sell houses for one year, just to learn the business, then move on to income-commercial properties. My career got off to a great start. My second day in the office an agent gave me a customer she didn't want. I showed them a few houses my first Saturday afternoon. Mr. and Mrs. Gray wanted to see more houses on Sunday so we went out again. They later told me they thought I was new because I was nervous but said I was more relaxed on Sunday. Monday morning I accompanied several agents in my office to tour a new listing. The minute I walked in the house I said to everyone (foolishly!) "Oh, this house is perfect for the Gray's! I'll have to call them when we get back to the office." Making the call, I described the house to Mrs. Gray.

"It sounds nice, Betty. We'll come by later this week and you can show it to us."

Novice that I was, my response was "Oh no, Mrs. Gray! Several agents in the office are showing it today and tomorrow. I know this is your house and think you should come in now." An hour later the Gray's were in my office and we quickly left to see the house.

"Betty, you are right. This IS our house," Mrs. Gray said

excitedly shortly after walking in the door. Mr. Gray nodded his agreement. We spent some time taking a good look at the house, inside and out, to confirm their first impression, then went back to the office and wrote up the offer. After one week on the job I had made my first sale. That was just the beginning!

Before Chuck and I married he'd said, very emphatically, "My wife will never work." After seventeen years of marriage his attitude had softened considerably and in the spring of 1973 after I'd passed the licensing test, he gave his blessing to work if I wanted to. It wasn't long before I heard from several friends that Chuck was very proud of me and often talked about my work in real estate

930 WEST FIFTH AVE.
ANCHORAGE, ALASKA

**Betty Halsey**
ASSOCIATE BROKER

OFFICE 279-8586
HOME   274-3034

214

# Chapter Thirty Nine
## Alaska - A Career Blossoms

During my second week working at Area Realtors, Kelly, the Residential Department Manager, walked into my office.

"Betty, Tom Christensen, manager of the Elmendorf AFB Exchange, called me. They are being transferred and want to sell their house. He and his wife are going to interview three Realtors. I made an appointment for Friday at 1PM and I'd like you to go with me and observe."

"I'd love to go. I'll make sure to be in the office at 12:30 and we'll go together."

"Good. Prepare a package of selling information for them, information about Area Realtors and about their property."

"I'll do that."

"Thanks, Betty."

The Christensen's had a typical 1960's style split-entry house. On entering the front door one immediately had to go upstairs or down. Upstairs was a spacious living room, dining area, kitchen, two bedrooms and two baths. Downstairs was a large family room, two more bedrooms, bath and laundry room. The house was a few years old, nicely decorated and well taken care of. After showing Mr. and Mrs. Christensen the folder of information I'd prepared, I responded only to questions directed to me, making few unsolicited remarks, letting Kelly do the talking, something he was quite good at.

My home phone rang late Saturday afternoon. "Betty, this is Anne Christensen. We'd like for you to list our house. Could you come about 2 o'clock tomorrow afternoon?"

"Yes, I can, Mrs. Christensen. Thank you for calling me. I'll see you tomorrow at 2."

Quickly, I called Kelly and related my conversation with Mrs. Christensen. "Kelly, I don't know how to list a house. You haven't taught me that yet. Maybe you better come with me."

"No, Betty, I don't need to come. She called you. You can handle it. Just take the listing form and fill in the blanks. If you have any questions, and I doubt you will, you can call me."

Sunday afternoon Tom and Anne Christensen and I enjoyed talking together about various things for half an hour or so and we really liked each other. I finally took the listing form out of my briefcase and we started filling in the blanks. Shortly before we finished Mr. Christensen answered the ringing telephone. Ending a brief conversation he turned to me and said "Betty, that was Jim Miller, the man who is taking over my job. I showed Jim and his wife the house yesterday and they've decided to buy it. When you finish here go by the Taku Motel, room #218, and you can write up the sales agreement. I told him we were almost finished here and you'd be there soon."

I could hardly believe it! Forcing myself to focus on the listing form, I completed it, the Christensen's signed it and sent me off to the Taku Motel.

The Millers were another nice family. They had three children still in school so they not only liked the Christensen's house they liked its proximity to schools. We wrote up their offer for the listed price. In both cases the Exchange System would pay selling and buying costs and there was no reason to haggle over price. After leaving the Miller's I went back to the Christensen's and obtained their signatures on the sales agreement.

A very excited real estate saleswoman leaped from her car and rushed into her house to share with her family the incredible story of the afternoon. The kids said "Congratulations, Mom" and went back to their own activities. After a hug Chuck surprised me when he brought out a bottle of champagne and a celebration began.

"I can't believe how easy this is! Selling real estate is one of the most fun things I've ever done! I'd do it for nothing and look how much I'm getting paid for selling two houses and my own listing the first two weeks! Isn't this incredible?"

Chuck and I became good friends with almost all of my

216

customers and many of us socialized together, attending dinners and parties at each other's homes. The good luck I'd had when I started working in real estate continued. I was introduced to George Adams, the top man at British Petroleum in Anchorage. George and his wife, Gail, and I really clicked and became good friends. You could buy a nice house in Anchorage in the early 1970's for $40,000 to $60,000. $75,000 was practically the top of the market and when I found George and Gail a spectacular property, beautiful house, five acres and a horse barn, and sold it to them for $105,000, my boss was ecstatic, as was I. My first sale over $100,000, but not the last.

In 1974 construction began on the first oil pipeline from Alaska's North Slope to its terminus at Valdez, a tiny town one hundred and fifty miles east of Anchorage on Prince William Sound. British Petroleum, Exxon, Alyeska Pipeline and related businesses opened headquarters in Anchorage and the city began growing rapidly. Houses could hardly be built fast enough. People were getting off airplanes practically waving money in their hands, needing to buy houses to have a place to live. For several years selling real estate in Anchorage was a lucrative business.

At the beginning of pipeline construction when George Adams came to Anchorage, he began bringing in friends and coworkers from Saudi Arabia, Texas and Louisiana. George expected me to find all of them the best house that Anchorage had to offer and every time I managed to find a house that each family was happy with. Having a natural affinity for people and a lifetime passion for houses, I loved what I was doing and almost always genuinely liked my customers whether buyers or sellers. From the start I worked almost exclusively from referrals so never had to make cold calls or knock on doors. I enjoyed meeting and having lunch with local bankers and other business people seeking any business I might send their way. Most of the time, on my desk, was a beautiful flower arrangement with a note of thanks for introducing a new customer or from a satisfied buyer or seller.

The first year I worked Chuck and I bought a house a block from the gate of Elmendorf AFB. The house was small and old but in excellent condition. The seller had just purchased it with a VA loan, nothing down and a low interest rate. Before moving in he

217

had decided to move back to Texas and wanted $1,000 for his equity and take over his loan. By digging window wells and installing larger windows in the basement, we turned the house into a duplex and rented it to two young Air Force couples. Within a year we sold it for $10,000 cash down which we used to buy two fourplexes.

My boss, the owner of Area Realtors, put together two groups with ten or twelve investors in each group, and purchased all of the land located between the old highway and new highway in the bedroom community of Eagle River, fifteen miles north of Anchorage. After eight years, the $14,000 Chuck and I invested over a three year period returned more than $100,000.

After investing in Les Pace's partnership I was seriously interested in obtaining a real estate designation called a CCIC that would qualify me to put together investment partnerships. Those letters stood for Certified Commercial Investment Counselor. Obtaining the designation required many classes, hours of study and the passing of lengthy examinations given after each of the six levels.

I began the process and periodically spent a week in Seattle for an intensive course and examination for each level. I completed the fourth level of study before my life in real estate and in Anchorage ended.

Working in real estate for eight years was one of the best things I did in my life. I made many good friends and was confident of my abilities in ways I had not been before.

Financially, the income I made during those years and the investments we made became the foundation for my financial life for the rest of my life

My original plan had been to spend one year selling houses but I enjoyed it so much I stayed in residential sales for two years. Finally, with some reluctance, I transferred into the Income Commercial Department. I knew that I would miss meeting new homebuyers but wanted to learn more about investing.

I listed and sold apartments and businesses. Hours would race by as I analyzed properties, working the numbers back and forth, figuring out what a property or business was really worth as

218

opposed to what the seller wanted for it. The bottom line was always "Return on Investment." Fascinating work for someone who'd always been a "numbers" person but I missed the rapport I had with my home buying clients. Going back to real estate school and passing the examination I obtained my Broker's license.

Good luck continued when Admiral Realty invited me to join them. Admiral was a small real estate brokerage with an office in the Captain Cook Hotel – the best hotel in Anchorage at that time. Six of us shared office space and expenses including a receptionist-general office helper. We all had Broker's licenses and each person was in business for himself. How much or how little I worked was my decision and everything I earned after my share of office expenses was mine to keep.

This was the perfect arrangement for me. I could usually schedule around important kids' activities and be home when Chuck returned from a trip, at least for a while.

# Chapter Forty
## Family Life and Travels
### 1972-1975

Winters we skied at Alyeska, twenty-five miles south of Anchorage and Arctic Valley, a few miles east of the city. We were all avid skiers. We started our kids skiing in Japan when they were barely more than toddlers. At Arctic Valley, Heidi and I rode in a huge Army canvas-sided troop moving vehicle, to the top of a mountain and skied down trails; always my favorite kind of skiing. "Hot dogging," aka freestyle, was the latest craze so we gave the boys lessons for Christmas and they spent their time "hot dogging" down the wide open slopes.

Summer temperatures, usually in the sixties and seventies, with a record high of eighty-six degrees, entice everyone outside. Anchorage summer days, dry and pleasantly warm, are rarely hot. Almost twenty hours of daylight help flowers bloom profusely all over the city and vegetables set records for size and beauty. Midnight baseball games are played on the 4th of July without lights.

Anchorage boasts many parks and lakes within the city. The lakes are too cold for me but the kids swam in them. Bicycle trails, with road underpasses and overpasses, go almost across the city. Chuck and I, now in our forties, started flyng kites again as we'd done so many years earlier. Frequently we took our pseudo-grandsons, Zack and Jonathon, with us. They were the sons of my nephew, Mike Tuck, and his wife, Rosemary, in the Army and stationed at nearby Ft. Richardson.

Anchorage Children's Theatre staged a couple of productions a year. Always well supported and attended by local residents, the children's talents were amazing. We saw a performance and Heidi was enchanted and joined the group. A natural actress, she enjoyed

220

acting in several productions. Heidi played violin and Steve played tenor saxophone in their school orchestras. All three children kept busy with school, friends and activities.

Chuck and I had a busy social life with old friends and new. We got together with JAL friends living in Anchorage for dinners at home or, occasionally, several of us would go to Elmendorf AFB Officer's Club. The club had recently begun serving Mongolian BBQ, a favorite dinner that we had eaten every Monday night for three years in Yokohama. It wasn't nearly as good at Elmendorf but it was the only Mongolian BBQ available so we ate it once in a while.

Frequently JAL friends still living in Japan passed through Anchorage. A couple of favorite friends we saw were Fernando Serra, originally from Chile, and Jan Guerts, from Holland. Passing through Anchorage, they often came to my office and took me to lunch. If Chuck was in town he'd join us. Jan Guerts was a dead ringer for Robert Redford, and just as charming as he was good-looking. Rosemary, our office receptionist, developed such a crush on Jan she'd practically faint whenever he walked in.

Deep sea fishing out of Seward, a hundred miles south of Anchorage, and salmon fishing in the Kenai River fifty or sixty miles south of the city, were favorite summer past-times. In a boat, out on the ocean, holding my fishing pole and waiting for a bite, while watching harbor seals and sea lions sunning on rocks near the shore, brought a feeling of contentment difficult to maintain back on land. Fishing for silver salmon we stood on the river bank or out in the river, wearing waders up to our chests, until we caught our limit of three fish each. We tried to see as much of Alaska as we could drive to and never tired of its awesome beauty, majestic snow peaked mountains, evergreen forests and roaring rivers.

Many relatives were motivated to visit us in Alaska and see part of the 49th State. Chuck's mother came from New Mexico for Chip's high school graduation in 1974. My parents came from Atlanta. Daddy had consented to fly only once before and that was to visit my family in Seattle in 1968. They flew Delta Airlines from Atlanta to New York where they were met by an escort from

Japan Air Lines who took them to the gate where they boarded a JAL 747 from New York to Anchorage, piloted by Chuck. A proud moment for them.

Selina, my brother Jimmy's daughter, the same age as Heidi, was twelve the year she came. My nephew, Ross, was Evelyn's youngest child and a few months younger than the girls. He came from California at the same time so I took the three kids to Mt. McKinley on the train. The lodge at the mountain had been destroyed by fire the year before and the resort brought in railroad sleeping cars to use as hotel rooms. The kids were excited about the accommodations but, of course, fought over which one of them had to sleep in a lower berth. Ross was angry at losing out to the girls. He ran off into the woods and we almost had to launch a search party before we found him.

Next day Ross redeemed himself by being first to spot almost every species of animals that lived in Mt. McKinley National Park. Most of us on the bus would never have seen some of the animals without Ross spotting them at great distances and pointing them out. The tour guide said she'd never had a tour quite like ours. Most of the time a tour was considered "successful" if they spotted three or four large animals but we saw everything from grizzly bears, brown bears, caribou, and Dall sheep, to wolves and the elusive red fox, almost never seen in daylight.

My nephew, Ken Chapman, flew up to visit us. He asked me to help him plan a different kind of trip back to New Hampshire. Planning trips was right up my alley! If I couldn't go myself, I'd do it vicariously by planning someone else's trip. "Ken, how's this for an idea? Take an Alaska Ferry to Prince Rupert, British Columbia, the western terminus of the Canadian Pacific Railroad. Then take the train all the way across Canada to Montreal. You could have a friend meet you there or take a bus the rest of the way home."

"That's an interesting idea," Ken responded. Let's figure out schedules, fares, etc. and see if it's feasible."

While Ken was taking the long way home, I was waiting impatiently to hear trip details. Arriving home, Ken called me. "Ken, tell me all about the trip, the ferry ride, the train trip across

Canada, everything! I've always wanted to do that. How was it?"

His brief answer, "It was long," was about all I ever got until I started this book.

*Ken's memories of his trip to Alaska:. "When I visited you in Anchorage, I flew Chicago-Seattle-Anchorage. While there we visited a homestead home, had trip to the Denali area. You took me to Alyeska for skiing, and to the Portage Glacier. We went to Homer Spit. I took a bus trip from Anchorage to Valdez, then a ferry to a small train that carried me through tunnels to the highway to Anchorage. From Anchorage, I flew to Juneau, had time to tour Mendenhall Glacier, Red Dog Saloon, then ferry to Prince Rupert, B.C. Spent the night there before the train to Montreal. Train trip was the least satisfying part of the travel. It was either three or four nights (I had a berth), but the most exciting part of the trip, the Rockies, was traveled at night, so I only got to see the scenery as the train was coming into Jasper. Then the trip was FLAT, and l-o-n-g. Train tracks do not travel through the scenic areas of communities. Finally decided that I should sleep during the days and read during the nights."

Chuck joined an indoor tennis club and when the snow melted he played golf. Once, while playing golf at Fort Richardson, he lost his wedding band. It was a wide white gold band, matching the one I wore. Both were inscribed inside "Love Always 3-17-56." The ring hurt his finger when he swung the golf club so he always took it off and put it in his pocket. He was visibly upset when he came home and said he was going to rent a metal detector and go back the next day and look for it. After more than twenty years of marriage I was touched that the ring meant so much to him. I thought it was probably a waste of time to look for it but didn't say so. Next day when he came in from the golf course with a huge smile on his face, I knew he'd found the ring. It had been run over by a lawnmower and had scratches and a small nick in one side. After being polished it looked just fine. When I saw it on his finger I couldn't help but think "How fitting that nick is. Just like the ring, the marriage has also suffered scratches and nicks but is as strong as ever."

A travel addict, always looking for an opportunity to take a trip, spring break, 1974, was approaching. Chip's senior year in high school, I was thinking it might be a long time before our family could all travel together again so we decided to go to Australia. Steve, because of allergies, had never gotten a smallpox vaccination and he'd been allowed to live in Japan and travel all over Southeast Asia with a letter from his doctor. Knowing Australia had strict immunization laws Chuck visited the Australian Embassy in San Francisco and asked if Steve would be allowed to enter with a letter from his doctor. They responded that coming from the United States, he would be admitted.

When spring break came, we left for Australia. Flying from Anchorage to Tokyo, we stopped for a few days in Yokohoma to visit JAL friends who were still there. Suziko, our maid while we lived in Japan, came to the hotel to visit us. Returning to Haneda Airport for the flight to Australia, JAL would not let us on the plane because Steve did not have a smallpox vaccination. The ticket agent didn't care what someone in the Australian Embassy in San Francisco had said, we could not get on the flight to Sydney. Disappointed and upset, we finally talked JAL into letting us on the flight to Manila. We'd stop there and go to the Australian Embassy to try again to obtain a visa for Steve.

At the Australian Embassy we explained that the Embassy in San Francisco had said Steve, coming from the U. S., would be admitted into Australia but JAL wouldn't let us on the flight. Patiently, it was explained to us that he *would* have been admitted had we traveled directly from the U. S. to Australia. We had just spent a few days in Japan so that disqualified him! He would have to be vaccinated! Before we left Anchorage all three kids and I had gotten the necessary immunizations, and, except for Steve, updated our smallpox. What to do? How could I solve this problem?

I've done things in my lifetime that I'm not proud of and, looking back, I'm surprised at my boldness. I have trouble believing I actually solved this problem the way I did. Chip was 16 months older than Steve so I bribed Chip to pretend to be Steve and took Chip-"Steve" to the Manila Immunization Clinic and told them I'd lost his shot record. Of course they asked to see Steve's passport. I pleaded ignorance and told the nurse "No one told me to bring the passport; my husband has the passports for safekeeping." The nurse shook her head at the "dumb American" but waved Chip–"Steve" in. After giving him the smallpox vaccine, she looked at me and said "If you're going to Australia, he'll need yellow fever and typhoid shots also."

Chip looked at me and said "MOM! I just had those!"

Looking at Chip, I responded, "Well, Steve, they have to be on your shot record." Turning towards the nurse I said "Give him the shots."

Chip–"Steve" scowled, the nurse gave him the shots and, nervous as I was, I could hardly keep from laughing out loud. Looking over my shoulder to see if someone was coming to arrest me, I was eager to leave Manila. That was only the first part of the story!

When our plane arrived in Australia, we proceeded through immigration, kids first, then me, Chuck last. The kids and I breezed through without a second look. Once you leave the area, you cannot go back so the four of us waited outside in a hallway for an hour wondering what in the world had happened to Chuck. Just as I was about to try to locate someone who could check on the situation, Chuck finally came straggling out with a look of astonishment on his face. "What in the world took you so long?" I asked.

"They almost didn't let me in! The ink on my shot record was smeared over my smallpox date stamp. See, right here. They couldn't read it clearly so they were not going to let me in! I had to wait while they called a supervisor. Finally, showing them all of my JAL ID and my shot record, which goes back a few years showing that all of my shots are kept current at all times, and my passport stamps showing all of the places I'd been traveling to that require smallpox immunization, the supervisor decided to believe me and let me in. He advised me to get a new shot record before visiting Australia again! I doubt I'll ever want to visit this (blankedly-blank) country again! Come on, let's get out of here."

Despite its inauspicious start, our visit to Sydney and environs was wonderful. Sightseeing tours took us to the most beautiful and interesting places in and around the city. The Opera House looks exactly as pictures depict it and the tour guide's talk about the architecture and how and why it came to be built was interesting. Heidi and I bought beautiful topaz rings in a mining museum.

One day was spent enjoying the warm blue ocean and a brilliant white sand beach north of the city. By the time we left I knew I wanted to return some day and see more of Australia. The people were so nice and friendly and loved Americans.

On the way home, Chip and I stopped in Manila for a couple of days to shop. Chuck and Steve and Heidi went on home. Showing up at the airport with a beautiful small blanket chest, wood inlaid with bone, caused us a little more worry. It was wrapped with heavy paper and tied with ropes but at check-in they gave me a hard time. Finally, they took it. Of course the chest did not show up in Anchorage when Chip and I did. I filed a lost baggage claim but despaired of ever seeing it again. A couple of weeks later, after being found in Paris, the chest arrived in Anchorage. Needless to say, our entire Australian trip has been good for many laughs through the years.

After returning home from Australia, my thoughts turned to Chip's graduation. A good student, he was looking forward to an independent life at the University of Colorado. Considered a very good school, even though we had to pay out-of-state tuition, we knew he could get a good education there. While it was nice to know where he'd be going, I was ambivalent about his leaving home at the end of summer. He was only 17 years old. I wanted him to have the experience of being on his own but wished he could be closer. Colorado is a beautiful state, a favorite of mine since I'd skied there many times when I lived in New Mexico. Chip would feel right at home with the outdoor life there.

Our busy lives continued through spring and summer. Real estate activities took much of my time. Hosting visiting family members, keeping an eye on three teenagers, and spending as much time with Chuck as I could when he was home, filled the rest of my hours. When Chip left for Colorado at the end of summer, I really missed him and wrote him frequently. He was good at writing often and we talked on the phone occasionally. He was making friends and things were going well. The other children, Steve, a junior in high school, and Heidi in ninth grade, kept

Chuck and I busy on the home front.

Spring of 1975 Chuck and I went to Spain and Portugal for a vacation. Our good friends since 1956, Ann and Gid Terry, were in Spain. Gid was stationed at Torrejon AFB, fifteen miles from Madrid. I wrote Ann and asked her to recommend a hotel in Madrid for us for two or three days. She wrote back giving us the name of the hotel where she would try to get a reservation. Her letter said she'd meet us at the airport. On arrival, after passing through immigration, Chuck and I looked for Ann. Going down an escalator, I thought I saw her standing near the bottom, wearing a beautiful blue suit. As we got nearer and the woman showed no signs of recognizing us, I said to Chuck, "No, that's not Ann." It had been eight years since we'd last seen each other at their home in Memphis.

Chuck and I took a taxi to the hotel and, surprisingly, learned there was no room for us. Our reservation started in a couple of days. Going to a lobby phone, I called Terry's number. Ann answered and could hardly believe we'd missed each other in the airport! She had been there but had not seen us so thought we'd probably come in later. When I asked her about our hotel reservation, she explained she had been unable to get one. There was not a room to spare in Madrid's hotels because of a special event in the city. Ann said she'd drive back to Madrid and pick us up. We were to spend a couple of days at their home on the AF base. When she arrived she was wearing the bright blue suit the woman I'd seen in the airport had been wearing!

We had a fun reunion with Ann and Gid and their younger daughter, Lisa. Their older daughter, Debbie, Chip's age, was in her first year of college in Texas. One evening Gid told us we were going to dinner at a very special restaurant in Madrid, Casa Botin. We'd leave the house around 9:30 PM. "Why in the world are we going so late?" I asked.

"Siesta," was the answer.

Siesta is one of the most famous aspects of Spanish life, that dead period in late afternoon when everything shuts down so people can rest. There are two periods of siesta in Spain, siesta for shops and businesses, from about 2PM to 4PM, during which time many people go to a bar or restaurant. Siesta for the restaurants, which obviously can't rest when everyone wants to come and eat, is from around 4PM to 8 or 9 PM.

Spain is a hot country, especially mid-afternoon, and the traditional reason for siesta is for workers in the fields to shelter from the heat. Refreshed after their sleep they would work until late in the evening, longer than they would have been able to without the siesta. In spite of air conditioning in modern times, another reason why the Spanish stop for siesta is not so much out of *need* but out of *want* - the Spanish *like* stopping for a while at lunch time. It allows them to stay up later in the evening. They enjoy a long lunch, lasting up to two hours or more. A rest before going back to work is essential after that. Spanish nightlife is an all-night affair. Visitors to Spain are surprised to see streets just starting to fill with people at midnight and are even more surprised to see people in their 60s and 70s still out at 3am. They wouldn't be able to do this without a siesta.

*The Guiness Book of World Records calls "Casa Botin" the oldest restaurant in the world, open continuously since 1725, and Ernest Hemmingway really did eat there, many times. Located in the Plaza Mayor, Casa Botin is popular with both locals and tourists. Ernest Hemingway is credited with making the place famous internationally. In "The Sun Also Rises," a novel he wrote in 1926, "We lunched upstairs at Botin's. It is one of the best restaurants in the world. We had roast young suckling and drunk riojo alta." In his 1931 book "Death in the Afternoon," he wrote "I would rather dine on suckling pig at Botin's than sit and think of casualties my friends have suffered."*

Plaza Mayor is equally famous. It began in the fifteenth century as a market place outside the city walls. Eventually, after many buildings and re-buildings, it became a very large square surrounded by arcaded buildings with entrances that lead to the interior plaza.

*"Plaza Mayor has been the site of executions, tournaments, weddings, bullfights and Inquisition trials. This very large square is surrounded completely by one very large building from which onlookers perch to view the festivities in the square below. Much of*

228

*the history of Madrid, and Spain, is tied to this 17th century plaza, and today it is still very close to the heart of Madridians. Visiting the square, you will not witness any executions, but you might witness a coin or stamp show on Sundays, a free concert, or residents taking their evening strolls." (Quoted from "aviewoncities.com)*

Ann and Gid took us to see a magnificent memorial to the million men who died on both sides of Spain's civil war. "The "Valley of the Fallen" is cut into a mountainside and has a huge concrete cross on top of the mountain that can be seen from miles away. They also took us sightseeing in Madrid and to a furrier where we bought large, heavy, thick fur blankets for $35 each. They were patchwork style, made from fur scraps. We bought several for gifts for family members and they are treasured to this day.

After our enjoyable visit with the Terry's, Chuck and I checked into the hotel in Madrid. A city tour took us to highlights of the historic and beautiful Spanish city. Wanting to see more of Spain, we rented a car, purchased a highway map and took off. My favorite stop was the city of Toledo, 45 miles south of Madrid.

Designated a national monument, Toledo, a former capital of the Spanish Empire, known for the peaceful coexistence of Christian, Jewish and Moorish cultures, has been the home of many world famous artists, including El Greco. Sitting atop a large hill, "Old Toledo" is encircled on three sides by the Tagus River. Retaining the medieval road plan, with twisting streets and irregular terrain, we lost our way several times. Wanting to visit the museum located in the Alcazar (castle), we persisted. The Alcazar, almost completely demolished by artillery during the Spanish civil war in 1936, has been restored and the museum within contains a collection of war memorabilia.Toledo's cathedral contains beautiful stained glass windows, delicate wood and stone sculptures and a large collection of paintings by Spain's most celebrated artists.

After just a couple of days of touring the countryside around Madrid, we returned to the airport and boarded a short flight to Lisbon, Portugal. The morning after our arrival and a restful night in a hotel in the middle of the city, we toured Lisbon's highlights.

St. George's Castle can be seen from almost everywhere in the city and looks over Lisbon from its highest hill, offering memorable views. Dating from the 6th century, it served as a Moorish royal residence until captured by Portugal's first King. Upon completing our city tour, Chuck then decided we'd rent a car, with a driver this time, to drive us around as much of Portugal as we could see in two days. A good decision, it turned out, as we were able to enjoy the natural beauty of the country without having to drive and navigate.

We especially enjoyed our brief visit to the world famous Casino Estoril, the biggest casino in Europe. Ian Fleming based his plot for "Casino Royal" on its glamorous and sophisticated atmosphere, inspiring the most famous of spies, James Bond.

As always when traveling, we left hoping to come back someday for longer visits in both Spain and Portugal.

Returning to Madrid, I kissed Chuck good-by at the airport. It was time for him to get back home to Steve and Heidi and to work. I returned to Terry's home at the AF Base. They had invited me to accompany them to Tangier, Morocco. Ann had organized the trip for the Officers' Wives Club and she and Gid were going. Thrilled to be invited and excited about the opportunity to visit another continent, Africa, even though Tangier is located on the northwestern edge, bordered by the Mediterranean Sea and the Atlantic Ocean.

Ann, Gid and I, plus about 25 others in the group, flew from Madrid to Tangier. Soon after takeoff the Captain instructed us to look down at the Rock of Gibraltar. There it was, something I'd studied in 4th grade geography, a spectacular sight! With the blue Mediterranean beneath us, lit up by brilliant sunshine, we had a wonderful view of marine traffic, from the tiniest sailboats to ships of all sizes. Pretty soon we landed in Tangier and were transported by bus to a hotel in the heart of the city.

Tangier has a rich history due to the historical presence of many civilizations and cultures starting from the 5th century BC. The multicultural communities of Muslim, Christian, Jewish and foreign immigrants attracted artists and writers from Europe and the United States throughout the 20<sup>th</sup> century. Our visit to the Tangier Casbah was the most interesting part of the trip. The casbah is a square facing the former palace of the Sultan, now a museum. Built on the highest point in the city and encircled by the walls of the Medina (old city), the walk was steep. After we entered the gate there was an amazing and intricate system of winding alleys, arcades, shops and open bazaars selling just about anything you could think of, from spices to jewels to brocaded fabrics, rugs and much more.

Outside the casbah were many shops catering to tourists and it was hard to decide which would get my money. Several people in our group were buying jellaba's, a loose cloak with a hood worn in the Middle East and northern Africa. Chuck had previously brought home a white cotton jellaba from Egypt that we had not found a use for, so I wasn't tempted to buy another one. Actually, I bought very little other than small souvenirs for the kids.

The most fun entertainment was the night we had a group dinner in a nightclub featuring belly dancers. Gid Terry didn't know it but he'd been set up by Ann and our tour guide to be picked by one of the belly dancers to get up and dance with her. He was a good sport and our group had a lot of fun with it. For his efforts he received a certificate proclaiming him a belly dancer. When the trip ended and we were back at Terry's, I left almost immediately for my home in Alaska. I'd had a fantastic vacation in Spain, Portugal and Morocco but I was ready to be with my family.

*Steve ~ At His Best*

# Chapter Forty-One
## Heartbreak Begins - Steve
### 1976

*B*y 1975 Chuck and I were seriously concerned about Steve. He was no longer the pleasant, easy to get along with kid he'd always been. All "A" report cards he'd always brought home were a thing of the past. Grades dropping, attitude changing, we thought it was just adolescence. He drove us crazy arguing about anything and everything. Drugs in schools were a problem in Anchorage as they were across the nation. We talked to the kids many times about the dangers of using drugs and were convinced they were neither involved with drugs nor kids who used them.

We began family counseling but it didn't seem to help with Steve. He would sit mute and refuse to cooperate and Chip and Heidi were angry about being there. Truthfully, Chuck and I resented being there also! Steve was the one causing the problems; if he'd just straighten himself out and do what he was supposed to do, everything would be okay!

By the time Steve was a junior in high school, he had become more and more difficult to live with and understand. Chuck and I gave the boys small allowances compared to many of their friends. $10 a week included school lunches. Steve asked us if he could get a paper route and brought the paper route manager to meet us. After discussing issues of responsibility in delivering the papers on time and collecting from customers and paying his bill to the newspaper, Chuck and I thought it might be a good idea. Things went fine for a while but then the telephone began to wake us early on weekends. Steve was not getting the papers delivered on time and customers were angry. After I'd awakened Steve three or four times to get up and deliver his papers, we told him he had to quit the paper route.

Soon after that, with Steve's behavior deteriorating, my suspicions were aroused. He kept one of his desk drawers locked and I decided to find out why. It was easy to jimmy the lock and, I guess you could say I was shocked and not surprised at the same time. I found a baggie of marijuana. Disappointed, we restricted his activities even more.

By summer of 1975, Steve was 17 and whenever he was home, chaos reigned. It was difficult for all of us but he constantly picked on Heidi, just turning 14, and it was taking a toll on her. We no longer knew where Steve was a lot of the time and we didn't like the looks of the "friends" he brought home. As a last resort, we practiced "tough love" and told Steve to leave. We were hopeful being on his own would shock him into changing his behavior. One friend after another took him in. In late summer, driving down Northern Lights Blvd., I saw Steve walking up ahead. Wearing the big, old Army coat he'd recently taken to, posture slumping, expression sad and dejected, it was as if a lightning bolt struck my heart. Suddenly, I knew something was wrong with my son, badly wrong.

When Steve came by the house later that day, I spoke more softly and didn't argue with him. I told him he could come home if he wanted to go back to school for his senior year, so he came home. Fall semester passed; Steve spent most of his time alone when not in school. He appeared to be struggling to understand everything but was less argumentative and we did not think he was using marijuana or other drugs so we let some things pass, just to keep the peace. Early in 1976 Steve began having more and more "sick" days; he just could not or would not get up and go to school. He complained frequently, his bones hurt, his head hurt. There were other symptoms but we couldn't convince him to see a doctor.

*A thorough physical at that point in time might have altered the course of his life. Ten years later we learned he had a baseball sized tumor on an adrenal gland that had been pumping massive amounts of corticosteroids into his system from the beginning of adolescence. It hurts me to think that Steve's life possibly could*

234

*have been different. Realistically, I know that in 1976 or in 2012, with the primary symptoms being behavioral and/or mental, it is unlikely a routine physical would have discovered the tumor. Too much cortisol produced in the adrenal glands causes multiple symptoms, physical and mental. It was not until he began suffering seizures in 1986 and twice was taken to the hospital by paramedics, that an endocrinologist accurately diagnosed Steve with Cushing's syndrome and he had surgery to remove the tumor.*

Ultimately, the morning came when I awakened Steve and asked him to get up and get ready for school. He responded, "Mom, I can't go to school any more. It's time for me to go out and teach."

"What are you talking about?"

"I'm Jesus Christ. I have to go out and teach."

"Steve, why don't you get dressed and come upstairs? I'll fix you breakfast and we'll talk about this."

This time the lightning bolt struck my head. I immediately knew exactly what was wrong with my son. I knew he had schizophrenia. Struggling to make sense of what was happening, I thought of Chuck, due home from a trip in a few hours. I'd have to tell him our world had changed irrevocably.

The mental pain could not have been worse. At times, sobbing, I screamed out to God, "Why did you do this to my child? His life is just beginning. I've already had 45 good years. Take me instead! It's not fair!"

It was important to me to find a psychiatrist who believed that mental illnesses were physical diseases of the brain and had nothing to do with toilet training. Not finding the right doctor in Anchorage I knew we'd have to take Steve out of Alaska for treatment.

I'd read an article by Linus Pauling, Ph.D. about orthomolecular medicine, the practice of preventing and treating disease by providing the body with optimal amounts of substances which are natural to the body. Studies indicated that some patients with schizophrenia and manic-depression were being helped by proper nutrition and large amounts of "B" and "C" vitamins.

I called International Society of Orthomolecular Medicine in New York City. They referred me to a doctor on Long Island, New York. I talked with Dr. Hawkins about Steve and the kind of treatment the doctor would give him. Dr. Hawkins said Steve needed inpatient treatment for a minimum of six weeks. He recommended we take Steve to Brunswick Hospital in Amityville, Long Island, where Dr. Hawkins would treat him. After talking to the hospital and completing forms they sent, I made an appointment to admit Steve.

Chuck and I took Steve on a JAL flight to New York City, rented a car and drove a couple of hours to Amityville. We had been telling Steve we were going there for him to have a thorough examination. He went along willingly. After arriving at the hospital, we were shown into a physician's office where the doctor talked to Steve. Chuck and I were tense, knowing what was to happen. When two burly attendants, dressed all in white, walked into the doctor's office, I had to suppress an urge to yell "*Stop. I've changed my mind!*" When they asked Steve to come with them, he looked at Chuck and said "Dad, what's going on? What are you doing?"

"Steve, go with these men. They're going to take you to a building across the street where you'll be examined. We'll be following right behind you." Chuck's voice trembled as he tried to reassure Steve.

Following the hospital vehicle half a block and into a guarded entry on the opposite side of the street, we parked the car and followed the attendants and Steve into a building. One of the attendants took out a key and opened a locked door and after we were all inside a long hall, re-locked the door. We were shown around the Intake Unit, Steve's room and the Day Room where we saw a dozen patients ranging from lethargic to agitated. Steve was extremely angry with us and didn't fully comprehend what was going on. He thought we were abandoning him and he didn't know why. We tried to reassure him he was going to be examined and evaluated and we would be staying in a motel nearby.

The Head Nurse asked us to leave, saying Steve would calm down after we left. Telling him we'd return later, we were escorted out. This was absolutely the worst day of my life. March 17, 1976 was also Chuck's and my 20th anniversary.

By the time we got to our motel room we were both crying and all we could do was hold each other and hope our precious child would be helped.

Returning to visit Steve a few hours later, we found him still very angry. We told him over and over we were not leaving him there forever, that he would be treated and when he was better, we'd take him home. His diagnosis was "paranoid schizophrenia" and the doctor was confident that it had nothing to do with marijuana and/or other drug use. I derived some comfort from a sign over the nurse's station: "The patients are not an interruption of our work. They are the reason for our work."

After a few days Chuck went home to be with Heidi and go back to work. I stayed close to Steve for two weeks, by which time he'd settled down and seemed to be accepting the situation. When I left I told him I'd be back in ten days or two weeks. Chuck asked for more flights to New York instead of other routes he'd been flying. Whenever he had a flight to New York he would visit with Steve for a few hours.

While shopping in the commissary at Elmendorf AFB one day, I heard my name on the loud speaker. Hurrying to the manager's office, someone handed me the phone. Heidi said Brunswick Hospital had called to tell us that Steve had climbed over the fence and was gone! Leaving my basket of groceries I rushed home trying to figure out what to do.

By the time I got home, my nephew's wife had called from California. Pee Wee said Steve had called from JFK Airport in New York. He asked her to buy him a ticket to California. She told Steve she'd talk to Alan, my nephew, and asked Steve to call back in an hour. I called her and asked her to tell Steve she'd make arrangements and he should wait near the American Airlines counter. Next, I called the hospital and told them where Steve was and asked them to send someone to pick him up. I then called airport security and asked them to detain Steve until someone from the hospital came for him. The plan worked smoothly and within a few hours of leaving Steve was back in the hospital. Little did I know this was the first of countless times over many years that I would have to figure out a way to rescue Steve from far-flung places, Hawaii, Florida, Maine, Chicago and Philadelphia, just to name a few. Our family journey with schizophrenia had begun.

Whether with Steve in New York or at home in Alaska with Heidi, I felt a need to be in both places at once. Stress was constant, not being able to fix everything and have us all home and happy. Chip, in college in Colorado, knew what was going on but wasn't living with it every day. I brought Steve home after six weeks with a restricted diet and medications plus mega doses of vitamins. Better, but not "well," he went back to school in a special program and completed his senior year and graduated. Always struggling to see that Steve took his medications and vitamins and stayed away from foods to which he was allergic was a full time job.

We returned to Amityville several times, twice for hospitalization, and other trips for outpatient visits with Dr. Hawkins. A new book, "The Amityville Horror" was released and a big hit. Supposedly a true horror story, about a family living in a nice waterfront house in Amityville, I stayed awake all night in the motel reading the book and scared myself half to death! The house was near the hospital so I drove by to see it. That night, in my dreams, I could see it all night! By the time the movie came out, filmed at the house, I'd lost all interest! I was still living my own "Amityville Horror!"

Many things I'll never forget happened on and around those trips. Tension was always high when traveling with Steve. He and I were leaving on a JAL flight to New York one night and after boarding and settling in our seats, a JAL representative came on and asked us to leave the flight. Not knowing why, we got off the plane. I learned that Steve had thrown up in the hallway at the airport shortly before we'd boarded and hadn't mentioned it to me. Humiliated, I feared embarrassing Chuck with his employer. Upset and crying, I called Chuck to come back to the airport and pick us up. After calling the hospital to tell them we'd be a day late I made a reservation on another airline for a flight the next day. I didn't want to travel with Steve on JAL again and didn't even want to use discount tickets, so paid full fare!

238

That was the flight that Steve spent introducing passengers seated near us to each other. He'd say *"Hi, I'm Steve. What's your name? Jim, I want you to meet ..."*and then he'd ask Jim's seatmate his name and proceed to introduce them to each other. Next Steve would say, *"Jim, have you ever heard the song 'The Lord's Gonna Be In New York City?"* Jim usually answered "No," after which Steve would say *"Well, when I get there, he will* be."

I've never been so glad to get off a plane in my life! Hurrying to the Avis Car Rental desk, I put my driver's license on the counter with my credit card and told them I'd reserved a car. The agent picked up my driver's license, told me it had expired and he couldn't rent me a car! We shared a van to Amityville with several people so I endured Steve's introductions and *"The Lord's Gonna Be In New York City"* for two more hours. We were the last ones in the van and as each of the others left, they wished us good luck! When I asked the van driver if he could please drop us off at Brunswick Hospital instead of the designated motel stop, he took us to the door. I used taxis all week and, first thing, when I got home, renewed my driver's license.

239

# Chapter Forty-Two

## Living With Schizophrenia

### 1976-1984

From the beginning Chuck and I were open about having a child with schizophrenia. Amazingly, people seemed to come out of the woodwork to tell us about mental illness in their family. Friends and coworkers revealed they also were dealing with it though they'd never mentioned it before.

Steve had good periods and bad periods, the bad ones usually precipitated by his not taking his medications, a common problem. For a year or more he ran his own janitorial service. He cleaned a few offices at night and a couple of apartment buildings we owned. Part of the time he knew he had schizophrenia and recognized that his delusions were "crazy" but couldn't stop the other side of his brain from believing they were real. The rest of the time he argued there was nothing wrong with him, the rest of us were crazy and picking on him! It was easy to see the "split in the mind" that Freud wrote about. One part of Steve's mind could see that the other part was irrational but the rational part couldn't maintain control. Advances in technology, particularly Positron Emissions Tomography, known as the PET scan, show the frontal lobes of the brain in people afflicted with schizophrenia, do not receive enough blood flow. The frontal lobes have to do with logical, orderly thinking leading to a conclusion. When they don't have enough blood flow, people affected have disorganized, illogical, impulsive thinking.

Over an eight year period Steve worked hard to be "normal." He accumulated almost three years of college credits, one or two classes at a time. The fact that Steve was very bright made his plight more difficult. No matter how well he'd do for a while, nor

240

how hopeful we'd be, inevitably the decline began again.

Steve went traveling several times. We always tried but could never prevent his going. He'd leave with very little money, no plans and no clothes except what he was wearing. He never wanted to be bothered carrying as little as a change of clothes. He quickly learned how to live on the streets, where to get a free bed or meals or a change of clothes. He worried excessively about world affairs and once spent several days at the Library of Congress doing "research." He wrote letters to world leaders advising them on whatever their current problems were. Amazingly, he received a few responses thanking him for his interest. He also made many phone calls to Russia and to Buckingham Palace when he believed he was a member of the British Royal Family.

Worn out from two years of traveling back and forth to New York, I tried again to find a psychiatrist in Anchorage to treat Steve. My ad in the newspaper searching for an "open minded doctor who believed mental illness is a physical brain disease, and willing to treat a patient from that perspective," prompted no replies from doctors. Many other heartsick people seeking help for a loved one responded. I received a dozen phone calls and several letters from people in all parts of Alaska asking me to share any responses from the ad with them.

When we first recognized Steve was ill, I called the Alaska Mental Health Association, listed in the phone book. The telephone had been disconnected and I couldn't track them down. Two years later, I learned they had opened an office again and went in and talked with Joyce Munson, the Director. The office had been closed for a year because the association was out of money.

I told Joyce about my ad and the heartbreaking responses I'd received from people desperate for help. We decided to start a family support group. We set a date and called the newspaper and The Anchorage Times wrote an article about the meeting. Besides Joyce and Chuck and I, there were seven others at the first meeting, Valentine's night, February 14, 1978. Two of the people at the meeting were battling depression but others all had a family member with mental illness. For all of us, it was like finding a long

241

lost relative. We met people who understood what we were going through, who shared our grief. It was a great relief to share our personal stories with others on the same journey.

We named our group REACH, "Reassurance for Each." A few months later we changed the name to SHARE, "Self-Help and Reassurance for Each." Later still, joining forces with a small group starting up in Michigan, our group became a charter member of the National Alliance for the Mentally Ill (NAMI).

As leader of the Anchorage group I spent hours on the phone with members as well as people looking for help. From a distance I helped groups get started in Fairbanks and Juneau. Becoming a thorn in the side of Alaska's Social Services Department, advocating for badly needed services for the mentally ill, I never gave up. I testified before Alaska's legislature by radio/phone hookup from Anchorage to Juneau. The state asked me to attend a mental health meeting in Yakima, WA about providing for services for people with mental illness in rural areas, and report back what I learned. In 1980 I attended the first national convention of NAMI in Denver and had my picture taken with Rosalynn Carter.

Taking advantage of every opportunity to advocate for the needs of mentally ill people, I was invited to speak before civic groups and asked to participate in a television program about mental illness. Four of us were on the panel, a psychiatrist, a psychologist, a representative from Social Services and me. Viewers called in with questions for the panel. At one point the psychiatrist was asked a question and he answered "I don't know."

Immediately, I spoke up and said "I'll answer the question," and I did. Increasingly, the calls were for "the doctor in the blue dress." Many people told me that I came across as knowing more about mental illness, needs and services available or not available, than the other three panel members put together! I don't mean to be bragging but simply to emphasize the disorganized mess that passed for mental health services in the 1970's in Alaska. Contacts in other states confirmed things weren't any better in other states.

When I was invited to join the Board of Directors of the Alaska Mental Health Association, I accepted. Natalie Gottstein was now Director of the association's office in Anchorage. Joyce

Munson had resigned to run for election to the state legislature. She won and became a strong advocate for services for mental health services in Alaska.

One interesting thing I learned was that when Alaska became the 49th state in 1959, the United States Congress stipulated Alaska set aside one million acres of land to be designated "Mental Health Lands" and all income from those lands was to be spent for mental health services. Land was set aside but any income from it never went to services for the mentally ill.

The Alaska Mental Health Association was formed to challenge the state on this issue. Jim Gottstein, an attorney and Natalie's son, representing AMHA, sued the state several times and in 1994, finally prevailed. Alaska Mental Health Land Trust was formed and all income designated for mental health services.

During my service on the AMHA board, part of the time as Vice President, I learned a lot about state government and I'll always be grateful for my experience. Natalie Gottstein became my lifelong friend. She once rescued Steve from the Alaska wilderness and sent him home to California. She visited me twice after I moved to California and even though she was receiving treatment for cancer, came to my wedding in 1985. She died a year later at her home in Anchorage

# Chapter Forty-Three
## Some Very Hard Years
### 1976-1981

The years from 1976 through 1981 were busy and difficult years. Chuck was working, having transitioned from the DC-8 to Boeing's 747. He enjoyed the airplane and felt proud to be one of the first JAL pilots to fly it. Real estate still took up some of my time. Meeting people and helping them find a home they'd love was enjoyable and a needed distraction. Having studied income commercial investment properties, I sold a couple of businesses. Working independently at Admiral Realty sharing space and expenses, allowed me to work as much or as little as I wanted to.

Chip, attending the University of Colorado in Boulder, knew what was happening at home but didn't live with it on a daily basis. After his sophomore year Chip told us he had every intention of finishing college but he'd like to take a year off to work and travel. Chuck and I strongly opposed that idea, fearing he wouldn't return to college. After his junior year, Chip didn't "ask" us but "informed" us that he was taking a year off. He took his year and worked and traveled, spending a couple of months in Taiwan. Then he went back to Colorado for his senior year, graduating in 1979. He accepted a job with U. S. Borax in Los Angeles.

Heidi finished her high school years and started college. She didn't want to go to school in the Northwest, as most of her classmates did. She wanted to go to a different part of the country where she'd make new friends and have new experiences. I liked her attitude; it reminded me of my eagerness to leave Atlanta for new places and people. She chose Northern Arizona University, Flagstaff and started there in the fall of 1979.

Steve continued his roller coaster pattern of bad times and better times. During the better times, which meant when he was

244

stable and taking his medications, he lived at home. When he stopped taking his medications and not doing the best he could for himself, he lived with friends or in his own apartment.

I took a class now and then at the University of Alaska, Anchorage. The one I enjoyed most and remember best was "Speed Reading." The first class the instructor gave us a reading test and when she had studied our results I was surprised to learn I already qualified as a "Speed Reader."

All of us managed to squeeze in a trip now and then. Chuck and I went to London with Bill and Pam Sundeen for a few days. Pam was from London and the perfect tour guide. We saw shows and Pam showed us some of London's lesser known but interesting sights. Heidi and I went to London with our friends Alice Huey and her son, Jeff, a couple of years older than Heidi. The "excuse" for our trip was shopping for school clothes. We saw a couple of shows and shopped till we dropped!

Shortly after Steve's first hospitalization, my mother got sick. Hospitalized and diagnosed with Multiple Myeloma, she passed away ten days later. I took Steve with me to Atlanta, grateful I was with her for her last few days.

July, 1979, shortly after Heidi's high school graduation and Chip's college graduation, Chuck's only sister, Yvonne, passed away suddenly from a stroke. She was 63 years old, 13 years older than Chuck. He was devastated by grief. Yvonne was the only family member living in New Mexico near their mother, in her 80's.

In the summer of 1980 Heidi told us she did not want to go back to Arizona to college. She had a good job and a boyfriend she didn't want to leave. We tried to change her mind but didn't succeed.

That same summer, a year after Yvonne's death, Chuck's only brother was diagnosed with cancer of the esophagus. Fryer, 65, was raising a 14 year old daughter alone. When Fryer was hospitalized Chuck took time off and flew to Florida. Their mother went to Florida from her home in New Mexico. Shortly after arriving, Chuck's mother suffered a massive heart attack and almost died. I took the next plane to Miami to be with Chuck and help him. Fryer died before I got there and Mother was out of danger and Chuck was very happy to see me.

Fryer's daughter, Alline, refused to move to Alaska to live with us and, fortunately, a family friend offered to move in with her and become her guardian. For all practical purposes, Alline was an orphan now; her mother had abandoned Fryer and Alline when she was a baby. Chuck was executor of the will and Alline's financial guardian.

Mother was in the hospital for three weeks and rehab for a couple of weeks. Chuck spent his time flying between wherever his job took him and Anchorage and Homestead, Florida. Finally, his mother recovered enough that Chuck was able to take her home to New Mexico. He hired a caretaker and left hoping she'd be okay.

A few months later, in November, 1980, I met Chuck at the airport when he returned from a working trip to Europe. He came home a couple of days earlier than scheduled and, not flying the flight, traveling as a passenger. Seeing him coming towards me in his uniform always caused my heart to do a flip-flop. After 24 years we were still "in love." He looked terrible, pale and gray at the same time. Hugging him, I said "You look really tired, Hon, are you okay?"

"No. I'm sick. I've been sick for two days. I told Operations I was sick two days ago and to find someone to take the flight I was scheduled to fly roundtrip from Amsterdam to Hamburg. They tried but one of the pilots in Europe had injured his eye and another was sick so I had to take the flight anyway. I flew to Hamburg, then went into the Ops Office and lay down until time to fly back to Amsterdam. Once back in Amsterdam I told JAL I was getting sicker and to get me on the next flight to Anchorage, so they did. After boarding I went to the upper cabin and climbed into a bunk and stayed there until we landed."

"I'm taking you to the hospital. You're never sick like this." After a few protests Chuck allowed me to take him to the emergency room at Elmendorf Air Force Base. They gave him an EKG which, we were told, was okay. They said he probably just had the flu and to go home and take it easy. We went home that

246

Sunday afternoon and Chuck went to bed. Wednesday, when the telephone rang, he was still there.

The voice on the telephone said "Is this Mrs. Halsey?"

Thinking it was probably a real estate call, I said "Yes, this is Betty Halsey. How can I help you?"

"Mrs. Halsey, this is Dr. Smith at Elmendorf AFB Hospital. I've just had a look at your husband's EKG that was done a few days ago and I'm not sure the EKG machine was working properly. Could you bring him in so we can do another one?"

"Sure. We'll be there within an hour."

Arriving at the hospital I let Chuck out of the car at the door. After parking the car, I went in and found Chuck sitting in a wheelchair in the Cardiac Unit. The doctor quickly said, "Mrs. Halsey, your husband has had a heart attack and needs to be hospitalized. I was just asking him if he wants to stay here or go to Providence Hospital downtown.

Realizing Chuck had been misdiagnosed for three days, I said "I'll take him to Providence."

Dr. Smith said, "I'd prefer an ambulance take him. You meet him there."

Driving to the hospital I realized this was another bombshell exploding in our lives. This was the end of Chuck's job with Japan Air Lines. What would we do? Where would we go? Those were questions for later. Right now the most important thing was to get the best cardiac doctor in Anchorage to take care of my husband.

In early December Chuck came home from the hospital severely depressed. Depression almost always follows a heart attack but in Chuck's case it may have been worse because the heart attack cost him not only his job but his license to fly. He'd been a pilot since he was 14 years old. It was all he'd ever wanted to do and he'd been able to spend his entire career flying, first in the U. S. Air Force, then for The Boeing Company and for the last eleven years for Japan Airlines. Mentally, he'd lost his ID. He didn't know who he was any more.

Financially we were okay. I was making good money selling real estate. The market was at its top. Home prices had escalated dramatically since I'd started in real estate in 1973 so commissions were much larger. I had all of the clients I could handle, working only with referrals. We also had savings and investments. It was just a matter of figuring out where we wanted to go and what Chuck wanted to do for his next career. At 51, he was too young to totally retire. Before he had time to figure anything out, life stepped in and kept him busy.

Frequent calls came from Alline's guardian in Florida, always needing more money. Household things broke down frequently, or Alline had school expenses, or she was causing problems. It was a difficult situation for everyone involved but there was no one else to oversee things.

The caretaker for Chuck's mother in New Mexico wasn't working out. His mother needed full time care. Chuck went to New Mexico to find a nursing home. When he couldn't get her into a nursing home in Albuquerque or Socorro, the two closest towns to Belen, where she lived, he took her to Grants, 60 miles west and too far for most of her friends to visit. Chuck made regular monthly visits to New Mexico and after a couple of months I went with him. We cleaned out his mother's house, sent a few things to storage in Albuquerque, had an estate sale for the rest and sold the house, all accomplished in one week!

Heidi had been telling us for several weeks that she had to leave Alaska to get away from the boyfriend she'd broken up with. He wouldn't leave her alone, was stalking her, and she was afraid of him. We thought she should just ignore him but after he started leaving threatening messages for all of us, we were convinced and early in 1981 helped her move to Phoenix. She moved in with a college friend and found a bookkeeping job. We gave her money for a used car but told her since she had completed her education, she was on her own financially, that we were not going to support her. After only a few months she asked if she could go back to school. She didn't want to work forever in a low-paying office job, so made plans to resume college in the fall.

March 17, 1981 was Chuck's and my 25th wedding anniversary. I convinced him to take a Caribbean cruise. He tried, for my sake, but was never able to arouse enthusiasm for the trip.

248

We flew to Miami and when Chuck saw his suitcase coming down the ramp in baggage claim, he said "Someone's been in my bag."

"How do you know? What makes you say that?"

"My shirt's hanging out the side! I didn't close it that way!" He opened his bag right there in the airport. At the last minute I'd added a couple of things to his bag, our camera, in its hand-tooled bag I'd bought in Morocco, and a bag of bottles containing vitamins. Both were missing. After getting to the hotel and our room, Chuck started to take a shower and discovered the hot water faucet was not working and we had to move to another room! I tagged along behind as he stomped off down the hall, barefooted, wearing his robe, following the bellman with our bags.

Despite our best efforts, we didn't have much fun. Chuck had always been full of life and full of fun wherever he was but now there was no joy left in his soul. One day as we relaxed in lounge chairs on deck, I noticed directly above us was a small black cloud in an otherwise cloudless blue sky. I couldn't help but exclaim, "Damn! That black cloud has followed us ever since we left home and there it is, still over us!"

# Chapter Forty-Four
## Alaska Heartbreak
### 1981

*A*nchorage had a wonderful bicycle trail system that stretched many miles across the city. A new section had recently opened from our area west to the water's edge. It was airport property but totally undeveloped. Each side of the gravel road was heavily wooded and it was a gorgeous ride toward the setting sun. I bought a neighbor's bicycle and began riding in the long spring and summer evenings. My friend, Alice, who lived on our block, had a bicycle and she and I rode together frequently. I was totally at peace when I was riding with my face to the sun and the wind ruffling my hair. If our husbands were out of town, we'd stop for dinner in an old rustic log cabin, after our ride. It was there I first tasted warm bread pudding covered with a rich cream sauce and it is still a favorite dessert.

For a couple of years I'd been going to the health club in the Captain Cook Hotel before going to my office. I'd go early in the morning and spend 45 minutes on the treadmill, then another 45 minutes swimming laps, which I estimated to be about a mile. I loved the exercise; it made me feel better mentally and physically.

After Chuck's heart attack I encouraged him to buy a bicycle and ride with me and to join the health club and share that also. I knew the exercise would be good for him. After enduring my nagging for a few months, he finally bought a bicycle but only rode with me a few times. His heart wasn't in it and his head wasn't in the right place either.

In June, 1981 Chuck and I went to visit Chip and meet his fiancé. Chip had given Jackie, his college sweetheart, an engagement ring and she had joined him in Los Angeles where

250

he'd gone to work after graduating from college in 1979. We flew to California and stopped to visit my sister, Evelyn's family before going to L. A. to see Chip. We met Jackie and liked her but my feeling was they did not have a lot in common. We borrowed Chip's car and drove Hwy. 1 north to Santa Cruz, exploring and looking for a place we'd like to live. It was important to me to be close to the ocean. We really liked a small village called Shell Beach, on the central coast 10 miles west of San Louis Obispo. We liked it so much we considered making an offer on an oceanfront lot in a new development but decided maybe we'd better think it over.

Next we flew to Arizona to check on Heidi. We met her roommate, a nice young woman, and they shared a comfortable apartment. New Mexico was our last stop to visit Chuck's mother for a couple of days, then back home. Steve was very sick again and living in his own apartment so Chuck and I rattled around in our house which was much too big for the two of us.

Still grieving over Fryer's and Yvonne's deaths, his mother alone in Grants, N. M., where she knew no one, his heart attack and the loss of his job, Chuck found it hard to even want to live. "They died so young! Why? All of my family is gone except Mother and she's too mean to die!" Frequently, if Chuck had a drink or two, he'd say, "I might as well die, too. I'm no good to anyone, anyway." Knowing alcohol is a depressant and seeing how it affected Chuck, I tried to get him not to drink at all. That, however, was impossible considering the culture we'd always lived in.

The years Chuck was in the Air Force, a certain amount of drinking with his squadron friends was encouraged. They usually had "Happy Hour" at the Officer's Club on Fridays after work and most of the guys felt like they "should" attend, at least for a while. The same was true the two years he worked at Boeing and while at Japan Air Lines crews spent a lot of their time away from home socializing in bars. Dinners out, or with friends in their homes or ours, everyone had a drink or two.

I had tried all year to get Chuck to see a doctor about his depression and he refused. Finally, I all but forced him to go. He saw a psychiatrist, didn't like him, and came home and said he'd never go again.

Early in September, longtime AF friends, Stan and Ruth Kibbe, flew to Anchorage in their plane and visited for a few days. Their neighbors were traveling in Alaska in a motor home and the four of them arranged to meet in Anchorage. We invited Kibbe's neighbors to dinner and enjoyed meeting them so we spent a couple of days showing the four of them some of Anchorage and the surrounding area.

Chuck had begun playing golf again and didn't seem quite as depressed as he had been. I was busy preparing for a two day conference in Anchorage put on by the Alaska Mental Health Association and Alaska Mental Health Services, with help from the Anchorage group of the National Alliance of the Mentally Ill. Mental health professionals lead seminars and the keynote speaker was to be Patricia Neal. I was scheduled to lead a seminar on the difficulties of families coping with mental illness. I spent most of Thursday and Friday morning at the conference.

At lunch time Friday I called home but there was no answer. I assumed Chuck was running errands, or maybe he'd gone to play golf. I went home hoping he'd come in before I returned to the hotel to lead my seminar. I baked Chuck a birthday cake and put it on the dining room table with his presents. It was September 25, 1981, his 52$^{nd}$ birthday. Chuck didn't come home while I was there so I returned to the hotel to prepare for my seminar. I left Chuck a note reminding him that we had a table for 10 people for the evening's keynote speaker and dinner. I said I'd be home as early as I could to get ready.

Some days later Chuck's golf buddy, another JAL pilot, told me where Chuck spent a few hours that fateful Friday. Don said he'd called Chuck to ask if Chuck would play golf but he said "No." Don played golf and when he finished his round, went into the clubhouse where he saw Chuck having lunch. Don sat down with him and, because it was Chuck's birthday, bought him a drink. Several others joined in the celebration, all buying drinks for Chuck. By the time Chuck left the golf course, he'd had way too much to drink.

Chuck's car was in the garage when I drove in about 5PM. The house was quiet as I entered. I looked around downstairs while I called him. When I didn't get an answer, I climbed the stairs and at the end of the hall entered our bedroom. My beloved husband was lying on our bed with a bloody hole in his heart and a shotgun standing upright between his legs dangling off the side of the bed. With one hand I grabbed the phone and dialed 9-1-1. With the other I cradled his head and begged him, "Please don't die! Please don't die! Please don't leave me!"

Very quickly my house filled with people, friends from different parts of my life brought together by tragedy. Chip arrived from California closely followed by Heidi, from Arizona. Evelyn and Dean and my nephew, Alan, came from California, and Lillian and Larry came from Atlanta. Numb with shock and grief, that entire period is a blur. Somehow, necessary things were accomplished and a service was held. The only part I vividly remember is Chip's eulogy for his dad. When a tear rolled down Chip's cheek, he lifted his hand and brushed it away and kept talking. All of our hearts were broken and our lives shattered. How would we live without Chuck, my husband, the love of my life, my children's father?

# Chapter Forty Five
## Aftermath

After several days at home, Chip flew to New Mexico to tell his grandmother that her third and last child had died. She had lost all three of her children in just over two years. Eighty-five years old, in frail health and living in a nursing home, I expected she wouldn't last much longer.

Heidi returned to her job in Arizona and other family members returned home. My oldest sister, Hazel, and her husband, Jack, came to stay with me for several weeks until I left to spend the holidays in California. Steve was hospitalized at Alaska Psychiatric Institute.

Just before Thanksgiving, I flew to New Mexico to visit Chuck's mother. We shared our grief and she thanked me for loving her son and giving him three beautiful children, and her, her only grandchildren. I was shocked but appreciated it when she told me I was still young and she wanted me to marry again and have a good life. At the age of 50, I didn't feel young. I felt like an old woman and I knew I'd never love anyone again. That part of my life was over.

From New Mexico, I flew to Arizona and was met at the airport by Heidi. She had rented and packed a U-Haul trailer with all of her things and had it hooked up to her yellow Pontiac Sunbird. We immediately headed west towards Riverside, California where we'd spend the holidays.

In early December, ten days after I'd visited her, my mother-in-law died in New Mexico. Chip and I flew to New Mexico and arranged a service at her church. The few relatives she still had in New Mexico came as did all of her local friends. After the service Chip and I, followed by a hearse, drove to La Junta, in

254

southeastern Colorado, to lay her to rest beside her late husband, Ralph Sale.

We drove my mother-in-law's car and after our brief graveside service, attended by Ralph Sale's relatives, we drove 175 miles north to Denver. Chip had already decided he did not want to live his life in a place he didn't like, Los Angeles, so he planned to move to Denver in January. We drove to the home of a college friend of Chip's where a few of his friends had gathered to welcome him back to Colorado. We left his grandmother's car there and someone drove the two of us to the airport for our flights back to California.

On my flight, I couldn't help but dwell upon the fact that my husband and his entire family, brother, sister and mother, had all vanished from the face of the earth in less than 2 ½ years. There's no way to prepare ahead of time for circumstances such as this. Numb with grief for all of them, I just wanted to get through the holidays for the kids' sake.

Steve joined us in California for a couple of weeks and I was glad to see he was better. I was grateful the hospital let him come because he needed to be with us, at least for a while. After Christmas, he returned to the hospital. Chip went home to pack his things for his move back to Colorado and Heidi and I flew to Atlanta to spend a couple of weeks with my large family.

When we returned to California, I put my fate and future into Heidi's hands because nothing made any difference to me. Still numb, I'd live wherever she found a college she thought she'd like to attend. Starting south of Los Angeles, we drove down the freeway, closest to the coast, getting off to visit several colleges. Heidi chose Palomar College in San Marcos, a small town 30 miles north of San Diego, 7 miles inland from the ocean at Carlsbad. She registered for classes that began in a couple of weeks. A few miles east, in Escondido, much larger than San Marcos, we rented a condominium and, within a few days, had moved in.

Jane, my niece who lived in San Diego, was going to Hong Kong in March with the "Back Street" gang. Back Street was a restaurant in Riverside that had a gang of regulars who had eaten there for many years; they were all friends and now called the

"Back Street" gang. Evelyn and Dean were part of the gang and Jane was friends with the restaurant's owners, Mac and Barbara, as well as most of the gang. Every year the Back Street gang took a trip together and in 1982 they were going to Hong Kong in March. I was invited to join them, so I stayed on in California. A nice, young, military couple, friends of Evelyn's, were staying in my house in Anchorage taking care of the house and Elke. They were saving money to buy a home of their own so they didn't care how long I stayed away.

The trip to Hong Kong was a good distraction. You can't travel with the Back Street gang and not have fun because they are all fun-loving people! A former member of the gang, who now lived in San Francisco, joined us on the flight when we stopped there. Bunny was near my age and she and I hung out together the entire week and became good friends. I was a crazy person that week, spending money with abandon, buying all kinds of things, art work, a diamond ring, and dozens of hand embroidered tablecloths for gifts. It took me years to give them all away!

When I got back to Escondido, I'd take Heidi to school and use her car to explore surrounding areas, looking for my new home. There are a large number of beautiful communities between San Diego and Escondido so it was difficult to choose.

One Sunday, returning from San Diego on the back roads that I always prefer, we drove into La Costa, an especially beautiful community built around a hotel and well-known golf course. It was pretty, but not for me. Three miles further up Rancho Santa Fe Road, approaching the small town of San Marcos, we saw the entrance to "Lake San Marcos" and turned in. At first sight I knew I'd found my home.

There was a tiny village, with a few businesses, a café and a restaurant on the lake, the "Quail's Inn." There was a large lake with homes around it, community tennis courts and swimming pools plus a country club and two golf courses.

Driving into "Sunrise Pointe," a duplex style condominium community on the lake, it looked perfect. Inside one of the model homes, located on the lake, I talked to a Realtor, asking when the models would be for sale.

256

She didn't know, but didn't expect them to be sold anytime soon. I told her I wanted one of the models and I'd be back in a couple of months. I had to go home to Alaska and sell my house and couple of apartment buildings, but I would be back. Jackie told me later, she knew I meant it. Beautiful, tranquil and peaceful, I could see that Lake San Marcos would be my healing place, where I could begin to build a new life.

Returning to Anchorage, I had a lot to do. First, I told my officemates I wasn't coming back to work so they should find someone to take my place. They decided to close the office as a couple of them were ready to retire and the other two couldn't afford to keep that space. I put my house on the market for sale and had a buyer the first week.

Then I started selling most of my furniture and packing the things I'd move to Lake San Marcos. A good friend, a real estate broker and investor, who shared our office, offered me a fair price for my two apartment buildings. Steve, out of the hospital and doing very well, lived with me. He was happy we were moving to California where we'd be with Heidi and Evelyn's family. He was a big help preparing to leave.

Two months after I'd returned to Anchorage, I left it for the last time, carrying Chuck's ashes and ten years of memories of my family growing up, Steve's illness and Chuck's death. It was a bittersweet ending.

# Part Four

## A New Life

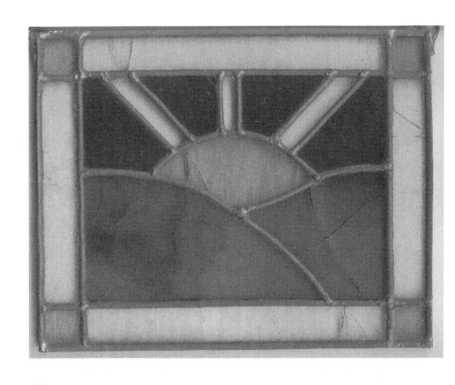

*Chuck's 1<sup>st</sup> Stained Glass*

# Chapter Forty Six
## The Healing Place

Arriving in southern California in May, 1982, there were several priority things to take care of. The most important was to make arrangements to bury Chuck's ashes in the Riverside National Cemetery. A couple of weeks after we got to California we had a beautiful military service complete with a 21-gun salute. All of our California family were there for a brief but moving service. I needed that because when we had services in Anchorage I was still in such a state of shock that I could hardly remember it.

Topping the list I needed to buy a car. I had left my car in Anchorage with a friend to sell for me. My brother-in-law, Dean Tuck, spent a day driving me to Buick dealers in the region. I had been happy with the Buick LeSabre I'd had in Anchorage and wanted another one. We finally found exactly what I wanted in a pretty redwood color at a fair price and after writing a check I drove it away.

Next, Steve and I took our things from my sister's house in Riverside to Escondido and moved into the condo with Heidi. Within a few days we rented an apartment for Steve nearby. He was doing very well and I wanted him to have help in maintaining that. We signed him up for a "Case Manager" and for the Mental Health Day Treatment Center. He had received a lump sum retroactive disability payment so we went shopping for a car for him, buying a small Subaru, only two or three years old. He was pleased to have an apartment and a car and promised to continue taking his medications.

I drove the eight miles from Escondido to Lake San Marcos, a small village of 4,000 people, built around a lake. I went directly to the model homes in "Sunrise Pointe," that I'd looked at two months earlier. Going into the real estate office, I saw Jackie, the same saleswoman I'd talked to earlier. "Hi, Jackie, remember me? I met you a couple of months ago."

"Yes, I do remember you. You told me then you wanted to buy one of the model homes when you returned from Alaska. There's good news for you! The models were just put up for sale a couple of days ago. Model #1, the smallest one, is already sold but #2 and #3 are available." Jackie handed me a brochure showing the details and selling price for each model.

"That's wonderful news! I'll look at them." Leaving the office, I said, "I'll be back in a few minutes and tell you which one I want."

The two models were similar in size – 1750 sq. ft, living room with fireplace, dining area, kitchen with eating space, den, two bedrooms and 2 baths, plus a good-sized double garage. I liked both but made a decision based on the view of the lake. In Model #3 the dining area and the kitchen faced the lake. In Model #2, the view was from the living room and the eating space in the kitchen. Both had small fenced patios overlooking the lake but #2 had another patio with access from both bedrooms, as well.

I went back to the office and signed a contract to purchase Model #2. I asked that some of the furniture be included and offered to buy other pieces as well. I also specified that I be allowed to move in within two weeks. We celebrated when my offer was accepted and spread the news to my Riverside and San Diego relatives.

Heidi and I went shopping for furniture I still needed. We bought a sofa and love seat for the living room; I'd shipped everything else from Alaska I'd need for that room. For my bedroom the only thing I needed was a new bed as I'd purchased the furniture in the model. A table and chairs for the kitchen eating area was also on our list. We found just what I wanted in a store in San Diego. It was light colored wood, heavy and substantially built. I bought it but when I learned they were going to charge $50 to deliver it 30 miles up the road to Lake San Marcos, I balked. "We'll take it with us. Where should I pull my car up so you can load it in?" Mouths agape, someone gave me directions.

On the way to move the car, Heidi said "Mom, I don't think

that table and chairs will fit into the car!"

"Don't tell them that! We'll make it fit," I responded. After half an hour and a lot of twisting and turning and taking out and starting over, the table and four chairs were resting comfortably in the back seat and the large trunk of the new Buick LeSabre. Heidi and I laughed all the way home as we kept remembering the astonished looks on the faces of the store employees who tried to convince me that it was impossible, that there was no way the table and chairs would fit into the car!

We moved our things out of the condo in Escondido and into my new home as well as an apartment Heidi rented in San Marcos, a mile from Palomar College, where she was a student. Chip and a couple of friends had purchased a condo in Denver where he had started his new life. Elke was the only family member living with me and though my private yard space was small, Elke was now 15 years old and not nearly as active as she'd been most of her life. I walked her several times a day and she was fine.

Intentionally, I didn't want Steve or Heidi living with me, even temporarily. After five years of turmoil caused by illness and death, I had a lot of healing to do and needed to be alone in my beautiful, serene place on the lake. If I was going to be able to help Heidi complete her education and get launched into adulthood, and be able to take care of Steve's needs for probably the rest of my life, I understood on a deep level that I had to take care of myself first. The most important thing for me was to heal myself and hold the remnants of my shattered family together.

When the moving company delivered my shipment from Alaska, I had them put all 101 boxes in the garage. I had packed most of the boxes myself and had a list of everything in each box and the outside of each box was clearly marked with the room where the contents were to go. Many years of moving experience had taught me to be organized. I easily found whatever I needed whenever I wanted something. Some of the boxes were marked with the kids' names and I'd keep them until each of the three were settled enough to want all of their "stuff" together.

Soon I'd established a routine. Mornings I'd unpack boxes. After lunch I rode my bike to the closest pool to swim laps, enjoy the perfect weather that region is famous for and talk with my new neighbors. In the late afternoons, on my back patio, I'd lie back in the big papa-san chair I'd bought in Taiwan in 1972 during my last shopping swing around Southeast Asia before we left Japan. With a cold drink on the nearby table, I'd watch the swan family float around the lake or wave at the occasional canoe or row boat passing by, or, sometimes, wave to a group of people on the pontoon boats that were popular at the lake. The speed limit on the lake was 8 miles an hour so there was no noise or disturbances from speed boats or water skiing.

Eight homes were on my block plus the developer's large home at the end of the cul de sac. Only mine and one other house had full time residents. The others were vacation homes so my block was especially quiet. I soon learned Lake San Marcos had a nickname, "Heaven's waiting room." Average age at the lake was 69. Several people asked my age and upon hearing that I was 51, would suggest I should move to a younger community where I could meet people my own age. They didn't understand that I had no interest in meeting younger people. I was content just where I was.

I'd been living there a few weeks when Evelyn and Dean, came by one day with their 5-year old granddaughter, Kiersti, they'd just picked up in San Diego. Kiersti's mother, my niece, Jane, was going on a vacation and Kiersti was going to stay with Evelyn and Dean for a couple of weeks. They were leaving for Texas in a few days to attend a military ceremony honoring my nephew, Mike. "Don't take Kiersti on that long drive! Leave her with me. I'll be glad to keep her!" Kiersti didn't know me well. She'd been around me during the Christmas holidays the previous year but that was about it.

Evelyn asked "Kiersti, do you want to drive to Texas with Grandpa and me to see Uncle Mike, or would you rather stay here with Bett?"

The quick response was, "I'd rather stay here with Aunt Bett." So, that was that. Kiersti fit right into my schedule. The first thing we did was buy her a life jacket. With the lake and my dock just outside the patio door, I wasn't taking any chances. I insisted she

264

wear the life jacket whenever she was outside alone. Next, we made a deal; if Kiersti entertained herself in the mornings while I continued organizing the house, after lunch we'd go to the children's swimming pool. We went to the pool every day and Kiersti swam like a fish and played with other visiting grandchildren. She was an easy child and good company.

A friend from the time Chuck and I were married lived in Fallbrook, a beautiful community in the hills 15 miles north of San Marcos. Natta Lee's husband, Dusty, was Chuck's flight engineer and they were one of the first couples Chuck introduced me to. Dusty had died at the age of 44 after hitting a home run. Rounding third base, he'd dropped dead of a heart attack. Natta Lee and I stayed in touch through the years and now we were living not too far apart. She called to say that she and Jim, her second husband, wanted to come spend July 4th with me. They would bring a picnic lunch and I shouldn't worry about a thing. I told them that Kiersti was with me but they came anyway and were delighted to meet Kiersti, even bringing special treats for her.

A few days after the 4th of July would be Kiersti's sixth birthday. One day she said, "Aunt Bett, could you give me a birthday party?"

"Heidi, Steve and I could give you a birthday party but it would be small. I just moved here so I don't know anyone else to invite."

"I know someone," she said, giving me a sly look. "We could invite those nice Fallbrook people." We didn't do that but Heidi and I took Kiersti to Oceanside to the theatre to see "E. T." We bought her a special book and E.T. doll but, suddenly, she started to cry because her mother wasn't there to share her birthday. We went home and had ice cream and birthday cake and Kiersti was happy again.

Another early houseguest was Brett, the 12 year old son of my nephew, Alan. They lived in Upland, about 60 miles from me. Brett spent a week with me and we played tennis, swam, rode bicycles all over the area and rented a pontoon boat for cruising around the lake. I was glad I'd kept Chuck's bicycle and brought it from Alaska. It came in handy as Chip and other visitors used it to go riding with me.

"Sunrise Pointe," where I lived, was a 124 unit condominium development within Lake San Marcos. A monthly newsletter advised residents on matters of interest to our community. Every couple of months Sunrise Point held a welcoming party for new residents so I decided to attend the August party. It was a potluck held in the lake's main recreation area adjacent to the tennis courts and main party room. I plucked up my nerve, prepared a dish to take, and went to join the party and, hopefully, meet some interesting people who might become my friends.

Immediately after arriving, someone took my dish and put it on the food table; someone else asked what I'd like to drink, and people began introducing themselves. I'd been thinking about adding a skylight in a rather dark hall/bathroom/laundry-room area and started asking if anyone living in the same floor plan had done that. Norma and Jim had been thinking of doing the same thing and soon we were talking to Bob and Jenny, who had installed a skylight in that spot in their home. They invited Norma and me to come over on Monday and look at their skylight. We set a time and Norma said she'd walk by for me and we'd go together.

Going to the welcome party was the right thing to do. From then on, walking through Sunrise Pointe or riding my bicycle, everyone always waved or we'd stop and chat. Lake San Marcos was becoming my home.

A strange thing made me feel I was where I was supposed to be. The year before, Chuck had taken a stained glass-making class. He'd made three pieces: I gave Chip one and Heidi one and I kept one. My piece showed the sun rising over mountains. From my kitchen table I watched the sunrise over what looked like the same spot.

*A New Life*

# Chapter Forty Seven
## Building A New Life

*A* few days after the Sunrise Pointe welcoming party, the telephone rang. "Hi Betty, this is Beth Conlin. I met you at the party the other night. Do you play tennis?"

"Hello, Beth. I used to play but not for the past ten years while I was living in Alaska."

"Well, I haven't played since college so that was a lot more than ten years ago! How about going to the courts and just hitting balls together? Would you like to do that?

"Yes, I'd love to! When would you like to go?" Beth said, "How about tomorrow morning around 9 o'clock? "

"That's good. I'll meet you there."

That was the beginning. After a few sessions of just hitting balls, I wanted more. "How about I see if I can find a tennis instructor who'll come give us lessons? Would you be interested?

"Sure, that's a good idea," said Beth.

Marcus came to our courts to give Beth and me lessons twice a week. He'd had a career as a tennis coach, was now retired, and happy to have paying clients now and then.

One day when Beth and I were playing singles, Adam and Carol stopped us and asked if we'd like to play doubles with them. We played and arranged a time to play again the next day. Adam and Carol had lived in Mexico for several years and had recently returned to the U. S. and moved to Lake San Marcos. Months later, after we'd become good friends, I learned that Adam had worked for my brother, Bill, a Regional Administrator for the U. S. Department of Labor. Adam had actually been to Bill's home for dinner! Small world!

Gradually, other people stopped, one or two at a time, and asked to play tennis with us. We had an informal group that played together on Monday, Wednesday and Friday. Whoever showed up played. Usually we had enough players to fill two courts. If there was an extra person, we'd take turns so everyone got to play. We all belonged to the Lake San Marcos Racquet Club and I began getting calls to play several days a week. I never said "no" even if I'd already played that day! One day I ended up playing three times, a total of nine sets!

Beth dropped out of the lessons with Marcus after a few weeks but I continued them for several months. Because I was playing so much it was only natural that I got better and better. Eventually, I was invited to join the LSM Ladies Tennis Team. For a few months each year, the ladies' team played teams from various clubs in north San Diego County. One year our team beat the Camp Pendleton ladies' team and won the North County championship! That was especially satisfying because the average age of the Pendleton ladies was about 25, while the average age of our team was close to 70! At that point, I was the youngest one. Personally, I have always been a fierce competitor. I like to win!

Besides tennis almost every day, I swam 50 laps in the pool, estimating that to be about a mile. My bicycle tempted me to ride it several miles a few times each week because I had such a beautiful, relatively flat area in which to ride. Gradually, I became more physically fit than I'd been for some time. Recovering mentally was slow and still painful. Most mornings when I awoke, unbidden, my first thought would be "Is this all there is?"

I'd met Norma and Jim at the first party. The next week, Jim died suddenly. I reached out to Norma and we began going to dinner together once a week. We went to nice restaurants and tried a different one each week. Soon, other widows asked if they could join us so we'd have anywhere from two to six or eight ladies dressing up and going out to dinner. We laughingly called ourselves the "Tuesday Evening Dining Club."

The first few months at Lake San Marcos, I played bridge with the Sunrise Pointe ladies and enjoyed it because I was getting to know people better but I really didn't like being cooped up inside.

Eventually, I dropped out of bridge because I enjoyed my active pastimes more.

Daily life filled the hours. The racquet club had a party in the recreation center every three months. Usually, the parties had a theme, Las Vegas night, or Halloween costumes, or whatever season or holiday we were celebrating. A local band usually played "oldies" for dancing and a good time was had by all. There must have been an unwritten rule because the parties were always over by 10 PM, which was fine with me.

Several couples invited me to dinner and I reciprocated. My first Christmas at the lake, I invited many friends to my house to watch the Christmas boat parade. Since most of them didn't live on the lake, they were delighted to accept. The boat parade party became my "event" of the year and it grew larger year by year. I never felt like a fifth wheel because it was common at the lake to include everyone, couples, and singles of both sexes. We went around together in groups. Frequently, a group from the racquet club would travel to Mexico for a week of fun. I declined the invitations; I just wasn't ready yet.

"Hey, Betty, got a minute?" George, a neighbor in the next block had waved me down. "The Sunrise Point Homeowners Association annual meeting is next month. We need a few more names for the ballot. We have to elect two new board members. We already have six people interested but we'd like to have a couple more names just to make the ballot longer. Would you let me put down your name?"

Hesitating only a moment, I replied, "Sure. You can use my name." I don't know where my brain was but I honestly didn't realize that I'd just agreed to serve on the Board of Directors should I be elected! I didn't give it any more thought until the night of the meeting when I was shocked to hear that I'd won and would be a new member of the Association's Board of Directors.

As head of the Architectural Committee, I enjoyed my work. With two other committee members, I inspected properties and made a decision about exterior alterations a homeowner wanted to make. I was easy to get along with. I didn't see why our homes shouldn't have our individual "stamps" on them, accomplished with tasteful and minor changes that didn't disturb neighbors. I almost always gave them a stamp of approval.

Friends and family members came to visit, from Washington, Arizona and Georgia. I went to Atlanta at least once a year to see my father and the rest of my large family. I saw my Riverside family and Jane, in San Diego, often. I hosted a party for the Backstreet Gang, with whom I'd gone to Hong Kong. Everyone came from Riverside except Bunny, the woman who'd joined the flight in San Francisco and who took me under her wing. Bunny flew down for the reunion and stayed with me for a few days. Everyone brought pictures of the trip and one man surprised us all with a movie he'd put together with music and sound.

A notice in the newspaper caught my eye. It was an invitation to attend the "Get Acquainted Party" of the San Diego "Over The Hill Gang." The original "Over the Hill Gang" had been started by a group of aging avid skiers so they'd always have someone to ski with. I was a skier with no one to ski with so I went to the meeting. It was a cook-out on a beach north of San Diego. It was fun and I attended a few more of their events and made a few new friends.

Soon after moving to California, I joined the Escondido Alliance for the Mentally Ill. My five years experience in Alaska qualified me to lead a discussion after the general meeting when we broke into small groups. Involvement with the group was satisfying. I liked comforting others newly struggling with mental illness in a loved one, while I struggled daily with my own son's schizophrenia. A year after our move to California Steve spiraled downward again. He stopped taking his medication and started traveling around the country. As always, I was his chief problem solver. Once, with the help of my dear friend in Alaska, Natalie Gottstein, I had to rescue him from Alaska and get him back to California and into treatment and new housing in Escondido.

No matter how busy I stayed, nor how many new friends I had, there was still a big hole in my life and I thought it could never be filled. Something vital was missing.

272

# Chapter Forty Eight

## Road Trip

### 1984

After attending Palomar College in San Marcos for a year Heidi moved to San Diego to attend San Diego State University. She enjoyed living in San Diego and we met for lunch or dinner often. Chip had moved from Los Angeles to Denver a few months after his father died. He'd started his own computer programming business. He came to visit every few months, once bringing home a delightful young woman that I thought might be "The One." She wasn't.

Sunrise Point Homeowners Association had a monthly newsletter. The woman coordinating it, typing it, and making a copy for each of the homeowners, had to give up the job. I agreed to take it on and it wasn't as time consuming as it sounded. Each block had a designated "Captain," who gathered news from residents and passed it on to me. After the newsletter was printed, the captains distributed them on their blocks. It just took a few hours work from me to lay it out and type it up and have it printed. No home computers in those days, just my trusty typewriter.

I'd been in California almost two years by the spring of 1984 and my traveling feet were itching again. Del Mar, a nationally famous racetrack, was only a few miles away. I wanted to see the races but did not want to drive in the congested area around Del Mar. An ad in the newspaper solved the problem for me. A travel agent was advertising a bus for group visits to the track. I went to their office and got the details. Then I gathered up 15 friends and contracted for a bus. The driver dropped us off at the entrance to the racetrack and when the races were finished, he was waiting for us at the exit gate.

During the races, we all had a hilarious time. We'd bet on horses because we liked the colors the jockey was wearing, or because we thought it was the most majestic horse or just because it was a long shot, or some other silly reason. I, along with a few others, had to learn how to go to the proper window, and make my $2 bets efficiently so as not to rile others in line behind me. In our group we had a winner or two in several of the races. Luck was with me and I left the track $30 ahead. The bus returned us to the country club where we all had dinner together, continuing the fun and laughter we'd enjoyed all afternoon. It had been a great day!

Dixie, the travel agent who arranged for the bus, talked to me about a two week Mediterranean cruise. If I could get ten people to sign up for the cruise, I'd get my trip free. I arranged for Dixie to come to the country club and give a cruise presentation. A number of people came for the talk but none signed up. Two of my close friends, Eleanor and Mary, expressed interest, as did a Sunrise Pointe neighbor whose husband didn't like to travel. With encouragement from me, the four of us made our reservations for the cruise in September.

I had met Eleanor and Mary playing bridge. When they heard that Norma and I were having dinner out once a week and trying different restaurants from San Diego to Oceanside, they asked if they could go with us. Eleanor and Mary lived three blocks from me. Their condos were side by side. They were both Italian so, while similar in some ways, they were very different from each other in other ways and neither of them was remotely like me. They didn't play sports at all, weren't adventurous, and had lived far different lives from mine. Even so, we enjoyed each other and became good friends.

Eleanor's husband had been a butcher in Chicago. They'd bought a Burger King franchise in Savannah and moved there. With a partner they acquired other Burger King franchises in the South. They did extremely well financially and were happy raising their two sons in Savannah. The reason Eleanor ended up alone in Lake San Marcos was because her husband was murdered in the Savannah Burger King. He didn't usually work in the restaurants but happened to be there the night a robber came in with a gun. Eleanor's brother lived in Vista, 7 miles from Lake San

274

Marcos, so she moved to California to be near him.

Mary had lived the life of a traditional Italian wife. Her husband owned a plumbing business and Mary was a stay-at-home mother. Literally, she'd never even learned to drive! After being widowed she took driving lessons. Her son lived in La Costa, only 3 miles from Lake San Marcos, with his wife and Mary's only two grandchildren. It almost seemed like destiny that Eleanor and Mary ended up side by side and were best friends until Mary's death many years later.

I talked the two of them into taking a road trip with me, something they'd never done before. We left in mid-June of 1984, heading northeast on I-15. The first night we spent in Las Vegas with Mary's daughter, who lived there.

Continuing up I-15, we arrived in Salt Lake City the second day where we had reservations at a downtown hotel with a swimming pool. I'd made all the reservations for the trip so we always stayed in places with a pool so I could get a little exercise while traveling. Salt Lake City is close to the Rocky Mountains on the east and the Great Salt Lake is to the west. The natural scenery is spectacular. The state capitol is the prettiest I've ever seen and there are many historic mansions dating back to the eighteenth century. We toured the Mormon Temple complex but were not allowed inside the Temple itself.

A good friend of mine from Air Force days lived in Provo, north of Salt Lake City. Jean and Charlie were from the area and after he retired from the Air Force, they'd returned home. Jean met the three of us for lunch. The last time I'd seen her had been a few years before when Chip and I visited the Jones family in Wiesbaden, Germany. In Utah we had a good visit and a good lunch while catching up on mutual friends.

From Salt Lake City, we traveled to Sun Valley, Idaho for a couple of days, staying in the well known Sun Valley Lodge. It had become famous in 1941 when Olympic skater turned actress, Sonja Henie, starred in a movie filmed there, "Sun Valley Serenade," also starring John Payne. I had a crush on John Payne for years! In the hallways hung framed, autographed pictures of movie and sports stars that had stayed there.

275

A few hours' drive on a scenic highway, with magnificent vistas of the Grand Tetons and pristine high altitude lakes, took us to Jackson Hole, Wyoming. The picturesque mountain village was a top ski area and still on my list of places I wanted to ski. We had a large room with two beds plus a half balcony above with another bed. Our view from the two story windows reminded me of museum paintings, depicting a snow topped mountain range of many colors. Throughout the day colors changed as the sun transited northeast to northwest. A few miles north was the small town of Jackson, population (at that time) 4,500 people. Millions of tourists pass through Jackson each year as a major gateway to the south entrance to nearby Yellowstone National Park, Grand Teton National Park and the National Elk Refuge, plus several ski resorts.

Located in the center of Jackson was a square park. Entrances at each corner of the park were marked by a large, thick arch make of elk antlers, certainly unique to Eleanor, Mary and me. Throngs of people crowded the streets, shops and restaurants and we soon learned why. The southern entrance to Yellowstone was closed due to blizzards. Many people had been waiting in Jackson for several days, hoping the weather would clear. Our plan was to enter Yellowstone at the south entrance and drive west across the park to Old Faithful Lodge and after a few days, exit at West Yellowstone. Within a few hours, Eleanor, Mary and I studied our maps and decided to drive 150 miles around to the west entrance to Yellowstone; reports were the weather was better there. It wouldn't be much out of our way to change our plan. We were headed north to Canada anyway.

We were in Eleanor's car and I was driving north in Idaho under a sunny sky. Suddenly, clouds masked the sun and began dropping big snowflakes on us! The road was ascending because we had to go over a mountain pass just before we'd cross the state line back into Wyoming. After an hour, snow was piling up on the sides of the road and we felt apprehensive because, naturally, we didn't have snow tires. Finally, we saw signs for a "rest area" and pulled in. A trucker coming from the opposite direction, pulled in beside us. I got out of the car and asked him, "How bad is the weather and snow at the top of the pass?"

"Same as it is here," he replied while giving me a strange look. I decided, if that were the case, we could make it over the pass. Less than a mile further up the road we passed a sign, "Summit." No wonder the trucker gave me such a strange look! We were there and didn't know it!

# Chapter Forty Nine

## Yellowstone and Canada

Shortly after crossing the state line from Idaho into Wyoming we finally entered Yellowstone National Park. Our reservation at Old Faithful Lodge was a stone's throw from the Old Faithful geyser I'd learned about in 5th grade. I was excited to be visiting another place I'd longed to see for many years.

The lodge was built in 1903, so well-heeled visitors, arriving by stage coach, could rest comfortably while touring the park and visiting the star attraction, Old Faithful geyser. The lodge is a celebration of natural wood and stone, a whole new style of "rustic elegance." I loved just looking at it.

Old Faithful was everything I'd imagined since I was ten years old. Eruptions typically shoot from 3700 to 8400 gallons of boiling water to an average height of 145 feet. Eruptions happen approximately 90 minutes apart but, on unpredictable occasions, the time varies. Tourists start crowding around the geyser half an hour before the expected eruption just to make sure they don't miss it. The day we were there the geyser performed right on schedule amidst "oh's and ah's from spectators. A day's bus tour of the park showed us views of much of the park's wildlife and fields of geysers and hot springs. The park's natural beauty has inspired artists from all over the world for more than a hundred years.

Yellowstone National park is one of our country's treasures. Thankfully, our leaders had the foresight to set aside those thousands of acres for future generations to enjoy. I had visited countries in Europe and Asia with documented histories thousands of years older than the United States. Most of them had not had the foresight to protect such vast areas for future generations to enjoy. The U. S. was a toddler, in age comparison to many other countries but that day I felt proud and grateful that I was born in this great country.

Eleanor and I had a problem we discretely discussed. We started the trip with each of us taking a turn driving. After Mary had her first turn, Eleanor and I weren't comfortable with her driving. She drove too fast and, seemingly, didn't pay enough attention to what she was doing. We had been stalling every time Mary offered to drive. Finally we were in Big Sky country, Montana. Traffic was sparse and the highway wide open and straight so we decided Mary could take her turn again.

We had discovered early on that Mary was "directionally challenged." She never knew which way was north, east, south or west and Eleanor and I had been trying to teach her, to find a way Mary would be able to remember, so she could figure out which way she was going. Calling from the back seat, I said "Mary, we're pointing directly to Canada. The Rocky Mountains are off to our right. The Pacific Ocean is way, way out to our left. What direction are we going?"

After a long pause, during which Mary appeared to be considering the question, she answered, "West!"

"No, Mary! Oregon and Washington are on our left, way out west of us!"

"Oh. Are we going north?" Clearly, she wasn't sure, so I picked up my book and read for a while. Eleanor was dozing in the front passenger seat. "Wee! This is fun driving in Montana!"

I rose and looked at the speedometer. "Mary, slow down! You're going 90 miles an hour!"

"Oh, my! I guess that is too fast, but it's so easy without much traffic." Pretty soon we stopped and changed drivers and, without discussing it, Eleanor and I knew that was the last of Mary's driving but we kept trying to teach her directions.

Continuing north into Alberta, Canada, we had lunch in Calgary and a self-directed tour of the city before proceeding west again on Trans-Canada Highway 1 towards Banff. Banff and Lake Louise were two more of my long dreamed of destinations. They were built by the Canadian Pacific Railway in the late 1800's and the Banff Springs Hotel and the Chateau at Lake Louise were now world class resorts. The closer we got the more excited I felt that I was finally going to see the famous Banff Springs Hotel I had heard and read so much about. My eyes and brain worked overtime trying to take in the magnificent scenery. When surrounded by the beauties of nature, or a man-made piece of art, I feel joyful and peaceful, which is probably part of the reason I've always been such an eager traveler.

Banff is Canada's "highest town" with an elevation of 4,450' and located within Rocky Mountain National Park. In 1883 when the transcontinental railway reached the formidable Rocky Mountains, three Canadian Pacific Railway workers tried to file a claim for the land when they discovered hot springs bubbling from the base of Sulphur Mountain. Their thwarted attempts led to the establishment of Rocky Mountain National Park, Canada's first.

Originally a sleepy summer resort with designer shops for international travelers, it closed in winter. Eventually, with the popularity of skiing growing rapidly and the building of the Trans-Canada Highway, Banff became a year-round destination. It 1985 it was designated by UNESCO a "World Heritage Site."

In 1984 when Eleanor and Mary and I visited, Banff was quite a small town but designer shops still lined the main street. A few hotels and motels were scattered throughout the town. We stayed in a small lodge a couple of blocks from the main street. Instantly, at first sight of the Banff Springs Hotel, I felt my heart sink because we were not staying there. It had a five star rating and their room prices reflected that. The Chateau at Lake Louise was the same and Eleanor, Mary and I had decided to splurge and stay at one of the two hotels but not both. In Banff our lodgings were comfortable but modest and I regretted our unnecessary frugality the whole time I was in Banff.

Banff Springs Hotel looks like a Scottish castle and is located on a bend in the Bow River so that it overlooks the river upstream for several miles. High peaks of the Canadian Rockies almost touch the back of the building. An image of the Banff Springs Hotel, from a couple of miles upstream, is burned into my mind as one of my favorite "most beautiful places in the world." Since we were not staying there we could only tour it and enjoy gourmet

280

meals in elegant, richly appointed surroundings.

I was drunk with happiness at being in such an incredible place. At dinner one evening I blurted out to my friends, "I'm going home and find someone to marry so I can come back here on my honeymoon!" My remark surprised me as much as it did Eleanor and Mary! I had not consciously had any thoughts of that nature but almost three years since Chuck's death, healing was happening and my subconscious must have had some desires I'd not allowed to surface before.

Our next stop was an hour away, the Chateau at Lake Louise. The two nights we stayed there I kept getting up all night to peer out the bathroom window at the full moon shining on the lake. Such an awesome sight, I couldn't get enough of it. Not wanting to disturb my roommates, I spent hours in the bathroom staring out at the moon, the mountains and the lake.

Still enjoying a natural "high" when we stopped next in Kamloops, B. C., I was exuberant, more open and friendly than usual. We were told the food at a restaurant near our hotel was excellent. Walking towards the restaurant, we saw a man alone leave and walk towards us. "Good evening, ladies. Are you planning to have dinner there?" he said as he nodded towards the restaurant.

"Yes, we are. Is the food good?" I answered.

"The best in Kamloops. Ask for a window table because the view of the river is as outstanding as the food."

Eleanor jabbed me in the ribs and muttered, "Ask him if he wants to go to Banff." Afraid he'd overheard her remark I quickly ended the conversation and we moved on. From then on, for the rest of the trip, every time a man smiled at us, or said "Good morning" or "Good evening," either Eleanor or Mary would poke me and mutter the same question. It was good for a lot of laughs.

Next day on the highway we narrowly missed a horrific accident. I was driving when suddenly, a quarter mile or so in front of us, I watched as a pickup truck crossed the highway and collided with a propane truck. The resulting explosion sent a massive fireball across the highway setting fire to several vehicles and scattering cars of a passing freight train as if they were matchsticks. There weren't more than a dozen untouched automobiles between us and the carnage. We couldn't help but shudder when we realized, had we not stopped briefly to change drivers a few miles back, we might have been involved.

Two more days of driving through the exceptional beauty of British Columbia, we were in Vancouver, my vote for the world's most beautiful city since I first saw it in 1967. We spent a few days there sightseeing, including a ferry to Victoria to see Butchart Gardens.

Continuing south in Washington we had dinner with friends of mine, Jan and Dave Robinson, in Seattle and stayed a couple of days with friends of Eleanor's in Lake Oswego, Oregon. From there we drove to the coast and Highway 1, one of the most scenic drives in the country. Eureka, CA was especially interesting with many restored Victorian homes.

We met Mary's friend for lunch in Sausalito then to Monterey to see the aquarium and the area made famous by John Steinbeck in his novel, "Cannery Row." We saw the original cannery row where the movie version was filmed.

After lunch in Carmel we continued down the picturesque coast highway through Big Sur before spending the night in San Simeon. Next day we toured Hearst Castle and the delightful faux Danish town of Solvang before spending our last night in charming Santa Barbara. The last day of our trip we toured the city and the landmark Spanish style Court House. We felt we deserved an award, or at least a bumper sticker, saying "I drove every scary mile of Highway1!"

While in Monterey we went into a shop that had a barrel of small brass items for $1.00 each. All three of us found a few things to buy. By this time Eleanor and I had pretty much given up on teaching Mary north, east, south and west. She just couldn't seem to get it. A couple of months after we got home, one day Mary said to Eleanor and me, "Remember that brass shop in Monterey where we bought some do-dads for $1.00?" We both said we remembered that. Mary continued, "Well, I bought a compass and I sat in the back seat the rest of the way home with it on my lap, and you never again asked me, 'Which way are we going?"

*Chuck Moorhead - After Tennis*

# Chapter Fifty
## Another Pilot Named Chuck

*T*he day after returning home from my long trip with Eleanor and Mary, I rode my bike to the courts to play tennis with three friends. Playing on the first court, I couldn't help but notice a twosome playing on the fourth court. Jean was a member of the tennis club, a 60 year old Barbie doll. She retained her high school figure, loved flirting with men and, after two divorces, was currently single. She collected men friends, but no one special. Jean was the type of woman that many women don't like but I liked her. I thought she was funny and she had always been nice to me so I had no reason not to like her. That day at the tennis court I saw that Jean was playing with someone new.

Bizarre though it may sound, I felt an immediate attraction to that man I couldn't even see very well three courts away! The magnetic pull was instantaneous. My first reaction to these feelings was shock and astonishment that I could be attracted to someone! My next feeling was gratefulness. I recognized I was capable of loving someone new. After our game ended Jean came over and introduced the rest of us to the new man. He lived at the lake but was much younger than most residents, in his late 40's. A retired Coast Guard Captain, another pilot named Chuck. His eyes twinkled; he smiled warmly and displayed the graciousness of southern gentlemen. When introductions were made Chuck Moorhead focused intently on each of us in turn, so I felt he really was glad to be meeting me. Yes! This was meant to be.

Riding my bicycle home, I saw Eleanor in her back patio, adjacent to the street. Stopping my bike, I called out, "Guess what, Eleanor, I just met the man I'm going to take to Banff!"

"You're kidding! What are you talking about?" Eleanor's eyes were large and her mouth hanging open.

"Believe it! I just met him at the tennis court. I absolutely KNOW I'm going to marry this man."

From that day I carried a picture in my mind of our wedding. It would be an outside wedding beside the lake, with our children and extended families. Chuck didn't yet know the joy and happiness that I already knew was in his future. It sounds like a fantasy in my mind but I was positive it was more than that. It would happen.

Everything I gradually learned about Chuck confirmed my first instincts. He was divorced in 1979 in North Carolina where he retired from his career as a U. S. Coast Guard Captain and aviator. He had three children. After his divorce and retirement he moved to Palos Verdes, CA to be close to his sister and brother-in-law, Michelle and Bart Earle.

Bart owned a "Red Onion" Mexican restaurant, originally started by his grandparents in Los Angeles. He planned to build and open one in San Marcos, thirty miles north of San Diego, and hired Chuck to work for him in coordinating and building the restaurant. At the same time Bart and Michelle also built a large home on the hill overlooking Lake San Marcos and Chuck bought a condo in the area.

A few months after the San Marcos "Red Onion" opened, Bart had some very bad luck in his businesses. First of all, the new restaurant in San Marcos was found to be the source of a case of hepatitis, traced to an employee. After a great start this was a huge blow to a new restaurant, not yet firmly established. About the same time, Bart discovered his partner in the Palos Verdes restaurant was "stealing him blind." The result of these two things was the beautiful "Red Onion" in San Marcos, that Chuck helped to build, was sold to a Mexican restaurant chain and Bart had to cut his losses in Palos Verdes and settle with his partner in court, with Bart retaining full ownership of that restaurant.

Chuck had worked in the "Red Onion as Host/Assistant Manager and sometimes bartender. When the job ended, he enrolled in a golf academy that would qualify him to work as a golf professional. That is what he was doing when we met. He started playing golf his first year out of the Coast Guard Academy, loved the game and was an excellent player.

Now that I was home it was time to start practicing for the 4<sup>th</sup> of July canoe race. Historically, only men were allowed to race. A couple of months earlier a group of ladies, including me, approached the resort's owners, Gordon and Don Frazier, and asked to participate in the canoe race. Gordon was my neighbor and Don played tennis with us frequently so we thought they could be persuaded. However, they said "No" and thought that was the end of it. Susan Frazier, Gordon's daughter, in her late 20's, managed the hotel at the lake. We enlisted Susan to help us change the antiquated "rule." She not only got the rule changed, she joined our team!

Barbie Doll Jean and another tennis friend, Virginia, were my partners and we started practicing rowing every day. None of us had any experience in canoes but we got the hang of it and I liked it so much I decided to add rowing to my list of activities.

On July 4<sup>th</sup>, about an hour before the race I bumped into Chuck. He was alone and had come to watch the race and see what other festivities were going on. We talked for a short while until I had to join my team to prepare for the race. Every time I was around him and talking one to one, it was all I could do to keep from laughing out loud because I knew a secret he didn't yet know!

The men and women racers had taunted each other for weeks. One of the male racers said to us, "I don't know why you're wasting your time. We'll probably drown you before you make the first turn!" That was a challenge our teams couldn't resist. There had been lots of advertising about July 4<sup>th</sup> events at the lake so there were many guests in addition to residents, quite a crowd. Many of our tennis friends were there helping the ladies team launch the canoes and cheer us on. Six male and two female three-person teams participated. Before my team rounded the first barrel, we'd fought off a male crew attempting to dump us but, instead, we dumped them! The men were all after us determined not to lose face by losing the race to the gals! The final result was that our team came in third out of the eight teams, losing only to two of the men's teams and beating four of them. At the end we all ended up in the lake. It was one of the most fun July 4th's I'd ever had!

Eleanor, Mary and I were going on a Mediterranean cruise in September, three months after our driving tour of the west. Elaine Boyd, a young woman I'd met when I hosted a cruise information party at the country club, would be my roommate. When I started thinking about clothes, and what I'd need to buy before the cruise, I took a good look in the mirror. I'd been very indulgent on our trip and got very little exercise, so I'd gained about 10 pounds. That, plus the extra 10 pounds I was already carrying, convinced me I needed to diet. Having met the man I was planning to marry in a year, even though he didn't yet know that, was an additional motivator. I took on the project and by the time we left for our cruise, I'd lost about 15 lbs.

# Chapter Fifty One

## Mediterranean Cruise

### 1984

Eleanor, Mary, Elaine and I flew from Los Angeles to Athens, Greece, with only a brief stop in London. The 21 hour flight was part of our cruise package so the plane was full. Crowded into a middle row without much leg room, we got off to an uncomfortable start. Our excitement about the places we'd be seeing helped us to just grin and bear it. We were glad we arrived in Athens in the afternoon because, after boarding the ship, we would soon have dinner and could get a good night's rest.

Our ship was the "Royal Odyssey" from Royal Cruise Lines. We had two cabins, next to each other. This was a much newer and more luxurious ship than the one Chuck Halsey and I had been on a few years earlier. The cabins were spacious, with twin beds and a large window. A shower was in the bathroom and we had plenty of closet space so we were pleased.

Next morning after a tasty breakfast we boarded a tour bus to the Acropolis. Chip and I had spent several days in Athens on our around the world trip in 1970. Fourteen years had made a big difference. The first time I'd visited the Parthenon, we'd hiked a foot-path up the mountain, with no crowd and no security to keep us from wandering around. Now there were masses of people and rope trail markers kept us within boundaries. The Parthenon was showing the ravages of time and weather but still of great interest and fascinating to realize again the cultural history dating back several hundred years before Christ.

Meals on the ship were scrumptious with a variety of entrees to choose from. Dressing well was expected for dinner as the service was more formal than other meals. Jane, my niece in San

289

Diego was a single young woman with a wardrobe that included several outfits for special occasions. She brought up several dresses for me to try and I borrowed three very pretty outfits for the cruise so I only had to buy a couple of special dresses. Dinner always ended with a choice of delectable desserts but I had to be satisfied with small portions so I wouldn't outgrow my new wardrobe before the end of the trip!

A variety of entertainers were on board for our evening's activity and every night a different show was presented. We could also choose to dance or listen to music in the piano bar. While we were sleeping our second night on board, our pleasure palace, as we'd come to think of it, was quietly and smoothly taking us to Istanbul.

Istanbul, formerly Constantinople, has a population in excess of 12 million people and is Turkey's largest city and cultural and financial center. In the third century A.D. Istanbul was the capital city of the Roman Empire. It is also the only metropolis in the world situated on two continents. It extends on both sides of the Bosphorus, thus being located in both Europe and Asia. The highlight of our day's visit was the Blue Mosque, an architectural gem built from 1603 to 1617. With its six minarets and multiple domes, the mosque is free to visitors. However, it is a working mosque and is closed to non-worshipers for half an hour five times daily.

We spent a couple of hours in the center of the city where we strolled through a vast, fascinating but confusing market place. I bargained for and bought a framed picture that had been cut from a children's book similar to "A Thousand and One Nights." The colors in the picture were bright and vivid with much gold leaf. I paid $100 for it and knew I'd enjoy it for years to come. I badly wanted to buy a silk Persian rug I fell in love with, a size that would have been perfect in front of my fireplace, but after considering the hassle of getting it home, I resisted but, to this day, I can still picture that rug in my mind.

Our next port was Ephesus, the best preserved classical ruins on the eastern Mediterranean. I was disappointed to wake up with a migraine and told my traveling companions to go on without me.

290

Elaine hadn't signed up for the day's tour so she assured Eleanor and Mary she would look in on me, as they left for the tour. After medication and a couple of hours, I was feeling much better so Elaine and I got off the ship and wandered around the small city. Gold prices were much lower than at home and I bought a gorgeous gold bracelet, too dazzling and, after bargaining, priced too low to resist. Next we had a day at sea, so by the time we visited the Island of Rhodes I was feeling fine again.

The Island of Rhodes is a Greek Island in the eastern Aegean Sea, physically closer to Turkey than Greece. Rhodes was famous historically for the Colossus of Rhodes, one of the Seven Wonders of the World and is now a World Heritage Site. I learned that the Statue of Liberty at the entrance to New York City's harbor was inspired by the original colossus that stood over two thousand years ago at the entrance to another busy harbor on the Island of Rhodes, both built as a celebration of freedom.

We spent a few hours on the Greek Island of Mykonos, where we did a little shopping in the small village and marveled at the brilliant blossoms in the many flower boxes decorating homes and businesses.

Our next stop was Santorini, a stunning, all white village built on a mountain top. The ship anchored a half mile from shore and a "tender" deposited us at the bottom of a cliff. To reach the city above we could ride either a tram or a donkey. Scared, but wanting the experience, I chose the donkey. The trail up the side of the mountain was three feet wide, at most, and extremely scary, especially since I am afraid of heights and edges! I kept trying to get my donkey to hug the mountain side of the trail but, being stubborn, he chose his own path on the edge and I expected to plunge off the side every second until I finally dismounted at the top!

The last Greek Island we visited was Skiathos, which wouldn't remember at all except that I have pictures showing we were there.

After a relaxing day at sea spent enjoying the pool, the sun and reading, the following day our ship docked at Tel Aviv, Israel's largest city, located at the center of the country by the

Mediterranean coast. It is a modern city that functions as the center of the commercial and financial life of Israel. Our bus took us through the city, while the tour guide pointed out landmarks en route to Jerusalem, the capital of Israel.

Before the tour, of all the places the cruise would take us, I was least interested in visiting Israel. I grew up in a family that attended church regularly but at home we never talked about religion and what it meant to each of us personally. While I was in my teens I began to study all kinds of religions, the many denominations in my own country, as well as religions practiced in other parts of the world. By my twenties, I was an agnostic, not believing in any one religion or way of worshiping but accepting the value of religion in the lives of others.

While visiting Israel, much to my surprise, the Bible came to life! I had thought of all the Bible stories I'd learned in Sunday School as just being stories of an ancient past in places that no longer existed. Seeing the Mount of Olives in Jerusalem, praying at the Wailing Wall and even inserting a prayer into a crack in the wall, visiting Nazareth and a re-creation of the stable where Jesus was born, and the tomb, supposedly, where he was buried, driving alongside the Sea of Galilee and wading in the River Jordan, re-awakened childhood feelings and memories, and made it all very real for me. I remain an agnostic but have a much deeper respect for the stories in the Bible and how that one book has impacted the lives of the world's people for more than 2,000 years.

Next we visited Egypt. The ship docked in the port city of Alexandria where we boarded a bus that took us to Cairo. Along the way, the modesty of the dwellings, the hungry appearing animals and people crowded together in apparent poverty, reminded me of India. Once again a reminder of just how lucky I was to be born in America, truly the land of plenty. In Cairo we were given two hours to view a few of the Egyptian Museum's vast collection of antiquities, when two weeks would not have been enough time. The brief oversight was interesting and I hoped that someday I could visit it again. In the museum shop I bought a necklace.

Re-boarding our bus we would soon head to Giza but before

departing, a merchant came on the bus and took orders for a personalized gold "Kartush Name Pendant." Ancient Egyptians believed that the person whose name is inside this special design will be protected. I ordered one for my niece, Jane, who had so generously loaned me some clothes for the trip, one for my daughter, Heidi, and one for myself. They would be delivered in Giza.

Located on the great Nile River, Giza is home to the complex of ancient monuments and three pyramids known as the "Great Pyramids," along with the massive sculpture known as the "Great Sphinx." While visiting the pyramids, I had to ride a camel. The opportunity was there and I just couldn't pass it by. I might never have another chance! It was a much scarier ride than the elephant ride I'd had in Thailand! The camel was slick and I felt like I was sliding off the whole two or three minutes I rode it. It was also a very bumpy ride!

After meandering around the pyramids and listening to the informative lecture we were taken to the small town of Giza and the "Great Sphinx," which is the only one of the original "Seven Wonders of the World" still standing. When our brief visit was finished and we were back on bus, the merchant met us with the kartushes we had ordered. Jane's and Heidi's were beautiful and, next to them, mine was disappointing! Egyptian artists translate your name into Ancient Egyptian hieroglyphics symbols. If I had known that the letters B-E-T-T-Y would translate into such plain symbols, I might have changed my name!

From Egypt, while we slept, our ship took us back to Athens where we had embarked two weeks before. We flew from Athens to London where Eleanor, Mary and I spent three days. Elaine had flown directly home so she wasn't with us in London. I'd been to London several times before so I had the pleasure of showing my friends a few of my favorite English places.

We'd had a marvelous cruise. We'd had fun, enjoyed meeting people, visited interesting and beautiful places we'd not been before and wouldn't have changed a thing! Even so, it is always good to go home again.

*Chuck and Bett*

# Chapter Fifty Two
## Still Dreaming

$B$ack home after our cruise, as time went by, I saw Chuck often. We played tennis together, and were in social settings with friends frequently. He always came without a date. As I got to know Chuck my initial feelings about him continued to be confirmed. A truly nice man, a caretaker by nature, he was always making sure single women had a drink and someone to dance with. He had a wonderful sense of humor and kept everyone around laughing at his off-the-wall remarks. I believed more and more strongly that we were destined to be together; he just didn't know it yet! I could be as patient as I had to be. Except for Eleanor and Mary, no one knew my secret wedding plans.

Halloween was becoming an "event" at Lake San Marcos. The first year I'd lived there nothing special was going on so I suggested to Eleanor and Mary that the three of us get costumes and go trick or treating. Eleanor wore a beautiful kimono I'd brought from Japan and a realistic geisha mask. With her black hair and petite size she could have passed for a real geisha. I had a pair of overalls I'd bought for some reason years before, so I bought a flannel shirt to wear with them and an old straw hat. My old man's mask, complete with corn cob pipe, totally covered my face and I added a red handkerchief around my neck. Mary dressed like a farmer's wife. We went trick or treating only in Sunrise Pointe, our neighborhood. Apparently there'd never been trick or treaters before so our neighbors were taken by surprise but, mostly good sports, they rushed around to give us something, an apple, a cookie, a cupcake, or whatever they had in the kitchen. They thought we were kids from the local high school!

The second Halloween I lived at the lake, a few friends asked if they could go trick or treating with us when they learned Eleanor, Mary and I were planning to do it again. We had a group of eight and started the night at a Halloween party at Mary's son's house in La Costa. The crowd was a generation younger and we decided we'd go back to the lake and crash the Quail's Inn, a very popular restaurant that drew diners from miles around because their food was outstanding and the view of the lake pleasant. The bar was downstairs so that was where we headed. The regulars and other guests were delighted to see us enter in our costumes ready to party. We livened up the place for a while and had a lot of fun.

In 1984, the year I'd met Chuck, the tennis club had a party and prizes were given for costumes and I won 4$^{th}$ place for my black cat costume.

Earlier in the year I'd joined the "Over The Hill Gang," a club originally started in Colorado for "aging" skiers. "Aging" was anyone 50 and over. The focus of the club was skiing and I wanted to start again because I'd loved it since I first started skiing in New Mexico when I was twenty-one. As the club began to attract members in all parts of the country, those living in warm climates expanded their group activities into tennis, horseback riding, golf and boating.

In November my friend Jean and I went on a three day outing with the San Diego OTHG. We went to a dude ranch in the hills northeast of Escondido. Jean and I were housed in a charming 1920's era cottage with a living room with fireplace, a bedroom and a tiny kitchen for preparing snacks. All meals were eaten in the main dining room. We swam in an Olympic sized pool with natural hot springs water and had a hayride one evening with a chuck wagon dinner out in the sagebrush.

On Sunday morning we rode horses for an hour to the chuck wagon for breakfast. I had ridden a few times but had always been a nervous rider so I was happy when I ended up with the slowest horse in the barn, Old Molly. We were comfortable bringing up the rear. The problem began on the ride back after breakfast; the closer we got to the ranch the faster Old Molly began to trot! As the horse galloped faster and faster my feet flew out of the stirrups and I felt like I was going to be thrown off, for sure! I held on for dear life, and yelled "Whoa! Whoa, Molly! Whoa!" She totally ignored me. As we approached the barn, a worker grabbed the reins and slowed

296

Old Molly down and helped me off.

Out of a group of about fifty people, there was one man I thought I could be interested in. Andrew was a retired ophthalmologist who lived in La Jolla. He was handsome, looked about sixty and his hair was a beautiful silver. He was interesting to talk to and I thought I'd like to get to know him better. However, he seemed more interested in Barbie Doll Jean than in me.

It had been a wonderful weekend and I realized even more that I was definitely ready to have a "special" man in my life again. I had already met the man and even though we were friends, there had been no signs from Chuck that he was interested in more.

My wedding plans were all in my head. Our wedding would be outside overlooking the lake. Our six children and many other family members would be there. Everyone in the tennis club would be invited as well as neighborhood friends in Sunrise Pointe and the Backstreet Gang. Chuck's Coast Guard friends would also be invited. It would be a perfect day – the events unfolded when I looked at the pictures in my mind. It would happen. The bridegroom-to-be wasn't in on the secret and I knew I had to start moving things along.

We had just played our big Christmas tennis tournament, enjoyed a few refreshments and were cleaning up the area. Most of the players had already left. "Hey, Chuck. Are you coming to the Christmas party? We're having a live band instead of a DJ this time. I've heard they're real good." *I already knew he'd made a reservation for one. Since I was President of the Racquet Club I had a copy of the reservation list.*

"I'll be there. Do you need help with anything? How about I pick you up and take you to the party?"

"That would be very nice. I need to be there a little early. Can you pick me up at six-thirty?"

"I'll be there with my Christmas trousers on," he replied enthusiastically with a big smile. *That was odd, did he really have Christmas trousers?*

Again, my heart was singing! Finally, a date, sort of. This was my chance to get Chuck to see me in a different light, a more romantic light. Those wedding pictures in my mind were more vivid than ever.

Chuck showed up on time, well dressed for a Christmas party and I couldn't see anything unusual about his trousers. Dinner was delicious, the band was very good, playing all the old favorites. Chuck clearly enjoyed the evening and while we danced many dances together, we both waltzed around the floor with others, as well. Men were dressed up in coats and holiday ties and many wore red vests. The ladies wore their prettiest holiday dresses. Festive decorations in the party room and the view of brightly decorated homes across the lake, added to the ambiance. Another successful party. Seniors seemed to have more fun–filled lives than other people. Maybe it was just that they had more time and had already learned how important it is to live life to the fullest as it can change in a heartbeat. Mine had.

At the end of the evening Chuck left me at my door with a quick kiss on my cheek. "I'll see you tomorrow night. What time is your party?"

"Why don't you come about seven and set up the bar the way you want it?"

"Okay, see you then."

Heidi had graduated from San Diego State in June and was now attending USIU working on her Master's degree. She and I attended a display of holiday trees at the museum in Balboa Park and saw one tree completely filled in between the branches with baby's breath. It looked like clouds or mist in the tree and caused the Christmas lights to shimmer.

We scoured flower stands and florist shops throughout North County buying all of the baby's breath we could find. Our tree was breathtaking. Everyone who saw it commented how unusual and how pretty it was.

Every year since I'd moved to Lake San Marcos, I'd hosted a party the night of the Christmas boat parade. It started the first year I lived there when I heard about everyone decorating their boats for Christmas. I invited eight friends who did not live on the lake to come over and watch the parade with me. It was no big deal, just

298

a small get-together.

The second year I'd invited around twenty people and we'd had a lot of fun yelling and waving to our friends out on the water. This year, 1984, thirty-five people were expected and Chuck had agreed to tend bar. I'd invited a few friends I'd made in the Escondido Alliance for the Mentally Ill, so it would be a mixed group.

Party night, my house filled with friends and good cheer, I couldn't help but remember Chuck Halsey and the many happy family Christmases past. It was more than three years since his death and I still loved and missed him. I knew I always would, but tonight, I was enjoying the revelry, the new friends and new life I'd made.

"Hey, Betts, it's time for me to leave for the airport. Danny's plane lands in an hour. Thanks for a great party." Giving me another quick kiss on the cheek and waving goodbye to everyone, Chuck was out the door.

Chip came from Colorado for the holidays and Steve and Heidi were at my house also. On Christmas Day after opening presents at home, we went to Riverside for dinner with Evelyn's large family, our routine since moving to California. Growing up with seven siblings I was always happiest surrounded by family. The kids and I made it through our fourth holiday season without their Dad.

# Chapter Fifty Three

## Making Progress

Chuck had started a new job not long before Christmas. A retired Coast Guard friend of his had called and offered Chuck a job too good to turn down. He'd dropped out of Golf School to take it and was now Field Operations Manager at Pacific Aerosystems, an Italian owned firm in San Diego. They built unmanned aerial vehicles, also known as over-the horizon drones or remote controlled spy planes.

For several weeks I didn't see much of Chuck at all. He'd been conducting field tests in the Mojave Desert and then went to Italy to meet the company's owners and learn more about the work he'd be doing, some of which was top secret. Working long hours and playing golf, his greatest passion, on weekends didn't leave much time for tennis.

By February I'd begun to have occasional thoughts that my wedding dreams were a fantasy. *What was I thinking?* But, each time those thoughts intruded I would just meditate more strongly than ever on what I was still certain was going to happen. In early spring I ran into the La Jolla ophthalmologist while helping the OTHG fold newsletters. A few days later he called and I accepted a date with him. Over lunch at the Quail's Inn he said he was leaving in a couple of days for a European tour but would like to see me when he returned. I told him to call when he got home. In my head I was still planning my wedding by the lake and wasn't yet ready to give up the dream.

In April the tennis club held its spring party. Chuck hadn't been around much since he'd begun his new job. The two of us arrived at the party separately and were sitting at different tables. I was sitting with my closest friends and we were all in a good mood and having some noisy fun. I happened to glance over to the table

300

where Chuck was sitting and he was staring at me intently, as if he were actually seeing me for the first time. I could swear I saw a light bulb go on over his head! Immediately he got up and came over and asked me to dance. We stayed on the dance floor while the band played several numbers until a young woman in her early thirties tapped me on the shoulder and asked, "May I cut in?"

"Of course," I responded, gracefully turning over my partner to Jerry. Her mother was in the tennis club and frequently brought Jerry to the parties. I sat down with my friends and Chuck danced a couple of numbers with Jerry but was soon back at my table asking me to dance again. The next time we sat down, Chuck sat at my table where he spent the rest of the evening. He said "I hear you're going to Mexico with the tennis group."

"We leave tomorrow. I've been here three years now and have turned down the invitation each year so this time I decided to go. Jean's going to be my roommate."

"Wish I were going," Chuck said. "That's the problem with working, I have to miss some of the fun. I'm not playing nearly as much tennis or golf."

"It doesn't take long to get used to not working, does it? You're still young, you just turned fifty so you probably should work a few more years."

As we said good-night, Chuck said "When will you be home from Mexico? I want to play tennis with you."

I told Chuck the date the group would return and said, "Call me when you want to play."

A group of us left for Mazatlan the next day. Previously I'd only been to the border cities of Juarez and Tijuana and a few miles south to Ensenada so I was looking forward to seeing part of Mexico's "gold coast." Dick Reed, owner of the real estate office in Lake San Marcos, was the acknowledged leader of the trip. He made all arrangements every year and the week proceeded according to Dick's schedule. We stayed at one of the older hotels on the beach but Dick had permission for us to use the tennis courts at the newer hotel next door so that is where we started our day. Apparently the trips were the same every year – same city, same hotel, same restaurants. Since this was my first trip with them, I enjoyed it but knew I definitely wouldn't repeat it year after year! Some members of the group had rooms that opened onto the beach so that is where we congregated after breakfast and tennis. The others all enjoyed just relaxing and playing cards. I was too restless for that and after the first day I dropped out of the card games and spent my time walking the beach and browsing tourist shops.

One odd thing happened that week. My roommate, Jean, had been telling me for months that I should date Chuck. I always responded nonchalantly "He hasn't asked me out." Jean was the type who would have taken the lead and asked him out! Actually, she had asked Chuck out a few times to see a movie or have dinner together but told me they were just friends. That wasn't my style. I didn't want to ask him out and I definitely wanted to be more than friends.

Apparently the fun Chuck and I had together the night before we left for Mexico hadn't escaped Jean's notice because she said to me while we were in Mazatlan, "Betty, I know I've been telling you that I'm not interested in Chuck and that you should date him. Well, I've decided I'm getting more interested in him. I might try to date him myself."

Having seen the light bulb go on over Chuck's head, smiling to myself, my only response was "Go for it, girl!"

My phone rang early Sunday afternoon. I'd gotten home Saturday evening after a long day of travel delays and cancelled flights. "Hey" Chuck said. Only Southerners use "hey" as a greeting and I loved hearing Chuck say the word and the way he kind of dragged it out.

"Hi, Chuck."

"Let's play tennis. Bill Duncan wants to play. Bev is in Iowa so can you find another gal?"

"I'm sure I can. Give me an hour and we'll meet you and Bill at the courts." Sunday afternoon wasn't the easiest time to find a single woman player. For many people Sunday was a day spent with visiting children and grandchildren. After making several calls without finding someone to play I began to feel a little desperate. I didn't want to miss this opportunity so kept calling

302

until finally, Helen, said she'd play.

Tennis was always great fun for me. I'm very competitive and hit the ball as hard and fast as I could, not "ladies tennis" at all, so most men enjoyed playing with me. When we finished we sat at a table adjacent to the courts and visited for a while. Helen hopped on her bicycle and headed home because her husband was waiting for her. Bill had errands to do so he left also. When I started picking up my tennis bag, getting ready to leave, Chuck said, "Betts, would you go to dinner with me?"

At last! This was IT! Now I knew it wasn't a fantasy at all. I was going to marry this man and pretty soon, he'd know it too.

*Chuck + Bett with President Regan*

# Chapter Fifty Four
## Engaged - Wedding
### Summer - 1985

$I$t had been ten months since we met when Chuck picked me up at six o'clock for our first real date. "Michelle invited us to dinner and I want you to meet her. Is that okay with you?"

"That would be nice. I've heard you mention your sister so often I feel as if I know her already." Five minutes later we were at Bart and Michelle's house on the hillside overlooking the lake. The house dominated the hill and because I'd always loved houses, I was almost as eager to see the inside as I was to meet Michelle.

Michelle was forty, looked thirty, was very pretty and petite and had the winsome, appealing way of a child. Bart was in his fifties and, though polite, came across as rather stand-offish. We had dinner in the family eating area adjacent to the kitchen. Michelle is a good cook and dinner was delicious. Her table with fresh flowers and beautiful place settings created a nice atmosphere, as it always did in their restaurants. She is a warm, gracious person and put me at ease so I was drawn to her instantly. I knew we'd be friends forever. We had a lovely evening and when he took me home Chuck gave me his usual kiss on the cheek when he said goodnight.

The following Friday evening, close friends Nan and Ozzie, had organized a picnic a mile down the lake next to the dam, away from all homes. The picnic area was only accessible by boat so friends picked up Chuck and me at my dock. Several people were already there when we arrived but Jean was the first person whose eyes met mine. Her mouth was almost hanging open and the look on her face was one of pure shock that Chuck and I were arriving together. It was a sweet moment.

The next night Evelyn and Rolf had a party at their house and again Chuck and I went together. We hadn't been there long when someone took out a camera and started arranging us for group pictures. Standing next to Chuck, when he reached over and put his arm around my waist, I felt like I'd been hit by a lightning bolt! I think he felt the electricity because we looked at each other and our smiles conveyed more than words ever could.

Saying goodnight at my door, Chuck apologized for having an early golf date and said he'd see me about 1PM. What he didn't know was that I could feel a migraine headache coming on. I'd had migraines since I was sixteen and they had increased in frequency and intensity through the years. Fortunately Steve was staying in my guest room temporarily. An hour later he had to drive me to the emergency room where I was given a shot for the horrific pain in my head.

When Chuck came to pick me up at one o'clock, I was lethargic and hung over from the pain killers I'd taken but .was up and ready to go. Neither rain, sleet, snow nor headaches would keep me from that date! Some sort of festival going on in San Marcos "restaurant row" and that was where we headed. After tiring of the festivities Chuck said, "Let's go to Vera Cruz for an early dinner. I want you to meet Kelly. She works there." I knew Kelly was Chuck's older daughter. She'd moved to California with him a few years earlier and lived in the area. He'd told me his son was married and lived in North Carolina and his youngest daughter, sixteen year old Jennifer, lived in Vermont with her mother.

Kelly was waitressing that day so Chuck made sure we were seated in her section. As soon as she could she came over and hugged her dad and gave me a warm smile when Chuck introduced us. Kelly was even more petite than Michelle and was a beautiful young girl. I liked her immediately.

Chuck and I were spending a lot of time together. He was living in an apartment at Michelle's. Bart had been forced to sell the San Marcos "Red Onion" because a case of hepatitis had been traced to an employee while the restaurant was still new and getting established, and he'd not been able to recover financially.

Chuck was out of a job and had decided to go to golf school so Michelle suggested he rent his home and move into their vacant maid's quarters to oversee the property when they traveled. Even though he now had a very good job, he continued to live in the apartment.

I was startled when Chuck called one day and asked me to go look at a place in Solano Beach that a friend of Bart's was selling. We met the owner at the entrance to the property which was in a pricy area but was strictly a run of the mill condo. On the way home I tried to pick Chuck's brain to see just what he was thinking. When we got to my house, we were still talking about the place we'd seen and Chuck seemed interested in it. For him to buy it just didn't fit into my plans so I realized the time had come, I had to take a major step.

Standing in my kitchen, I put my arms around Chuck's neck, looked into his eyes and said "If you want to move, you can move in with me." Without a moment's hesitation, Chuck responded,

"I wouldn't move in with you unless I knew we're getting married."

"Did you just propose to me?"

"I believe I did! Will you marry me?"

"Of course I will. I thought you'd never ask!"

A while later I asked Chuck what had taken him so long to really notice me. "For ten months I've been sending all the signals I know! I've been across the net from you, waving my arms in a big arc and pointing to myself, mentally saying 'Here I am, the perfect one for you!' You were totally oblivious!"

"If you were sending signals they were more like this," he said as he crooked an index finger and made a small "come here" signal with it.

He may have been slow to pick up on it but finally we were together and both of us were giddy with excitement. I was almost embarrassed that I felt like a teen-ager again! I felt like renting a billboard alongside the freeway to announce the news!

We were eager to tell our children we were engaged. Sitting in my living room talking about what kind of wedding we wanted and

307

when, Heidi surprised me when she dropped in. She hadn't known there was anyone in my life I was seriously interested in and had only met Chuck casually a couple of times. When I announced our happy news Heidi was shocked! It seemed all too sudden to her. Looking at Chuck she responded, "Well, I hope you have good sense of humor!" Then she turned and left.

Chuck looked at me questioningly and asked, "What did she mean by that?"

"Who knows? That's Heidi. I probably should have told her something sooner. She was caught totally off guard and said the first thing that came to mind. Don't worry. She'll be okay."

The next day I called Chip and told him I would be getting married soon. He had many questions, how long I'd known Chuck and about his background, but soon said "I'm happy for you, Mom. I'll be looking forward to meeting him when I get there in a couple of weeks. I'm glad we've already planned my visit! Good timing."

Chuck wanted me with him when he called his son in North Carolina so I met Danny over the phone. He was cheerful and sounded genuinely happy for his father. Danny said he and Karen would definitely come for the wedding. Then we called Jennifer, Chuck's sixteen year old daughter in Vermont. She was delighted to hear the news also and especially happy when we told her we wanted her to come for the wedding. Jennifer sounded as nice and sweet as Michelle and Kelly and I looked forward to meeting her.

Chuck's mother lived in Sunrise Pointe just a block from me. I had been introduced to Doris one day when she stopped by the tennis court on her daily walk. A few days after he'd asked me to marry him Chuck surprised me with a beautiful engagement ring and we walked over to see Doris and share the news with her. She was happy her son would have someone to share his life with.

My sister in Riverside invited us to come for dinner. Evelyn and Dean had concerns that I might be vulnerable to a certain type of man who preyed on single women who appeared to be financially better off than they were. They warned me about this kind of predator when I moved to California so they were especially eager to meet the prospective groom. During our visit to Riverside they found Chuck to be a really nice southern gentleman.

308

Plus, he was a retired military man, as was Dean, so they welcomed him into our family.

After Heidi got to know Chuck, she told me, "Mom I really, really like him. He's a nice man and it's obvious he cares about you so I'm happy for you. I'm glad you'll have someone to share your life and I'm glad that when Chip and I have children some day, they'll have a grandfather."

Chip came from Denver in June and he and Chuck took to each other immediately so we had his whole-hearted approval. Steve was spending time with us and I deeply appreciated Chuck's obvious compassion for Steve. Even though he didn't understand Steve's behavior, he accepted it and loved and cared for Steve because he loved me.

The next few weeks were hectic. We had many invitations to dinner, a significant one to Al and Holly's house. Chuck's best friend, Al, was also a retired Coast Guard Captain and had known Chuck since they were cadets at the Coast Guard Academy. He and Holly lived in San Marcos and Chuck and Al played golf together frequently. The night they invited us to dinner, two other Coast Guard couples were there and I felt I was under scrutiny. They had all been friends with Chuck's wife for many years but I passed muster and eventually became friends with all of them.

As we prepared for the wedding, every now and then scary thoughts invaded my mind. *Was I doing the right thing? What if Chuck got sick? What if he died? Could I handle the pain again? It was risky but nothing in life is ever certain and whatever happened in our future, I knew I was strong enough to handle it. I'd already been tested. I'd had twenty-five years with Chuck Halsey and now I wanted at least twenty-five years with Chuck Moorhead. He was only fifty and I was fifty-four so I thought we should have at least that much time together. We both appreciated our second chances and I vowed to myself that we'd take life as it came and enjoy this gift of time together.*

*September 1, 1985*

# Chapter Fifty Five
## A New and Happy Life
### 1985-1988

We were married on September 1, 1985. Just as I'd envisioned it, the wedding was held on the lawn beside the lake. The weather had turned unusually hot with Santa Ana winds pushing hot air from the desert down onto the coast and a fire was raging just a mile from us.

Chip came from Denver for several days and Steve was well enough to be with us. All of my California family and friends were in attendance as were Chuck's three children. Danny and his wife, Karen came from North Carolina, Jennifer came from Vermont and Kelly from San Diego. Most of Chuck's family from around the country plus many Coast Guard friends celebrated with us. My dear friend from Alaska, Natalie Gottstein, being treated for cancer, flew down to share the happy day just as she'd shared the pain of Chuck Halsey's death with me. About 200 wonderful people came together for the joyous occasion.

We said our vows under a rose covered arch given to us by Michelle and Bart. Heidi was my maid of honor and Bart was Chuck's best man. During the ceremony when Bart pretended to have lost the wedding rings we got tickled and all of the guests laughed. We wanted a joyful day and that is what we had, capturing it all on video, the food, the champagne fountain, the dancing, the toasts, the cutting of the cake and Chuck's mother who celebrated so much she had to be taken home before I threw the bouquet, caught by Cathy, Chuck's niece. We never got to eat the food everyone said was fabulous before it was time to leave for our honeymoon at the Hotel Del Coronado. We only stayed there three days because we wanted to go home and share the time with our visiting children and other family.

After our wedding and honeymoon Chuck and I settled into a routine of sorts. He had resigned from his position as Manager of Field Operations for Pacific Aerosystems a few weeks before our wedding. He didn't want to start off a new marriage by having to travel frequently, and he especially didn't want to travel in Egypt, the proposed trip that prompted his resignation.

Before our wedding I told Chuck I'd prepare dinner most evenings but he was on his own for breakfast and lunch. I had regular tennis games scheduled on Monday, Wednesday and Friday mornings at 9AM and I was still swimming a mile's worth of laps several days a week, the fitness program I'd started in Anchorage. But now I could swim outside. Both early risers by nature, we'd start our day with a forty-five minute walk around Lake San Marcos. Frequently walking around the 18 hole golf course we'd see coyotes that had come down from adjacent hills for water. We kept a watchful eye on them, giving them a wide berth and they never bothered us.

Chuck had regular tennis games or golf dates four or five days a week. He'd also begun studying for a real estate license. I'd talked him into that because I'd enjoyed selling real estate so much in Alaska and in that time and place it was easy to be successful. We played tennis with other couples frequently and Chuck was teaching me to play golf on the par three course at the lake. In those days, for me, a perfect day was when we walked, I swam a mile of laps, played three sets of tennis and eighteen holes of golf. Truthfully, although I didn't often have a "perfect" day, I did try to fit in at least three of my favorite things.

Many friends lived close by so there was frequent group socializing. The first year we were married, between Thanksgiving and St. Patrick's Day, we went to fourteen parties. We also traveled. A few weeks after we married we went to Corpus Christi, Texas for a meeting of the "Ancient Order of Pterodactyls," an organization of U. S. Coast Guard aviators, retired and active duty. Chuck was proud to introduce me to several long-time Coast Guard friends. He'd signed us up to play in a golf tournament, novice that I was. He was a very good golfer so he must have made up for my lack of experience and ability. It was a fun three days.

312

Shortly after the Texas trip we went to Atlanta to introduce Chuck to my extended family. He fit right in as he was southern born and raised himself and had extended family he kept in touch with. We went to visit a few of them, the most memorable being Chuck's Aunt Sara.

At the age of 75, Aunt Sara was a newly-wed (her first marriage) and so happy and full-of-life it was great fun to be with her. The bridegroom, Milton, and his first wife had been best friends with Sara for fifty years. When Milton's wife died, he and Sara continued eating out several times a week at their favorite restaurants. One day Milton said to Sarah, "I'm tired of being alone, I want to get married. Unless you want to get married, I'll have to look for someone else."

Sara quickly said "Yes! I want to get married." A few days later, they did just that.

Stan and Ruth Kibbe, who lived in Truckee, CA. flew down to Palomar Airport in Carlsbad and picked us up in their beautiful twin-engine plane. The four of us flew to Matazlan, Mexico to join Jim and Dee in their time-share condo for a fun-filled week. We played golf one day, Chuck went parasailing even though I chickened out. The six of us were going deep sea fishing and early one day we took a taxi to where the boat was docked. After the taxi left and we saw the small open boat that the two Mexican men planned to take us out in, Ruth, Dee and I said "See you later!" We were several miles from town with no one around, no taxis, and no buses so we had to use foot power to take us back to an area where we could get a taxi back to the hotel.

The day we left Matzalan we flew north along the coast to a small town with many American expatriates near a Club Med – popular resorts in many locations around the world at that time. We hired a car, stopped for lunch at a country club, then went to the Club Med and they gave us a tour. It had everything anyone would want at a beach resort, primarily geared for young singles.

Next we flew across the Gulf of Mexico and landed at a small airport an hour north of Cabo San Lucas, Mexico, at the southern end of the Baja Peninsula. We had wonderful lunch in a hotel restaurant with an incredible ocean view. We had the hired car take us on a tour of several small towns north of Cabo, then spent the night in a hotel in one of them. We headed home the next day and barely made it to the fly-in border station, just a couple of minutes before closing time.

Chuck obtained his real estate license and went to work at the small real estate office at the lake. To me it seemed the perfect job. He would only show properties within Lake San Marcos which would be easy. He would still have time for a lot of tennis and golf. However, before long I could see that Chuck wasn't quite as easy-going and laid back as he appeared. Working in real estate was stressful for him. He didn't like having to depend on another agent to take care of details for his half of the transaction, either buyer or seller. The escrow companies didn't always handle the paperwork quickly and accurately either. There were just too many things Chuck had to accept that he couldn't control and it was difficult for him. Even though customers always liked him and became friends, six months of real estate was all he could take and he gave it up. I was disappointed it hadn't worked out for Chuck but understood why.

While I happily went my way playing tennis and working hard to improve my golf game, Chuck tried a couple of other jobs that weren't a good fit for him either and he soon quit. It appeared to me that any level of responsibility caused him a great deal of anxiety.

In my mind I was having trouble reconciling the Chuck I knew with the man I knew he had been in the past. As a graduate of the U. S. Coast Guard Academy, he had served twenty-three years on active duty as an aviator flying both fixed wing airplanes and helicopters. When he retired in 1979 at the age of 44, he had attained the rank of Captain and was Commander of the Elizabeth City, North Carolina Air Station. Besides search and rescue the station was home to the Coast Guard's largest aircraft maintenance and repair station and Aviation Training Center. Obviously he had been a highly capable man who could carry huge responsibilities. I puzzled over it without real concern, never dreaming these were clues that something was happening in Chuck's brain.

The first three years of our marriage flew by. Reading an ad

314

for production line workers at Taylor Made Golf, Chuck decided he'd like to learn to build his own golf clubs. He made an appointment, went for an interview and came home smiling. He told me he'd had to convince the manager that production line work was what he wanted. Looking at Chuck's resume the manager offered him a job in management but Chuck refused, explaining that he didn't want another career. So, Chuck started working on the production line learning to build golf clubs. Within a week, the boss convinced him to "manage" the line and Chuck accepted because he'd already noticed ways in which he could make improvements. A few months later Chuck was talked into another position and became Quality Control Manager. The work was enjoyable because he visited factories making the various parts of golf clubs for Taylor Made – the grips, the shafts, the club heads, etc. Chuck met many of his golf heroes; professional golfers who used Taylor Made clubs frequently toured the plant.

As always, Steve continued to have problems and required help. Chuck was there, loving, kind and helpful with never a negative word. Our wedding pictures show Steve at his highest weight ever. He had a moon face and a thick neck and it had happened very quickly. He'd always been thin so we attributed the weight gain to the medication he was taking for schizophrenia.

About a year after Chuck and I married, Steve suffered two seizures, something he'd never had before. Both times he was in a public place and taken to the hospital by paramedics. An endocrinologist took an interest in Steve and his history and determined to find the cause of the seizures. Tests revealed Steve had a grapefruit size tumor on one of his adrenal glands and diagnosed him with "Cushings Syndrome." The doctor scheduled Steve for surgery. He explained to us that the tumor had probably been growing since Steve was a young teen-ager. He was now 28 years old. It was pumping so much cortisol (steroids) into Steve's system that it might even have something to do with Steve's schizophrenia. The doctor said Steve's other adrenal gland had withered because it wasn't needed and that after surgery Steve would have to take Prednisone for at least a year, during which time the withered adrenal gland would probably regenerate. If all went well, Steve would be healthier.

A week before the surgery date Steve had a verbal altercation with a bus driver who wouldn't give him a free ride when he didn't have money for bus fare. Steve was put in jail and I had to figure out the best way to handle the situation. I could have posted his bond and gotten him out but I was afraid something else might happen to prevent surgery and maybe I should just leave him in jail. I made an appointment with an Assistant District Attorney and went in and explained Steve's situation. He agreed to drop the charges and release Steve to me if I promised to commit him to the Psychiatric ward in the hospital where the surgery would be performed. I'd already made the arrangements with the hospital to keep Steve until his surgery. Finally, the operation was performed and Steve did well. He came home with Chuck and me for a week to recuperate before going back to his apartment. For a brief period Steve almost seemed cured of schizophrenia, totally normal. Unfortunately, it didn't last. He began taking the Prednisone his body required and his symptoms gradually returned.

Heidi had graduated from San Diego State and spent a year at United States International University in San Diego working on her Master's Degree. She had gotten a job in Roseburg, Oregon in Children's Services. We filled her small Toyota Tercel with most of her belongings and I drove to Oregon with her. We rented an apartment and toured the area for a couple of days before she drove me to the airport in Eugene, Oregon for my flight home.

Chip was living in Denver and doing well. He came to visit at least once a year and we always had a good time together.

In the summer of 1988 I wanted to make another dream of mine come true. "Chuck, you don't really need to work for the money. Between your income and mine we have plenty to live on. I know you enjoy your job at Taylor Made but if you quit, we could buy a motor home and go traveling for two to three months at a time. I'll sell my place and we'll move into yours because it's easier to leave."

"Let's do it! Sounds like a good plan to me." In a very short time I put my house up for sale at a price above what a Sunrise Point home had ever sold for. A couple of real estate agents laughed at me but I had the last laugh. Within two weeks I sold the

316

house myself for the asking price. We gave the tenant living in Chuck's condo a 30-day notice to move and started packing. Between the tenant's moving out and us moving in we had his place totally redecorated and it looked beautiful. We had a swimming pool and Jacuzzi and a garden area, plus a tennis court. What more did we need?

*Motorhome ~ 1988*

# Chapter Fifty Six
## First Motorhome Trip
### 1988 - 1989

At last, it was November; Chuck and I excitedly packed the motorhome for our first lengthy trip. We were glad we'd bought one with a "basement." Basement models were taller than standard models and underneath the living area was empty space with access doors on both sides. There was plenty of room for everything we might need for two or three months. We'd be in Atlanta in December where we'd wear winter clothes and in Florida later and we'd need summer clothes. We took a small grill for outdoor cooking and lightweight outside chairs. We planned to be gone until late January or February. Hoping to avoid winter storms we took the southernmost route to Atlanta with minimum stops along the way.

My brother, Bill, was undergoing treatment for kidney cancer. He'd been retired for only a couple of years when the cancer was discovered. His treatments had been long and arduous and, most recently he'd commuted to Boston to get the newest treatment. He wasn't doing well and I was eager to see him.

We stopped in Tucson for lunch with Chuck's sister, Nancy, and her husband. After lunch they gave us the short version of a sightseeing tour as neither Chuck nor I had ever been to Tucson. It was the first time we'd seen Nancy in quite a while and we enjoyed our visit because she was sober. Alcohol was a problem for Nancy and caused friction between her and Chuck, so they hadn't been on good terms when she and Monty moved from California to Tucson.

We didn't stop again, except for overnights in RV parks, until we got to Mississippi. My nephew, Billy Chapman, lived near Starkeville, with his family. Billy was the younger of my sister

Lillian's two sons. Billy and Janet had seven children that I heard much about from Lillian, who kept me informed about their activities and sent pictures I always welcomed. They lived in a rural area and the children raised sheep, goats, chickens and a garden.

Chuck and I were impressed with the kids, who were homeschooled and seemed ahead of their peers in many ways. From a young age they had regular chores, including planning menus, shopping for groceries and cooking all the meals. I don't remember who cooked that night but I do remember the delicious stew and homemade bread. After dinner the movie camera was brought out to record our visit and passed from child to child, even the youngest, who was only three. We enjoyed a musical performance by the children and they told us about their many activities. We delayed our departure the next day while the older kids finished a special Christmas wreath they'd made for us. It was large, made with dried corn husks, a little greenery, red berries and bows. Unique and beautiful, a special present we enjoyed for many years.

Arriving in Atlanta in early December we parked at Maxine and Danny's and the next day went to see Bill and Georgia. Bill was still able to be up and dressed and enjoy visitors even though cancer was rapidly destroying his body. He'd been a good big brother and I was sad to know he was nearing the end of his life. He died in January while we were in Florida. His death, at 62, seemed even worse because my youngest brother, Jimmy, had died a year earlier at the age of 52, and my visit to Atlanta was my first without Jimmy being there.

After a couple of weeks with my big family, replenishing my heart's reservoir of love, Chuck and I turned south to Florida. Our first stop was in Live Oak for an overnight with Chuck's uncle's family. Chuck had been close to them while growing up. I enjoyed meeting them and we had a good visit.

A three hour drive across north central Florida took us to Disney World. After arriving at our site and hooking up to utilities we went exploring. Fort Wilderness RV park was a full resort within Disney World and only a cable car ride from all the other

320

activities. Walking and biking trails wound around lakes, beaches, and forests and a rustic log lodge contained all the support facilities campers and RV guests could possibly need.

After our exploring was finished Chuck urged me to relax on the beach in the warm sun for a while. Imagine my surprise and delight when I returned to see our awning open and the motorhome festooned with Christmas lights and the wreath handmade for us in Mississippi by loving children's hands, proudly displayed on the grille. Inside were more decorations I didn't know Chuck had packed. He was so thoughtful to plan ahead for this moment, I felt loved and appreciated and was so glad we'd married!

Chip arrived from Denver the next day; at least I'd have one of my children with me for the holidays. We enjoyed everything Disney World had to offer. The entire park was decorated for Christmas and couldn't have been more festive. We took the cable car from Fort Wilderness every morning after breakfast to the middle of Disney World and returned after the evening fireworks. Chip had accepted a dare from a friend to have his picture taken with as many Disney characters as possible so we all stayed alert for Mickey Mouse or Donald Duck or any Disney characters that roamed the park. When we'd spot one we'd chase him down to take a picture of my oldest kid, who would be 32 in a few days, hugging his Disney friend. It gave the three of us extra laughs and fun we wouldn't have had without Chip along.

We rented a car for a few days and explored Orlando. One day we visited two sisters I'd gone to school with in 1946 – 1947, my one year of high school in Florida. We'd kept in touch and seen each other occasionally through the years. We met for lunch and within ten minutes it was if Vivian and Marian and I had been together the day before.

A visit to NASA, the IMAX, museum and launch pads from where we'd sent men into space, was interesting and inspiring. Mt. Dora, the small town where Chuck grew up was an hour north. Many artists were drawn to the beautiful lakes area of central Florida and Mt. Dora was now a tourist destination. Chuck showed us the house he'd grown up in, his grandparents' home overlooking a lake where he'd learned to swim, his schools, and other places dear to his heart. He even talked to a few people around town who remembered him.

After a week in Orlando, Chip still with us, we drove to Pompano Beach, where Chuck's brother, Robert, lived with his family. We hadn't seen them since our wedding three years before. They welcomed us with open arms and we rang in the New Year, 1989, with Robert and Jan. Robert gave us a boat ride on inland canals to West Palm Beach so we had a close view of some of that area's costliest real estate. A seafood lunch at "The Fish Shack" was another treat.

I wanted to go to Key West and Chuck was willing to drive the overseas highway but I just couldn't do it. I'd been scared of bridges, even small ones, since I was quite young and the thought of being on a bridge a hundred miles long was terrifying to contemplate. So we drove around the western edge of Miami, and then crossed Florida and the Everglades on the Tamiami Trail, fondly referred to by the locals as Alligator Alley. Driving up the west coast of Florida our favorite stop was Sanibel Island, where we soon had the "Sanibel Stoop" from bending over to pick up so many beautiful shells that washed up on the beaches. We rented bikes and rode around the island and fantasized about living there.

Next we stopped in Tampa to visit Don Bellis, and Mary Ann, Chuck's friends since Coast Guard Academy days. Don is a world class story teller and he entertained us for two days on land and water as he took us sailing aboard his boat on Tampa Bay.

From Tampa we drove back to Orlando stopping by the Alligator Farm, enroute to drop Chip off at the airport. It was time for him to go home. We then drove to a lake just north of the city to visit my friends since the 1960's when Bob Huey and Chuck Halsey worked together at Boeing in Seattle and went to Japan at the same time to fly for Japan Airlines. In Anchorage, the Huey's had lived across the street from us. Bob and Alice were happy to meet Chuck Moorhead and treated us royally for a few days, taking us boating and sightseeing and Alice and I had a wonderful reunion.

Driving on two lane highways, we went back to the west coast. I wanted to see Cedar Key, a very small town where Mama

322

and Daddy had a vacation trailer for several years. I'd heard about the place and while I was in Florida I wanted to see it. The village was very small, rather isolated, and I could see why Mama never enjoyed it nearly as much as Daddy had.

We meandered up the coast until we got to the Pensacola area. It was my first visit to Florida's panhandle and it had a lot of appeal for me. Not only was it beautiful, compared to Florida's east coast, it was sparsely populated. We visited the National Aviation Museum in Pensacola and were impressed to see so much aviation history preserved.

We took the northern route around Lake Pontchartrain to bypass New Orleans, intending to stop there on a later trip. After stops in Marshall, Texas to introduce Chuck to my close friends, Ann and Gid Terry and in Fort Worth to see Diana Hull and meet Bill, her companion of several years, we were ready to go home. Gid Terry and Diana's deceased husband, Randy, were in Chuck Halsey's AF squadron when he and I married in 1956 and we'd stayed in touch and seen each other once in a while through the years.

Arriving home after two and half months on the road, we started planning our next trip. One of the first things we did was trade in my '82 Buick on a small Honda station wagon, easy to tow behind the motorhome. Now that we were seasoned RVer's, we wanted the Honda for sightseeing when we stopped for a few days.

# Chapter Fifty Seven

## The Pacific Northwest
### Spring 1989

*H*eidi had moved from Oregon to Tacoma, WA. Where she had a "special" boyfriend she was eager for us to meet, so we were going to Washington soon.

The middle of April we received thrilling news! Jennifer and Allan, living in Vermont, had a baby girl, Alanna. We were grandparents! To say we were overjoyed is putting it mildly! We would visit them in the fall when we planned to go to Connecticut for Chuck's class reunion.

A few weeks before we were to leave for Washington, Steve vanished. He left the group home where he'd been staying and no one knew where he was. Since I had control of his money, by necessity, he'd kept in close touch, even when he went traveling, so when I didn't hear from him for a week or two, I knew something was wrong. I called hospitals around southern California and didn't find him, then called law enforcement in counties all over California but there was no record of him. He didn't have Chip's or Heidi's phone numbers so I couldn't leave town unless I could figure out some way for Steve to reach me.

I made arrangements with a small local answering service that understood how important my calls were and promised not to fail me. Calls to our phone number would be forwarded to the answering service. They would keep track of callers and if Steve called would give him a message to call Chip and give Steve the phone number. I knew Chip would somehow solve any problem Steve might have or find me. I instructed the answering service to call both Heidi and Chip and let them know Steve had called. Heidi would then find me, wherever I was.

At the end of April we left to go to Washington. Our route was Hwy 1, along the coast, wherever it was available. Otherwise we were on Hwy. 101.Dinner in Santa Cruz was with Bunny and Bob Holcomb. Bunny was the friend I'd made on the Hong Kong trip with the "Back Street Gang" in Riverside in March, 1982, a few months after Chuck Halsey died.

Longtime Air Force friends of mine, Bob and Adele Danielson lived in San Jose where we had a fun visit. Bob took us to his workplace for a tour of NASA-Ames Research Laboratory where he showed us pictures taken from outer space and the ER-2, successor to the U2 spy plane. Our timing was perfect and we watched as the ER-2 took off. Bob and Adele also took us to the Winchester Mystery House and on a narrow gauge train ride through a redwood forest.

In Sunnyvale we saw Ben and Willie Dooley, my neighbors in Rome, NY from 1964–1966. We played golf and then had dinner at Lover's Point, a favorite spot of mine. I'd become enchanted with it the first time I'd seen it in 1981 when Chuck Halsey and I explored the California coast looking for a place to live.

North of San Francisco in Novato, we had dinner with the Sundeen family, Bill and Pam and their daughter and granddaughter. Bill had been a JAL navigator and I hadn't seen them since they'd left Alaska a couple of years before I did. Visiting old friends I haven't seen for while has always been one of my favorite things to do. I guess I learned that from Mama. When I was growing up, her favorite Sunday recreation was to have Daddy drive us from one relative's house to another in counties in northeast Georgia.

Once we entered Oregon, the glorious profusion of wildflowers was stunning. Bright yellow scotch broom, delicate pink wild roses, and wild azaleas from white to pink to red, colored hillsides and the further north we went, the more rhododendrons we saw. The brilliant colors and the craggy, rocky coastline thrilled me.

In Seaside, we found a note on Dorie Shannon's door directing us to her mountain cottage 20 miles away. Following directions we found Dorie and her daughter basking in warm sunshine on their deck. After a picnic lunch we followed them home and later met Jim and Jean Clune for dinner. The Shannon's and the Clune's were Coast Guard friends. The nice thing about Chuck's friends and mine from our earlier lives was that they were either military or aviation related and were practically interchangeable. We'd all lived somewhat similar lives with several moves and a lot of travel, so had common interests. My friends immediately took to Chuck and Chuck's friends to me so neither of us ever felt left out.

From Astoria we crossed the bridge into Washington and took back roads and two lane highways until we reached Olympia. When we got to Tacoma we parked the motorhome in the RV park at McChord AFB before driving to Heidi's. Happy to see us, she introduced Jesse, her "special" boyfriend. We liked Jesse, he seemed to be a very nice young man. They took us sightseeing around the area and to Mossyrock to meet Jesse's parents. Jack and Yvonne were nice unpretentious people, native Washingtonians who'd grown up in that region.

Leaving Heidi's we went to Gig Harbor to see one of Chuck's closest friends, Arne Soreng. Arne and Doris had left California a few years earlier to return to their home area. They'd built a beautiful house overlooking Puget Sound and Point Defiance. In 1989 Gig Harbor was a peaceful, small village with magnificent scenery in every direction and we could picture ourselves living there. Next we traveled west on the Olympic Peninsula to the small town of Sequim to visit Don Aites, another of Chuck's CG friends. Chuck was already so taken with the northwest, especially the small town of Sequim, that he was ready to move! We ordered a subscription to the local newspaper for a year to keep up with what was going on there.

After dinner at the famous "3 Crabs" restaurant, we'd only been at Don's house a few minutes when Heidi called. It was such a relief to hear the news that Steve was okay; he'd called Chip. I spoke with Chip who said Steve was in Needles, CA and needed money to return to Escondido. Chip wired him money and asked Steve to call him every couple of days to keep in touch until I returned home. I felt the tension draining from my body. For now, it was enough to know Steve was all right. The details could wait until later. As it turned out, we never got the details of Steve's

326

whereabouts for those seven weeks. He insisted he'd not been in a hospital or jail, that he'd simply walked to Needles and it was a long way!

We had lunch in the beautiful lodge at Lake Crescent with another CG friend in Port Angeles, Jim Butler and his wife, Ann. Jim took us to Hurricane Ridge to see the spectacular snow-covered peaks of the Olympics, then gave us a sightseeing tour of the entire area. Next we spent a couple of days in Port Townsend at an old military facility, Fort Worden, adjacent to the Sound.

I just had to show Chuck Vancouver, British Columbia, the city I consider one of the most beautiful cities in the world. Driving north we stopped in several of Washington's small towns and when we reached Vancouver, Chuck totally agreed with me about its beauty. I had been there several times before so was able to give him a good tour. Vancouver's Convention Center, built for Expo '86, was spectacular. Built to look like a huge sailing vessel, it dominates the downtown waterfront.

On our way south, we took a ferry from Anacortes to Lopez Island where we had lunch with Rosemary and Max Beasley. Rosemary was our office secretary in Anchorage. She and Max showed us what life is like on a small island in the San Juan Islands. Nice, but not our cup of tea.

Dave and Jan Robinson lived at Lake Morton, near Kent. They had been friends since 1956 when I married Chuck Halsey. Robinson's invited us to their beach house in Ocean Shores. We accepted and had a great time with them at the beach. Then, with the motorhome parked at Robinson's, we took a few day trips. We had lunch in Issaquah with Dave and Jan Irons, CG friends. Dave Irons had several interesting stories to tell. One was how they'd gotten rich by starting a very small cable TV firm and later selling it to a larger one for $6,000,000.

Another day we were invited to lunch with Chuck and Kathy Larkin at their waterfront home south of Alki Point. Chuck Larkin is a retired CG Admiral and they were very gracious people. One of the most delightful days was spent with Chuck's classmate, Joe Smith and his wife, Shirlee, in Mercer Island. While enjoying a drink with Joe and Shirlee on their patio, Chuck mentioned how much he'd enjoyed the rhubarb pie Jan Robinson had baked. Next thing we knew, Shirlee had disappeared and I found her in the kitchen making a rhubarb pie for Chuck!

After spending a couple more days in Tacoma with Heidi and Jesse, we headed home. While parked at the Valley of the Rogue State Park, near Medford, Oregon, we had dinner with CG friends, Norm and Lucille Horton, in the historic town of Jacksonville. We also took a jet boat eighteen miles down the Rogue River for dinner at a riverside restaurant. If you ever do that, carefully choose your seat! Even though we got wet, it was a lot of fun.

From Mt. Shasta, in northern California, we headed east to Reno where we parked in Bally's Camperland, for an evening of gambling. Our last stop was in Cameron Park, near Sacramento, to see Rhoda Stewart, a friend I hadn't seen since Chuck Halsey retired from the Air Force in 1967. Her husband had been killed in Vietnam and she'd had a new companion for several years, Dick Pottinger. We played golf at their club and had lunch before saying good-bye.

We arrived home after seven weeks and 3609 miles on the road. It had been a wonderful trip. Now I'd turn my attention to Steve and preparations for our next road trip, to the northeast for Chuck's class reunion in Connecticut and to see our first grandchild in Vermont.

# Chapter Fifty Eight

## The Aborted Trip

Between trips, we tried to catch up on routine things such as doctors' appointments and important paper work. We applied for a life insurance policy for Chuck and he made an appointment with our doctor for a checkup and to have him sign the medical section of the application. Dr. Lucas said, "I'm not going to sign this. Do you remember last year I asked you to make an appointment for an angiogram? You have a family history of heart disease and it's important we get a baseline exam for you. You haven't done that and I'm not signing the form until you do."

"How quickly can I get it done?" Chuck responded.

"You can probably get it next week. See the receptionist on your way out and she'll schedule it for you."

A few days later, following an angiogram exam of Chuck's heart, we got the bad news. The major blood vessel in his heart was 95% blocked! The only reason Chuck hadn't shown any symptoms was because he was so active, getting a lot of exercise every day playing tennis and/or golf, plus vigorous walking. His heart had formed a collateral network of blood vessels that looked like spider webs in the scans. They had been doing the job the major vessel could no longer do. "You're a walking time bomb," Dr. Lucas told Chuck. "You need an angioplasty right away." Angioplasty is a procedure where a balloon is inserted in a blood vessel in the groin, and threaded up to the heart where it is inflated to open up the blockage. Chuck had it done at University Hospital in San Diego. Two weeks later he had a follow-up appointment for a treadmill stress test that he passed with flying colors. The surgeon cleared Chuck to leave the next day on our trip to the Northeast.

The motorhome was packed and ready to go, with the tag-along Honda close behind. We planned to see many friends and relatives along the way but the most important reasons for the trip were Chuck's Coast Guard Academy Class of 1956 reunion in Connecticut and to see our five month old granddaughter in Vermont.

Excited to be on the road again we stopped the first day in Apple Valley, CA and spent the night with Joyce McCloskey. Joyce and I had worked together at the Bank of America in Victorville, back in the mid '50's. Mac was in Chuck Halsey's AF squadron and Joyce and Mac married a few months after Chuck Halsey and I married. Joyce and I were still friends even though Mac and Joyce had divorced and Chuck Halsey had died.

The next morning we went out for our usual early walk but Chuck cut it short because he wasn't feeling very well. We only had a four hour drive to Laughlin, Nevada, a gambling town on the California–Nevada border, so climbed into the motorhome and pointed it east. In Laughlin we played the slot machines for a couple of hours, then decided to have an early dinner and call it a day because Chuck's back was hurting and I noticed he was beginning to drag his right leg a little.

When we stopped in Arizona late the next afternoon, I begged Chuck to let me take him to an emergency room because he felt worse every day. "No! I don't need to go to the doctor. I'll be okay in a couple of days. If I'm not, I'll go to the doctor in Albuquerque."

The fourth day, after driving through the Painted Desert we stopped briefly at Meteor Crater, the world's best preserved meteorite impact site. The crater is 2.4 miles around, one mile wide and 550 feet deep. I first saw it in 1953 when there was nothing to see except a hole in the ground. Now the site boasted a marvelous visitors' center, a theater and education center to host millions of tourists every year.

Continuing across Arizona and half of New Mexico, Chuck was using his hands to pick up his right leg to move it from the accelerator to the brake pedal. We had made a serious mistake leaving on this trip without me ever having driven the motorhome!

330

By the time we were settled in the RV park at Kirtland AFB in Albuquerque, it was Friday afternoon of Labor Day weekend. Chuck was in a lot of pain and let me drive him to the base hospital. Physically, a beautiful, brand-new facility, it was a combination VA and AF hospital celebrating its grand opening. We told the ER doctor that Chuck had an angioplasty less than three weeks earlier and his back had been hurting him a lot the past four days, as well as his right leg, and now he had a slight temperature. *Without ordering any blood-work,* the doctor told Chuck he'd strained his back and he should go to the base recreation center and sit in the hot-tub as often as he could over the weekend. He sent us home with a bottle of pain-killers.

During the next week I took Chuck to the ER three more times, literally screaming in pain. My feeling was that the first doctor had made a diagnosis of a strained back and the following three doctors rubber-stamped the same diagnosis, never considering other possibilities. On the fourth visit, I finally backed the doctor against the wall and specifically asked, "If he's hurt his back, why does he have a fever?"

The response was, a shrug of the shoulders and the words, "I don't know. We'll just have to wait and see what develops."

I wanted to take Chuck to a civilian hospital but he refused. Desperate for any kind of help, he did let me take him to a chiropractor three times. After paying the doctor more than $800 for three or four treatments and tests, we were both starting to panic.

Calling from the RV park office, I got in touch with Maxine and Danny and Barbara, (Jimmy's widow). They were on their way to stay in our condominium while visiting Mexico and California. When I reached them, they were in Denver. Maxine and Danny had a car telephone years before cell phones were available and, when traveling, calls to their home phone were routed to the car. They agreed to detour to Albuquerque and drive us home. Barbara had a motorhome and had been the driver for years after Jimmy developed MS so she drove us, following Maxine and Danny.

The day after we got home, I took Chuck to our doctor. When

he heard our story he was clearly worried and sent us downstairs to a laboratory for blood tests and a CT scan. He said it would take a few hours for results and he would call when he got them. We'd hardly gotten home when Dr. Lucas called and said to come in immediately. When we arrived at his office we were escorted right in. Dr. Lucas said Chuck's blood was so thick the lab technician could hardly get it out of his arm. Chuck had a serious staph infection and the doctor asked what hospital Chuck wanted to go to, University Hospital where he'd had the angioplasty, Scripps Hospital, or Navy Balboa, an outstanding Navy hospital. Ever the military man, Chuck said, "Navy Balboa."

After calling the hospital and making arrangements, Dr. Lucas looked directly into my eyes and said, "I want you to drive carefully but I want you to get him to the hospital as quickly as you can. Don't stop for gas or anything else. Go directly there. If the mass of infection in his groin ruptures......they'll be waiting for you."

Someone was waiting just inside the door with a wheelchair. By the time I went back out and parked the car, then found Chuck, there were eight doctors surrounding him discussing procedures to be done. They told me they were waiting for the most senior surgeon who was on his way to the hospital and they began to prepare Chuck for surgery. About 10PM, while Chuck was still in the operating room and I was waiting alone, I looked up and saw my nephew, Alan, and Natalie, his wife. They lived in downtown San Diego, and my sister, Evelyn, had called them.

To make a long story shorter, Chuck spent 35 days in the hospital on intravenous antibiotics, and underwent two more surgeries to drain and clean the infection from his abdomen. When he finally was discharged, he was on intravenous antibiotics for three more months at home. The infection destroyed 90% of the cartilage in his right hip and the lowest three disks in his back. For a man who'd never had a pain in his back in his life, prior to the infection, he was left with a chronically aching back and it was a sure thing he'd need a hip replacement within ten years. He had physical therapy three times a week for several months and when all was said and done, he'd lost eight months before he began to reclaim his old life.

332

How do you figure it out? Did applying for life insurance almost cost Chuck his life? Or did it save his life by forcing him into a situation where he had a procedure that may have prevented him having a heart attack but also caused the massive infection. The life insurance company made Chuck wait one full year after recovery before issuing him a policy.

# Chapter Fifty Nine

## The Northeast, At Last
### Spring 1990

In the middle of April, 1990 we set out again in the motorhome to complete the trip we'd aborted in New Mexico the previous fall. We'd missed Chuck's class reunion in Connecticut but we could still see our first grandchild, Alanna. We also had our second grandchild by now, Bobby, born in December in North Carolina to Chuck's son, Dan, and his wife, Karen and we would visit them also.

Five days after leaving home we arrived in Hot Springs, Arkansas, a small historical city surrounded by the first and smallest national park in the United States, predating Yellowstone National Park by forty years. The region is picturesque with low mountains and many lakes. A popular vacation spot, dating back to 1832, the city and the park owe their existence to an array of thermal springs that still supply naturally heated water to the bathhouses. The city of Hot Springs has always been known for its opulent spa bathhouses, horse racing and gambling. Surviving are eight architecturally significant bathhouses built between 1912 and 1923, two of which are still operating. While there we toured Hot Springs Village, a huge retirement town fifteen miles north of the city. Boasting five huge lakes, five golf courses, multiple tennis courts and swimming pools, it was a planned community in a gorgeous natural setting but, somehow, didn't strike the right chord with us.

We drove north and east on the Natchez Trace Parkway, built on a network of ancient Indian trails in Mississippi, Alabama and Tennessee. The natural beauty is outstanding, with a cypress-filled swamp, waterfalls and towering trees hanging over the parkway.

334

We drove to Boone, N. C. to visit Dan and Karen and Bobby. Boone is a beautiful college town in the Blue Ridge mountains in the northwest corner of N. C. Chuck and I actually held a grandchild! Bobby was a happy, healthy boy, five months old and we could tell from his smiles and laughs, he liked us!

As we drove north on the Blue Ridge Parkway colorful vistas surrounded us. The Shenandoah Valley was pristine with many prosperous appearing communities. Further north in Pennsylvania, the region was not quite as scenic, especially when we reached the tri-state area where New York, New Jersey and Pennsylvania meet, along the Delaware River.

The drive across part of New York State, Connecticut and Massachusetts on many two lane highways was beautiful with spring colors bursting out all over. Chuck handled the motorhome like a champ through congested areas. I wished I could help him more with the driving but I was happiest driving in the wide open spaces in the West. It was comforting to know I could drive if I needed to, though.

We went as far north as Brunswick, Maine where we visited my nephew, Mike and his wife Rosemary and their two sons, Zack and Jonathon. They had lived in Alaska for four years when the boys were very young and they became like grandsons to Chuck Halsey and me. I hadn't seen them for a long time and we had a joyous reunion. The boys were now in high school!

On our way south again we stopped in Freeport, Maine to visit the L. L. Bean store. Freeport is a factory outlet town and you can buy almost anything you want there so it attracts millions of visitors each year. Back on the highway we laughed thinking we were probably the only people ever to visit Freeport and buy nothing but lunch!

In New Hampshire we visited my nephew, Ken, my sister Lillian's older son. I had lived with Lillian and Ken and Billy in Florida my junior year of high school, after Elmo, Ken and Billy's father, was killed in a plane crash. Ken and Billy had always been especially close to me. Ken and Carol live in a beautiful area of N. H. and they showed us several scenic and historic sites. We enjoyed seeing the Kankamaugus Country Store they owned; it is a well-known stop on the Kankamaugus Scenic Highway. With Ken we climbed to the top of Artist's Bluff for a spectacular regional view.

It was only an hour's drive from Ken's house to Jennifer's, in Vermont. Jennifer is Chuck's youngest child but the first one of our combined six children, to give us a grandchild. Alanna had just celebrated her first birthday; she was absolutely beautiful with dark, wavy hair and big blue eyes. She took to Chuck and me immediately and Jennifer let us babysit her in our motorhome one day when she had to work. We enjoyed a few days with Alan and Jennifer and enjoyed meeting Alan's family.

When we left Vermont, we decided to cross New York on the Southern Tier Parkway. I had already traveled the New York Thruway from one end to the other so I wanted to see the southern part of New York State. It was the right choice as we passed through the beautiful Finger Lakes region and between two mountain ranges, one in the north and one south of us. When traveling in the motorhome, just as at home, we started each day with a long walk. We stopped overnight in Bath, New York and close behind the RV park was a steep trail to the top of a ridge. We made it to the top and were rewarded with a wonderful view of mountains and lakes in southwestern New York.

In Ohio we stopped to see Bill and Carol Ruffer, Air Force friends of mine since Chuck Halsey and Bill were stationed in El Paso in the late 1950's. We were traveling on old two lane highways and even though it was Memorial Day weekend, there wasn't much traffic. We spent two days with Ruffer's, played golf at their club, visited their favorite restaurant and had a great steak and the house specialty, homemade potato chips, crisp with soft centers, and very good.

Traffic in the Chicago area was horrendous with several rude drivers showing us their displeasure at getting behind a big motorhome towing a small car. The only reason we braved those congested freeways was to see Chuck's sister, Michelle, and her husband, Tony. Michelle and Bart had divorced several years earlier and Michelle was remarried. We had a happy, fun filled three days with them even though they were still unpacking,

336

having just moved into their new home.

Crossing Iowa we wanted to stop overnight in Newton, a town we'd heard mentioned so often by our good friends at Lake San Marcos, Bill and Beverly Duncan. The only RV park in Newton was closed so we gave ourselves a driving tour of the town and spent the night in a small town in the middle of Iowa's famous corn fields.

Helen Gould was a friend I'd made at Lake San Marcos playing tennis. Helen lived in Omaha but spent winters in Lake San Marcos. She was also a golfer so when Chuck started me playing golf, Helen was kind enough and patient enough to play with me. Helen lived in a high-rise condominium and insisted we park the motorhome in the secure parking area and stay with her. She rolled out the red carpet for us; took us to dinner in one of Omaha's most elegant steak houses; played golf with us at her club; and took us to a baseball game. The National College League championships were underway and we saw Stanford defeat Georgia Southern. Georgia Southern should have won – there was an admitted mis-call early in the game but the score was not corrected!

West of Omaha, Nebraska is flat. Many pretty wayside state parks with small lakes bordered the interstate. The lakes were created when sand and gravel was removed for highway construction; a brilliant idea other states might use. We bucked a fierce headwind all day one day, which was not only scary, it was very tiring for Chuck.

Under a clear blue sky, we arrived in Denver on June $3^{rd}$. We parked the motorhome at Lowry AFB, not too far from Chip's apartment. He was a great tour guide, accompanying us on a drive over Trail Ridge Road, the highest paved road in the United States, through Rocky Mountain National Park. The scenery was magnificent and there was deep snow at the summit even though it was a warm, sunny day. I took Chuck to Central City, an old gold mining town, I hadn't seen since my Colorado skiing days in the mid '50's. It was more touristy thirty-five years later but the Opera House was still there, and the famous painting, "The Face on the Barroom Floor," in the Teller House Hotel barroom.

Dick and Frieda Housum were friends when we lived in El Paso from 1958–1960. They lived in a remote area in the mountains west of the tiny town of Lake George, Colorado. After a wonderful visit with them that included a lot of catching up on each other's lives and efforts by a bear to break into the closed in porch while we were sleeping, we drove to Colorado Springs. We toured the Air Force Academy and the Broadmoor Hotel, where Olympic ice skaters trained for many years, then headed south to New Mexico.

In Santa Fe, we had a delicious Mexican dinner at "The Pink Adobe," my favorite after ski restaurant in 1953-1954. I not only hold onto my friends forever, I also hold onto my favorite places and enjoy visiting them again even though years have gone by.

Next we went back to Albuquerque and the RV park at Kirtland AFB. We had bad memories of this place but it was the only conveniently located RV park in town. We had brunch with my old friend, Dana, with whom I shared a house in 1953-54, when we both worked at Sandia Corporation in Personnel and both of us attending classes at the University at night. Dana, and her husband, Don, were both professors at the University of New Mexico. I was glad we'd kept in touch.

Now on the homestretch, we drove west through Flagstaff, then turned south towards Phoenix, stopping for two days in Sedona. Sedona is in Arizona's "Red Rock Country," surrounded by amazing red rock monoliths, bordered on the north end by Oak Creek Canyon, a spectacular wild chasm

After two months on the road, and 7,743 miles driven, $3,339 spent, we were happy to be home again.

*On Board Falcon ~ Alaska 1991*

# Chapter Sixty

## The Last Motorhome Trips
### 1990-1992

A second trip in 1990 took us back to the Northwest. Heidi and Jesse were married in a beautiful wedding and Chuck was one of the groomsmen. It was a happy, festive occasion. Chip came from Denver, Heidi was radiant and we were all very happy.

Another highlight was being invited to go sailing for a few days with our friends, Jan and Dave Robinson on their boat, "Wayward Wind," and with Alan and Natalie aboard "Falcon." We went as far north as Big Bay and also put in at Sidney, British Columbia for a couple of days. From time to time we rendezvoused with other friends on other vessels. Being on a sailboat out in the wilderness is the most peaceful place I've ever been. It is like being off duty. No errands to run, no telephone unless I make the call when it's convenient. My entire being is totally quiet, all is right in my world.

In June of 1991 Chuck's daughter, Kelly, gave birth to a handsome baby boy, Gaither Rosser IV. We couldn't have been more excited because this baby lived a twenty minute drive from us, so we saw him often. When little Gaither popped out his father caught him and I cut his cord. What an exciting day! Within a few months I put Gaither into his stroller and walked him all around Lake San Marcos, ringing doorbells of many friends, to proudly show him off.

A few weeks later we drove the Pacific Coast Highway north again to Semi-Ah-Moo, near Blaine, WA. Alan and Natalie were living there and had invited us to spend two months sailing with them to Alaska. We knew we were lucky and felt grateful for such an opportunity when we sailed out of the harbor for what turned into the adventure of a lifetime. Alan's boat was a 51' Mapleleaf sailing vessel, Canadian built and the epitome of quality and luxury.

I can't imagine a more comfortable way to see and explore southeastern Alaska's coast. We watched bears salmon fishing, whales in their bubble-net feeding circles, putting on shows better than anything I ever saw at Sea World. In remote bays off the inside passage, the main traffic channel between Alaska and Washington, every day we saw nature at its best: walrus, sea lions, otters, dolphins, whales and bears and eagles in their natural environment. At times, almost surrounded by icebergs and rugged mountains with hundreds of waterfalls and dozens of glaciers, scenery that almost took my breath away, I'd pause and wonder, "How did I ever get here? I am so lucky!" I'd have fleeting memories of a little girl who dreamed of new places and new adventures.

Every night we anchored in peaceful bays, frequently the only boat there. After anchoring we'd drop the crab pots and before long we had Dungeness crabs and prawns. Along with king and silver salmon, halibut and sea bass that we caught frequently, we feasted on fresh seafood almost every day. After two months we kept in close touch with weather forecasts. In September we knew the weather could change suddenly and dramatically so it was time to head south.

The last place on our "must see" list was the "Misty Fiords National Monument," located on the back (or eastern) side of the island on which Ketchikan is located. We motored for two days on mirror like waters before entering the Behm Canal that would take us south through the Monument and eventually to the Inside Passage that would take us home.

Close to shore watching eagles, we hit an uncharted rock that stopped "Falcon" like a car hitting a brick wall! Alan, Chuck and I were in the cockpit and were thrown to the floor. Natalie had just gone below to take a shower and when Chuck found her, she had a cut on her forehead and thought her arm was broken. An inspection determined no water was coming in and even though the engine mounts broke and the engine moved forward two inches, it was still secure and the boat was running okay. The galley and salon

342

were quite a mess. One inch marble had come off the countertops and broken up, and the stove and refrigerator had moved forward and dumped their contents.

Alan radioed the U. S. Coast Guard to report the accident and request that a float plane be sent to take Natalie to the hospital in Ketchikan. The rescue plane arrived, tied up to our stern and Natalie and I took our first float plane flight. She was checked out at the hospital; her arm wasn't broken and the cut on her forehead wasn't serious. We checked into Ketchikan's best hotel, located on top of a hill overlooking the city and the inside passage and from our window a few hours later, we saw Falcon approaching. After almost two weeks out of the water for temporary repairs, we headed home again with feelings of relief and satisfaction for having made the trip, mixed with a tinge of sadness that it was almost finished.

In February, 1992, my granddaughter, Paige, was born in Tacoma, WA. I was there within 24 hours rocking her in the hospital room she shared with her mother, Heidi. I was sure there wasn't a happier grandmother on the planet! I said right then, "I've waited a long time for a grandchild and this little girl is going to know me!" From that time on, I was in Tacoma every three months for a visit, sometimes with Chuck also, but not always.

That summer we explored Glacier National park in Montana and Waterton National Park in Alberta, B.C. enjoying the magnificent scenery and spectacular hiking trails. After finally taking my bridegroom to Banff and Lake Louise and Jasper we continued west to Vancouver and south to Washington for a few days with Heidi and Jesse and our granddaughter, Paige. While there, Paige was christened. She was almost seven months old and I'll never forget her huge smile lighting up her face after she surveyed the audience. Next we went to Seaside, Oregon for a meeting of the Coast Guard aviator's association, the Pterodactyl's, where we had a great time visiting with many Coast Guard friends.

A nice drive down Hwy. 101, a detour through Napa Valley, then I-5 south took us home again. 4,301 miles. What a life we were living in those years! We recognized how fortunate we were and enjoyed every moment of every day!

# Chapter Sixty One

## Valley of the Flowers

Lompoc, California is located on designated California Scenic Highway 1 on the central coast, one hour north of Santa Barbara. The area is known as the "Valley of the Flowers." For decades it has been the flower seed capital of the world. Boasting a moderate climate, flowers bloom, vegetables grow and outdoor sports are enjoyed year round. During our first exploring trip I went into the Chamber of Commerce to gather local information. "Well, if you're considering moving to Lompoc the first thing you have to learn is how to pronounce the name! It's Lom-poke," said as the clerk poked me in the arm with a finger. In 1993 it was a charming small town of 30,000 plus another 10,000 in the hills north of the city. We added two more in January, 1993.

Just as planned, we sold the motorhome after traveling all over the United States and a large portion of western Canada. We replaced it with a "conversion" van we used for trips.

We lived a different kind of life in Lompoc. We rented a house in the city while searching for a house to buy in the golf course community five miles north of town. Life was easy and peaceful. The closest four-lane road was 20 miles away, Hwy. 101. We walked and rode bicycles all over town, including to the tennis courts several days a week. We made friends easily and enjoyed tennis and socializing with a sizable group of wonderful people. After a few months we bought a house and moved in October but continued playing tennis downtown. The house, near the top of a ridge of hills provided a terrific view of regular rocket launches from nearby Vandenberg AFB.

We made a new circle of golf friends at Vandenberg golf club while playing there regularly and after we moved into our new home we joined the nearby country club where we enjoyed not

344

only golf and tennis, but many social events.

Happily surprised at how often our two guest rooms were occupied, we learned local history of the area and enjoyed acting as tour guides while showing off the picturesque central coast. Always busy, our lives filled with activities shared with family and friends, we were happy and content the years we lived in Lompoc.

Steve had many ups and downs and hospitalizations during those years. Unless he decided to "go traveling" again, he mostly lived in Santa Maria, half an hour from us. We saw him frequently and helped solve one problem after another, which was normal life with Steve.

Our other five children were living adult lives and we saw them all as often as we could. As our grandchildren multiplied and grew up, we felt even more compelled to visit so they could know us and we could get to know them.

Suddenly, in April 1999 I awoke with a lump on my neck, then diagnosed with cancer! What a shock! It took almost three months and every possible test to my entire body looking for the primary tumor. Treating cancer with an unknown primary tumor most often has a bad outcome. Finally, Lisa, my niece who worked for the American Cancer Society at Loma Linda Hospital, an outstanding cancer hospital, got me appointments with two of their doctors. I took my scans and test reports from my doctors in Santa Barbara and the doctors at Loma Linda were experienced enough to see the tumor under a fold above the vocal cords. I was sixty-eight and while initially scared, I determined to beat the cancer.

While taking radiation treatments twice a day five days a week for seven weeks in Santa Barbara, Chuck and I stayed at a motel one block from the Cancer Center, only going home on weekends to get mail and check email. It was then I realized what a great community of friends we had. They must have organized it well because every weekend different friends brought food to last the weekend and sometimes even take to Santa Barbara with us. I was unable to eat and living on Boost, a nutritional drink, but Chuck surely feasted well. All of the gifts, food and flowers created warm feelings in both our hearts. A large group of friends and relatives from California to Georgia were praying for my recovery and I mentally visualized myself well and strong, playing with my grandchildren.

My treatment ended the last week in August, leaving me so depleted it was difficult to walk out to our mailbox. Heidi was expecting her second baby the end of September and I determined to be strong enough to be there and be able to dispense with the painkillers so I could help Chuck drive to Tacoma. I began building my strength by walking to the mailbox, then the first corner, then the next corner and gradually regained my strength. We got to Tacoma in time for Riley Ty Redmon's birth on September 27, 1999.

In the back of my mind was a growing suspicion that something was wrong with Chuck and it seemed to be getting worse.

Thanksgiving, 1999 Heidi, Jesse, Paige and two month old Riley flew to California to spend several days with us. Chip had come from Denver and Steve lived only thirty minutes away in Santa Maria, so my part of our family was all there. After my cancer treatment that year, we had a lot to be thankful for, happy to all be together. We took advantage of the opportunity and had professional photographs taken.

Paige's eighth birthday was in February, 2000. As always, I flew to Tacoma to share it with her. Chuck stayed home and joined some Coast Guard buddies for a golf trip.

While in Tacoma Heidi told me they had been concerned about Riley's hearing since he was a few weeks old. She noticed it first because when she walked into his room talking to him, he never turned and looked at her until he could see her. They'd asked his doctor to have his hearing evaluated and had an appointment to learn the results.

Paige and I were dropped off at the Children's Museum where we had fun playing in the creative environment provided there. I had expected Heidi and Jesse to return for us in an hour or so and after two hours went by, I began to worry. The museum was closing at 5PM and Paige and I were about to be turned outside to wait when we finally saw the car approaching. Paige climbed in back with Jesse and Riley and I got in front with Heidi and asked

346

"How did it go? What did you find out?" Heidi's face was grim and she just shook her head. I understood that she didn't want to discuss it in front of Paige. I turned and looked at Jesse and tears were rolling down his cheeks. I knew the answer to my questions and it was bad.

Shocked and devastated that Riley, this precious baby boy we all loved so much was deaf, all four of us, including Paige, determined that somehow we'd see that Riley had a happy life and every opportunity to make it fulfilling and productive. We had so much to learn! We didn't even know what we didn't know!

Heidi and Jesse immediately started investigating resources available for deaf children. Hearing aids were ordered for Riley and he had them before he was six months old. We learned that from six to twelve months of age is when hearing babies brains develop pathways to connect sounds and speech and learn language skills. This is a critical time period and babies who miss it have more difficulty learning those skills later.

Chuck and I drove to Tacoma in July to visit. Riley was responding well to all of the sounds around him. One problem had been keeping his hearing aids in his ears! He was skillful enough to take them out and Heidi had designed and had a seamstress make helmet style hats for Riley with mesh earflaps and ties under his chin. Besides frequent doctor appointments, Riley had appointments for music therapy, play therapy and various evaluations for services benefiting deaf children. "I wish we lived closer," I said to Chuck. "We could be a big help with Riley."

"Well, let's move! I'm ready for a new adventure." His response was instantaneous.

"We haven't actually decided to move here but we'd like to see a few houses so we'll know what's available and what prices are, in case we do decide to move."

"That's fine," the Realtor I'd called replied. "I'll be happy to show you some homes tomorrow. I'll meet you at my office at ten o'clock."

After looking at two houses neither Chuck nor I liked, the Realtor took us to Danbridge, a medium sized community off Chambers Creek Road in University Place. Hundreds of trees

347

throughout the area shaded a multitude of blooming shrubs and flowers of every color in the rainbow. When she took us into a brand new house with 16' ceilings and windows all around filling the house with light, Chuck and I looked at each other and both of us said, more or less at the same time, "I could live here."

The next day we made an offer to buy the house. It was accepted and we'd agreed to close in forty-five days. We soon headed home to sell our house in Lompoc and it was almost unbelievable the way everything came together. The day after we got home Chuck told a neighbor we were moving to Washington and Bertha said "Don't sell your house until my friend has seen it. He's been looking for a place in this area." That night I called Bertha to tell her that her friend should come immediately if he wanted to see the house before it was listed with a Realtor. The prospective buyer came the next morning and before he left, he'd agreed to buy the house for cash and close within thirty days.

Six weeks after we saw the house in Danbridge, we moved in and started a new life in Washington. Another adventure! Many of our family and friends said from the time it was a thought in my head, to moving into our new home, was so fast and smooth, it was obviously "meant to be." The way Chuck's health problems were increasing, I could only agree. Whether or not we were "meant" to be in Washington I soon recognized we were where we needed to be, close to family.

*Christmas at a Friend's*

# Chapter Sixty Two
## Our Life in Washington
### 2000-2005

We moved into our new home in September, 2000 and spent the first few weeks shopping for new furniture and decorating the house. We joined the Lakewood Tennis Club and played with a couples group twice but both times Chuck fell on the court so he quit playing. I played with a ladies group once a week for a few months before I had to quit.

By Thanksgiving Chip had arrived from Denver and moved in with us temporarily while he looked for a job and then a home of his own. He'd planned his move long before we did but we were first to arrive. We welcomed him to stay with us as long as he wanted because he was a big help. Steve also arrived in Washington in November and since he was doing well at that time, I soon had him set up in an apartment and with a Case Manager.

When we decided to move to Washington, we recognized that climate-wise we were spoiled. Our plan was to travel in the winter months, mostly international travel, and we had a long list of places to go. Before moving we made reservations for a trip to the French and Italian Riviera with three other couples; early in December we flew to France to join our friends for a ten day tour. We had a wonderful time in the beautiful south of France, Monaco and northwestern Italy.

With all three of my children living nearby, plus two grandchildren, and my recovery from cancer the year before, Christmas of 2000 was a time for thankfulness and rejoicing. It was the first time since Chip left for college in 1974 that we were all living in the same place.

A few weeks after the holidays I said to Chuck, "You know,

351

ever since we've been married and Brian and Joyce came from New Zealand and visited us, we've talked about going to New Zealand. I think we should go now."

"Make the reservations. I'm ready."

So that's what I did. We flew to Christchurch on New Zealand's South Island to join a tour group for three weeks. By the end of the tour we felt we'd learned a lot about the country. We had covered most of the north and south islands and had fallen completely in love with the magnificent scenery and the warm, welcoming people.

When our tour ended in Auckland Chuck and I flew to Wellington where we were met at the airport by Brian and Joyce Mountjoy. They took us to their home in the delightful resort town of Paraparaumu Beach, an hour north of Wellington. The highlight of our visit was dinner with Mountjoy's neighbors – the Hann's. John was a collector of flags and during our visit with Mountjoy's, John flew the American flag in our honor. After we got home Chuck arranged to buy a Washington State flag that had actually flown over the Capitol and sent it to John with the certification.

Mountjoy's drove us all around their beautiful area. They located a shop where Chuck bought sheepskins to send home so he could have seat covers made for our new Sienna van. He had wanted those skins ever since his trips to New Zealand in the late 1960's. I was pleased they made him so happy and the seat covers turned out beautifully.

Once home we were as busy as ever. Paige was now nine years old and playing soccer and softball and we went to all of her games. Riley was eighteen months old and we kept him frequently. He brought such joy into our lives. Chuck loved classical music and he would play music and dance with Riley who always had a look of rapture on his face. Our best days were those spent playing with Riley. We took a three day "Signing Exact English" course and began learning to sign to Riley. Heidi and Jesse and Paige were signing every word they spoke. Within a few months, as Chuck's health was deteriorating and Riley was learning to talk, it didn't seem as essential for us to learn to sign. We stayed busy with family and were happy to be near them.

352

Our calendar began filling with doctor appointments for Chuck. We knew something was wrong with him and we needed to find out what it was. The falling had become dangerous; twice in New Zealand he fell while crossing the street.

Several doctors who examined Chuck were as baffled as we were. He was given a different diagnosis with each new doctor. Chuck had a bad hip as a result of the staph infection that had almost taken his life in 1989. New scans showed that most of the cartilage was gone and he almost had bone on bone. While he was not having pain in his hip, he was told he would soon and that the hip problem may be the cause of his falls. The orthopedic surgeon recommended a hip replacement and Chuck agreed to have it done.

We didn't have a crystal ball to show us that we were, in fact, embarking on the beginning of the end. Chuck had hip surgery in May 2001, two months after we returned from New Zealand. The surgery went well but afterwards Chuck's other problems were worse. He lacked the ability to cooperate in his recovery. He was supposed to use a walker for six weeks and not go down stairs plus a few other restrictions. If he fell and broke the new hip, he'd be in a wheelchair for life. Chuck didn't seem to "get it." He'd leave the walker in one room and go to another and when I'd see him he'd say, "Oh, you caught me!" It was as if he was a naughty child! Twice he went outside and fell and laid there until I found him. I wondered if the anesthesia had affected his brain.

Chuck's life was never the same. He never drove again and it seemed strange that he didn't complain about it. I also thought it odd that he never mentioned tennis or golf. I started dropping him off at the driving range when I went to the commissary or BX and he always said he enjoyed hitting balls.

Doctors' appointments multiplied as Chuck was referred from one specialist to another. He endured psychological testing and intelligence testing. The results showed that his brain was deteriorating. He was sent for a CT scan of his head but while being put in place for the test, he panicked and the test was cancelled. A neurologist diagnosed Chuck with Parkinson's disease because he had several symptoms that were consistent with that diagnosis. After starting on the prescribed medication his bizarre behavior and confusion accelerated. One morning at 4AM I awoke and Chuck was not in bed. I found him dressed, keys in hand, ready to go out the door. I asked, "What are you doing? Where are you going, Chuck?"

"I forgot to make arrangements for someone to pick up the birdies, so I have to do it."

I'll never forget that chilling answer. By this time Chip was upstairs with us and Chuck gave him the car keys. I coaxed Chuck back to bed, telling him we'd take care of everything in the morning, but I knew that things were much worse than I'd feared. What in the world was wrong with Chuck? If I hadn't been praying before I certainly began to pray now, begging God to help us find out what was wrong with my husband. I knew he had something far worse than Parkinson's disease and I began to wonder if the medication he was taking for Parkinson's was, in fact, affecting his brain negatively.

Doctors, tests, diagnoses and treatments multiplied while Chuck continued to get worse. In the spring of 2002 he began having sudden episodes of severe paranoia. If we were in the car, demanded to be let out wherever we might be. He seemed afraid of me. The first couple of times it happened, after a while he got back in the car and we proceeded home. The last time it happened, Chip was talking us out for Mother's Day dinner. We were on Ruston Way in Tacoma where we were going to eat in one of the waterfront restaurants. We had barely turned onto Ruston Way when Chuck unbuckled his seatbelt and demanded to be let out of the car. Chip stopped and Chuck got out and started running away from us, down the greenbelt between restaurants. After an hour spent trying to keep up with Chuck and get him back in the car, we finally called 9-1-1.

By the time the police and paramedics arrived, he was up a small hill standing on the railroad tracks. Once they got Chuck into the ambulance, they took him to a hospital emergency room. Chip and I spent the rest of the night there with him while Chuck was fighting off Indians and the medical personnel were trying to find a psychiatric facility to take him.

Having finally found a private facility that agreed to take

354

Chuck, the next morning he was put into an ambulance to be transported there but he fought so vigorously he had to be taken back into the ER. When left alone he ran and jumped through a window into some bushes and was transported to another hospital for examination of his minor cuts and bruises. From there he was taken to the county Psychiatric Crisis Center for an emergency three-day commitment. When I saw him there he was so overwrought that he feared for my life and insisted I leave.

Two days later there was a court hearing at the crisis center and the judge signed a commitment order for a thirty day hold at either the Veterans Administration Hospital at American Lake or Western State Hospital. The VA Hospital did not have the ability to care for a patient in such an acute state of crisis so he was sent to Western State Hospital.

When I walked into the unit where Chuck was, I was horrified! I had seen many psychiatric units previously with Steve, my son, but my first look at the Geriatric Medical Unit at Western State was the worst I'd ever seen. The patients were mostly elderly but a few were middle age. Many of them had Alzheimer's disease. They all seemed so much worse than the mentally ill young people I'd seen with Steve. I was appalled to see one middle age woman scooting around on the floor. I hoped they had some magic psychiatric medication for Chuck and I'd be able to take him home in a few days. If I'd had that crystal ball, I wouldn't have believed what it was showing me was our future – both Chuck's and mine

# Chapter Sixty Three

## The Long Slow Dying

$C$huck had been in Western State Hospital for three days when I was summoned to a meeting with several staff members, the Chief Psychiatrist, the doctor in charge of the Geriatric Medical Unit, the head nurse and others. At that meeting a doctor said to me, "Your husband won't ever be coming home again."

"Are you people nuts? Of course he'll come home in a few days. You must have some medication that will help him! We don't even know what's wrong with him yet! How can you say that?"

Chuck had entered Western State while his last medical diagnosis was Parkinson's disease so the doctors assumed he had dementia associated with that disease. By this time I was certain Chuck did not have Parkinson's and was determined to keep trying to find out what was wrong with him. I was sure he wasn't suffering from mental illness but from some other brain disease.

Eventually, after I convinced the doctors to take him off all medications, symptoms of paranoia vanished, along with most of his bizarre behavior, but not all of it. While he seemed perfectly all right most of the time, he continued to show occasional symptoms severe enough to keep him hospitalized. For example, one day when I arrived on the unit, the nurse told me that Chuck had bitten another patient. When I was with Chuck, he said, "See that man in the blue shirt? I bit him."

"Chuck, why in the world did you do that? Why did you bite him?"

"I don't know. I guess I just felt like it at the time."

Chuck became a favorite patient on the ward. Staff members

enjoyed talking with him and hearing stories of his Coast Guard career. Sometimes when nice music was played or came on TV, he'd get up and dance and even flirt with the attendants and try to get them to dance with him. Everyone enjoyed his sense of humor; he was the only patient like that in the unit.

I spent several hours with Chuck every day. We talked about the things we'd do after he came home and trips we'd take. Talking, listening to music, playing games and working puzzles, days, weeks and months passed. For the most part, Chuck seemed content but, once in a while, he'd say "Why did you dump me here?" That broke my heart because he had no memory of the circumstances that led to his hospitalization. Chip visited Chuck several times a week even after he bought a house and moved to Olympia. Holding on to Chuck's arm, Chip took Chuck outside for walks, something I wasn't strong enough to do. Occasionally he took him for a drive in the car.

Over the course of time I realized that Chuck was in the best possible place he could be. Everyone who worked on his unit was caring and compassionate and, in spite of my first impression, I soon grew to love those who were taking care of Chuck. He received excellent care. Every six months Chuck was taken to another building on the campus for a Court hearing and I was always with him. Every time there was enough evidence to convince the judge that his commitment should be renewed.

Chuck's physical abilities also deteriorated slowly but constantly. He had increasing difficulty getting out of a chair and walking without falling. I continued to take him to outside doctors, with the hospital's total cooperation. He was sent in a van with an attendant while I drove myself.

A neurologist at Harborview Medical Center diagnosed him with Lewy Body Disease, a brain disorder similar in some ways to Parkinson's, but that diagnosis was soon discarded also. The consensus of opinion was that a doctor at the V. A. Hospital in Seattle doing research on brain diseases and running a clinical study on Alzheimer's, was the doctor Chuck needed to see. In the fall of 2004, after almost two and half years at Western State Hospital I took Chuck to see Dr. Jim Levernz at the Seattle VA

357

Medical Center. Dr. Levernz diagnosed Chuck with a rare brain disease- Progressive Supranuclear Palsy, PSP for short. Brain scans done before Chuck retired from the Coast Guard showed abnormal spots in his brain that could not be explained, but now was thought to be the beginnings of PSP. After his death, the diagnosis was confirmed by researchers at Mayo Hospital.

During the two and a half years Chuck was in Western State Hospital Chip and I saw him almost daily and he had many other visitors. His children and three of his grandchildren when they could; his sister, Michelle, came often and his niece, Kimberly, as did his Uncle Dave. Heidi, Jesse, Paige and Riley saw him regularly; Chuck especially loved to see the kids. Several of his Coast Guard friends also visited. We took Chuck out for drives and even to eat at his favorite restaurant until he became too disabled. We also took him home for birthdays and holidays. It was a really sad day not long before he passed away when Chip took him for a drive. Chuck asked to go to Steamer's, his favorite restaurant. After Chip drove past it, Chuck managed to say, "You didn't stop." By that time he had great difficulty swallowing and speaking and was almost totally incapacitated.

Not long after the diagnosis, Western State Hospital decided Chuck was no longer a threat to anyone as he needed assistance to move at all. He couldn't even turn over in bed. He was losing strength every day and now that he no longer qualified for care at Western State, he had reached the point where I couldn't care for him at home. The VA Hospital at American Lake said they did not have room for him. The VA would pay for his care and gave me a list of "approved" nursing homes. I visited a dozen nursing homes in the Tacoma area and didn't find one that I was willing to let Chuck go to so I started visiting nursing homes in Olympia. I found one there I liked and Chip said he'd visit Chuck every night and I would continue to spend the days with him. Chuck was transferred to Olympia in early October, 2004. We owed Western State almost a quarter million dollars for care for two and half years but they had not pressed for payment. More than two years after his death, with help the hospital bill was paid.

Through Chuck's uncle Dave, I was introduced to a man who was in the highest echelons of the Veterans Administration in

358

Washington, D. C. I contacted him and after three weeks in Olympia, the VA Hospital in American Lake arranged to transfer Chuck there.

For the last year of his life Chuck was unable physically to talk ninety percent of the time. He communicated with his eyes and I always thought I knew what he was thinking. When he could speak he talked as if there was nothing wrong with him.

Two weeks before he died, Chuck had three great mornings talking to everyone with totally normal conversation. He showed the chaplain his book (similar to a high school yearbook) about his seven month voyage to Antarctica, identified all of the officers and explained the voyage in detail, even telling where most of the pictures were taken. The depth of his conversation that day was astonishing.

Another example, less than a week before he died, Chuck called out to a maintenance man mopping the floor in the hallway where he was in a reclining wheelchair. "Hey Jim, come here a minute." When the man got close Chuck said "You want to see a pretty nurse?" This was said while he was smiling flirtatiously at Rosie, a very pretty nurse, indeed. He still had his sense of humor even though he was rarely able to show it.

After sixteen and a half years of love and adventure and happy times, plus three more years of a long, slow dying, Chuck's life ended peacefully on March 25, 2005. He was seventy years old. We held a beautiful memorial service in the American Lake VA Chapel. All of Chuck's children and two of his grandchildren, and other relatives came plus several Coast Guard friends. It was a moving and well deserved tribute. The United States Coast Guard distributed his ashes at sea.

# Epilogue

After Chuck's death I felt terribly alone, even with my children nearby. I needed friends to enjoy movies, theatre and lunches or dinners together. During Chuck's last few months I'd taken two writing classes at Tacoma Community College. I looked around but couldn't find a current class to attend so went to a writers group in a local church that a member of my last class had invited us all to join. The group was quite small and I didn't feel I was learning anything to improve my writing skills so continued to look for a class. Not finding anything else I joined a group in a nearby library where most of the people were writing history pieces and long ago stories of their lives in the local area. They were interesting but, again, I didn't feel I was learning so I continued to look for a class.

Almost a year after Chuck's death I registered for a class at Clover Park Technical College. They had a Senior Center on campus and that was where the writing class was held. The first day I attended there were about a dozen people. Each one read something he/she had written and the group critiqued it. They were friendly and invited me to go to lunch with them. During lunch I learned many in the group had been together for more than five years and all were good friends. By the second or third week I knew I'd found my "home." These lovely, fun-filled people all became my friends and without their motivation, critiques, proofreading and friendship, I'm not sure my story would have made it to print.

I have continued traveling as much as possible. A friend with a condo in Maui invited me to visit. Heidi, Riley and I went with Chip to Vietnam in 2007 for his wedding to Lan. That was such an exciting and happy event.

I took many trips in the U. S. with Paige and Riley or alone to visit friends and relatives. In 2007 Paige and I went to Russia for a

360

cruise from Moscow to St. Petersburg. In March 2011 Heidi, Riley and I went to Argentina to watch Paige's Florida Tech softball team play. Paige started college in 2010. The happiest and most exciting event of these years was the birth of Michael Vo Halsey, Chip and Lan's son and my grandson. Mikey was born June 28, 2009 and has brought great joy to our family.

In June 2012, Paige and I went to Eastern Europe for three weeks. We had a fantastic time. Starting in Prague, Czech Republic, after three days there we drove overland in a small bus with about a dozen other people. We were all going on the Viking River Cruise. On the bus we traveled through Slovakia to Budapest, Hungary. After three days there we boarded the ship for a week. The ship made stops for one or two days of touring in Croatia, Serbia, and Bulgaria. Disembarking in Bucharest, Romania we spent six days in that country, traveling in Transylvania for two days. The highlight of our visit was touring Bran (Dracula's) Castle. Our last trip was to the Black Sea area. Fantastic adventure!

Riley celebrated his 13th birthday in September 2012. He has left the strong support system at Northwest School for Hearing Impaired Children he attended for ten years. He's in seventh grade at Harrison Prep in Lakewood where he is mainstreamed, the only deaf student in the school. He got a cochlear implant in 2011 to replace the hearing aids that no longer met his needs. He loves his new school and is doing very well there. He also is a great hockey fan and is playing on a recreational team.

Steve is currently living on the streets or staying wherever he can find shelter. He says he doesn't want a place of his own. I see him when he chooses to come to see me or calls and arranges for us to get together. When I'm no longer able to look out for him and help solve problems Chip will lovingly take on the responsibility.

Chip works for the state in the Department of Enterprise Services and lives in Olympia. Alexander Vo Halsey, Chip and Lan's second son was born on November 14, 2012. I am thrilled to have another happy, healthy baby in the family. I spend as much time with them as I can because the two little ones make me so happy.

Heidi has been in private practice as a Child and Family Counselor for many years and has accumulated many accolades from her clients.

I hope to enjoy many more adventures with my family. My bucket list is still long!

*Family Spring 2012*

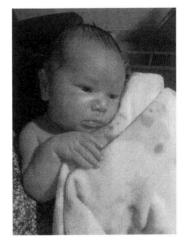

*Alexander, November 14, 2012*

# Acknowledgments

Without the time, patience and critiques from the members of the Lakewood Senior Center Writing Group from 2006 through 2012, this book might never have made it to print. Many writers have and come and gone from the group and all helped in one way or another.

I have to especially thank our current teacher-leader, Jean Chase, who has been generous with her time and help outside class. Jean has been a true motivator. I also have to especially thank Bill Abbott, Don Gray and Margaret Herzog who willingly took the time to read and edit many chapters in this book.

At a very low point in my life, you people took me in, lifted me up, taught me to write and gave me your friendship. You taught me to live for Mondays because that is the day we have so much fun together and good lunches everywhere.

I'll never forget you, my friends.

Much love and thanks to Chip for many hours of technical help. I couldn't have done it without you.

**Cover Picture**
**Fisherman's Bastion, Budapest, 2012, Paige Redmon**